Also By Cheryl D. Broussard

The Black Woman's Guide To Financial Independence;
Smart Ways to Take Charge Of Your Money, Build Wealth and Achieve Financial Security

Sister CEO; The Black Woman's Guide to Starting Your Own Business

Published by MetaMedia Publishing, Inc. Oakland, California

Visit our website at www.sisterceo.com

Printed in the United States of America

First printing: October 2002

Library of Congress Cataloging-in-Publication Data

Broussard, Cheryl D.
     What's Money Got To Do With It? The Ultimate Guide On How to Make Love and Money Work In Your Relationship/ Cheryl D. Broussard, Michael A. Burns. −1st ed.

p. cm.

Includes bibliographical references and index.
ISBN 0-9720094-1-8   2002109861

1. Man-woman relationships.   2. Finance, Personal.   3. African-Americans I. Burns, Michael B.   II. Title

MetaMedia books may be purchased for educational, business, or sales promotional use. For information please write: Special Markets Department, MetaMedia Publishing, Inc., 6114 LaSalle Avenue, Number 724, Oakland, CA 94611-2802.

Illustrations by Michael A. Burns
Cover Design by Brian Bouldin, Bouldin & Bouldin Graphics, Oakland, California

DISCLAIMER

This Publication is designed to educate and provide general information regarding the subject matter covered. However, laws and practices often vary from state to state and are subject to change. Because each factual situation is different, specific advice should be tailored to the particular circumstances. For this reason, the reader is advised to consult with his or her own advisor regarding that individual's specific situation.

The authors has taken reasonable precautions in the preparation of this book and believes the facts presented in the book are accurate as of the date it was written. However, neither the authors not the publisher assume any responsibility for any errors or omissions. The authors and publisher specifically disclaim any liability resulting from the use or application of the information contained in this book, and the information is not intended to serve as legal advice related to individual situations.

Cheryl

For my son
John Hasan Broussard——
you mean everything to me.

Michael

For Treneta, Rusty, Khephra, Vicki, Cheryl,
Alvin Moore and Sabrina Polk.

Acknowledgments

This book has taken four years to write and many people encouraged us during the entire process. There were times when it seemed like we'd never get through it. We had to learn how to make love and money in our own relationship first. However, with persistence, will power and focus, it is finally complete. We want to acknowledge everyone who participated for his or her help and support, without which this book would never have been finished.

Mary Ellen Butler, thank you for your total dedication and immersion in this project. Your editing skills have produced a superior product. Heartfelt thanks to Brian Bouldin of Bouldin & Bouldin Graphics, who put up with last minute cover changes and crazy deadlines, you truly are a Godsend.

To Susan L. Taylor and Khephra Burns, thank you for your tremendous leadership in the world of publishing, and for being a powerful influence and mentors.

To Brenda Ferguson-Hodges, a wonderful mastermind partner, without your continued encouragement we would have never finished this book.

To Treneta and Rusty Burns, thank you for being great parents. Thanks to Shirley E. Jackson, for being a surrogate mother and wonderful typist. To Sisters, Vicki and Cheryl Burns, thank you.

To our dear sisterfriend and exercise partner, Autry Henderson, thanks for keeping us in shape. And Imani Kei our masseuse, thank you for your healing hands that worked magic on our spiritual and physical body.

Thanks to our families and friends: Jeff Adkins, The Barnes, Battles, Binions, Bozemans, Richard Brooks, Broussards, Denise Brown, Robert Brown, Browns, Cheryl Crawford, Barbara Cruse, Douglass, George Fraser, Gordons, Tisha Greene, Hills, Linda Jamison, Jordans, Beverly Kimins, Lagniappe Bed & Breakfast in New Orleans, Lampkins, Mancils, Bola Mohammed, Paula O'Farrell, Pointers, Polks, Patricia Rambo, Attallah Shabazz, Pamela Thompson, Shaws, Wagners, Robert Schaefer and Ernest Priestly.

Thanks to our B-Healthy and Starlight Family: Toni and Bill Hanson, Gail Moody, Margaret Burns, Jeanette Hood, Pamela Ladd, Tanya Shepard, Yvonne and Brian Coleman, Evelyn and Troy Jackson.

Thank you to Revered Eloise Oliver and The East Bay Church of Religious Science for our weekly spiritual message that uplifted our spirits during those stressful writing periods. It was only through your messages that we were able to learn the truth and keep the faith.

To the Co-founders of the NPN Cruises, William Tedford, MD and Madeleine Moore, thanks for allowing us to put on our first Making Love and Money Work seminar for your cruise attendees. It made us realize we were truly heading in the right direction with this book.

To our clients and survey participants, thank you for your valuable input and recommendations, for without them this book would not be possible.

To the reader, thanks for reading this book. I hope you enjoy reading it as much as we enjoyed writing it.

Cheryl D. Broussard & Michael A. Burns

Contents

Foreword

Money talks. Mostly it talks about us. It tells the world that we are privileged or not, educated or not, foolish or wise, generous or miserly, secure, insecure, compassionate or indifferent. And much of what it says has less to do with how much or how little money we have than how we use what we've got or allow ourselves to be used.

Money is the great weaver of dreams and deceptions. It is Aladdin's lamp and Midas's touch, a good servant and a bad master. It is a passport to everywhere but paradise, the provider of everything but happiness. But it is hardly the root of all evil. There are far more worthy candidates for that dubious distinction, including ignorance, fear, and greed.

Ignorance, or a lack of understanding of money—how to make it, how to apply it, and how much weight to give it in our lives—is easily the cause of more suffering than great wealth that is wisely used. Fear of what might happen to us without money is the source of a great deal of anxiety, many a desperate and ill-advised decision, and worse—lying, cheating, believing that doing whatever it takes to get money is justified, even poisoning the earth. The selfishness and greed engendered by avarice and the fear of being without are spiritually corrosive. Understanding money and the role it plays in our lives and communities is therefore essential to our health and happiness. But fear not; it is our Creator's great pleasure to shower us with all that we need and want.

As a couple, we have had money, been without money, wasted money, dreamed about money, strategized and worked hard for years to get more money, invested it, lost it, made more, argued about it, worried about it, freely given it away—in short, experienced the gamut of circumstances and emotions common to people everywhere where money is the medium of dreams made real.

But we have found a balance in our lives, in what for most couples are overwatched and worried scales gauging who contributes what and how much. And this is often the heart of the divide in relationships between men and women. Clearly, income is one way to measure our respective contributions to our intimate relationships. But it is not the only measure; nor is it the most important. Susan has a higher profile and earns more money than I do…. Khephra brings an intellect and nonsexist attitude that enriches my writing and allows us to work together and build something greater than either of us could alone. I wouldn't think of writing an editorial or book without his eye and input…. Nor would I without Susan's wisdom and insight. And the management of our finances is a shared responsibility. We each bring strengths to the relationship that are applicable to some aspect of our lives; we each have gifts to share that help us both to grow. It all nourishes the relationship and, ultimately, impacts the bottom line.

Every couple that is serious about working in partnership must find a balance that works for them. But so many who are struggling to find that balance are bound by outmoded gender-defined roles and expectations that dictate a man should be the primary bread winner, that he should make most of the money and most of the decisions, and that a woman who works outside the home should also cook, clean and care for the children inside the home *and* look eternally 22.

Too many women and men today have unrealistic expectations, of their mates. Many women feel that if their men were more motivated, then together they could earn the money to create better lives and secure a brighter future. It's a major frustration among some black women who feel that they are carrying too much of the weight in their relationships. Young black men complain that black women only want them for the things they expect men to buy them. And both the larger culture and the music videos of our young people glorify conspicuous consumption in support of an image of wealth and a fantasy lifestyle. Rather than actually building wealth, too many of us—black, white, Hispanic, young and old enough to know better—pursue mere symbols of wealth that are of questionable value to begin with and which very quickly depreciate to nothing. Too many are caught up in cycles of instant gratification and debt, poor credit, limited opportunities and, in an attempt to find some pleasure in life, further squandering of limited resources on instant gratification.

There is no dearth of examples in America of financially successful black couples and families, nor of those who are working well together to secure their financial future. They're not well represented in the media, but they're not invisible either. We see them in the fruit of their labors—in thriving middle-class communities and the thousands of young men and women who enter our colleges and universities each year. Cheryl Broussard has been writing and speaking about their financial challenges—in many ways unique and in others typical of the challenges encountered by American men and women of every background—and offering strategies for their personal economic growth for more than a decade. Now she and Michael Burns, a marketing consultant and Internet technology specialist (and Khephra's brother), take an honest and insightful look at how money issues are affecting intimate relationships among American women and men. This book represents an important step in helping to heal these relationships and set us on the road to financial security.

– Susan L. Taylor and Khephra Burns

Introduction

What's money got to do with love and relationships? Everything! Money is one of the leading issues that impact Americans. So when you add Enron, Worldcom, AOL-Time Warner, other Wall Street accounting scandels, terrorism and a slowing economy, the picture can look pretty bleak for individuals and couples trying to obtain the ultimate American dream--financial freedom.

While these turbulent events affects all Americans financially, they really hurt the African-American family who is already behind the financial eight-ball in this country. In fact, the African-American family is in a state of economic crisis without these events going on with an ever- widening income and wealth gap between black and white families. Studies show the median wealth of black households is less than 10 percent of white households. Why? There are various reasons— racism, poverty, unemployment, lack of financial savvy resulting in rampant consumerism, no financial planning, not owning businesses and the big one— disjointed relationships.

> *Anyone who tells you money can't buy happiness, never had any. When you're dodging bill collectors and worrying how the kid's tuition is going to be paid, there's no comfort zone. And if there is no comfort zone, there is no time to deal with each other.*
>
> —
>
> Samuel and La Tanya Jackson,
> Essence Magazine May 2002

The evidence clearly shows that couples that stay together get wealthy together. According to the latest census data here are the facts: The median income for white married couples is $45,000 versus $39,150 for black married couples. But the problem is that black families aren't staying together. The latest study (2002) released by the Centers for Disease Control and Prevention which surveyed 11,000 women states that black women are the least likely to marry and most likely to divorce, with more than half splitting up within 15 years. The Asian marriages were the most stable, with whites and Hispanics in between. This issue leads to far too many single black women as heads of household. And since the median income for black women is a little over $16,000, it's very difficult to accumulate much wealth when you are struggling to just survive.

This cycle of economic and relationship disparity needs to come to an end and soon because our freedom and economic power is at stake. The African-American community must "**get real**" with their money and their relationships. It's time to break the cycles of single parenthood, divorce, money mismanagement, too much debt and lack of investment assets. *What's Money Got To Do With It: The Ultimate Guide On How To Make Love and Money Work in Your Relationship* is your answer. Our goal is to assist the African-American community with breaking these cycles and keeping the family intact. Why? An intact family works better at producing income. The income from a couple working together will translate into an enormous advantage when it comes to accumulating wealth. *What's Money Got To Do With It: The Ultimate Guide On How To Make Love and Money Work in Your Relationship* will help you to accumulate that wealth –together with your partner. It contains the tools and steps to put you and your partner on the path of a wealth creation journey.

Where did we get these steps and tools? We surveyed over 300 single, married and divorced men and women. Some were clients. We also researched and read hundreds of relationship and money management books and articles on the Internet. We were determined to know the secrets and the formula to make love and money work in relationships.

How were partners able to "create" their own financial paradise in a world of fast money and fast living? How are relationships that are Making Love and Money Work able to build this inseparable bond in regards to money when you have the advertising boom in the African-American consumer market helping to further divide black men and women over the issue of money and material means? The ads encourage us to ignore the internal qualities of a potential partner and instead evaluate them by the value of how much money they have, their career, the type of car they drive or the clothes they wear.

Many of us are no longer looking for a partner to work with us but a partner to take care of us. Many of the relationships in the African-American community are made of up of two half people with unresolved childhood money wounds trying to find the other half to make them whole. And we are finding that doesn't generally happen so we get a quick divorce and continue are search for the "so call" right brother or sister.

Just as relationships take work so does Making Love and Money Work take work. The grass isn't greener on the other side as many of us are led to believe. The perfect partner is not out there. To make it work we must first each become the whole partner before we enter into the relationship. We must each go way back and find out what our money wounds are and heal them. We must determine what are values are and what we want money to do for us as an individual as well as in our relationship, then we can really contribute to the family and to the community. Now we don't want you to have fairy tale expectations thinking that the money will always go smoothly in your relationship. It will not, as many of you already know. And guess what? That's Ok. The key is knowing how to deal with the financial bumps and challenges when they come up. You and your partner must learn how to become a team so that you can take the money in your life to the next level. African-American families must get on the same financial page with a financial plan to create wealth and accumulate assets.

One thing we know for sure, completing this task can be confusing. Our roles as men and women are no longer clearly defined, when it comes to relationship—getting married, having children, raising them, dealing with money, there is no rule book, there is no guide, there is no five-hour class; we're just expected to " wing it". Is it any surprise that over 50 percent of all marriages end in divorce? We don't believe it has to be that way. In fact, we know it doesn't have to be that way. There are people out there that are making love and money work. And doing quite well, thank you very much. We share some of their stories throughout the book.

Why Is Making Love and Money Work So Important For the African-American Family?

We mentioned a few facts earlier but here are a few more. How about the mere fact that relationships where love and money is working have a lot more money at retirement than divorced and never married persons? A Purdue University national survey of more than 7,000 households found that marriage has a lot to do with wealth accumulation. Getting and staying married provided benefits that greatly impacted long-term economic well-being. The survey found that people who had never married had only 14 percent of the financial assets that married persons had accumulated. And divorce people who did not remarry had only 15 percent. Isn't that reason enough?

Thomas J.Stanley, Ph.D, author of the two best-sellers, The Millionaire Mind and The Millionaire Next Door concurs with these findings. In his book The Millionaire Mind, he mentions a study where over twelve thousands respondents were surveyed (Janet Wilmoth and Gregor Koso, "Does Marital History Matter? The Effect of Marital Status on Wealth Outcomes Among Pre-retirement Adults") that found consistent participation in marriage results in significantly higher wealth. Conversely, those people who are not married, only over time, were able to accumulate lower levels of wealth during their adult cycle.

Dr. Stanley found that there were 6 key success traits of couples that were Making Love and Money Work:

1) Partners Making Love and Money Work were unselfish, caring, forgiving, patient, understanding, discipline, and virtuous. It also helped if the partners had similar interest, activities and opinions.

2) Early in the marriage, the partners made trade-offs between buying expensive consumer goods like clothes and cars and funding their investments and small business. Business and wealth-building was their first priority.

3) Partners Making Love and Money Work also had no need to use consumer goods as status symbols. Their six or seven figure investment portfolio says enough.

4) The partners that have a shared interest related to accumulating wealth are much more likely to reach millionaire status. Preparing a household spending plan, planning and making investments, setting financial goals, and owning and operating a business are important habits in a Making Love and Money Work relationship.

5) When these couples did make expensive purchases, the money used was from their wise investments not their earned income.

6) The 5 qualities that contributed to a couple becoming millionaires were:

1. Being Honest
2. Being Responsible

3. Being Loving
4. Being Capable
5. Being Supportive

These 6 success traits aren't rocket science. Anyone can put them into practice.

Our goal with this book is to help you and your partner make these traits and habits a part of your daily regime.

What If I'm Not Married or In A Relationship?

Don't worry; this book is for you as well. We cover topics such as the Singles Money Scene; How to Play by the New Rules. We'll show you how to find a comparable money partner with our fun money compatibility chart in chapter 5. Based on your money style we tell you who is your best partner and which one to avoid. For single women; we show you how to stop looking for a Money Prince Charming and to focus on your own financial empowerment. We also discuss why work, money and power are so damn important to men. Women need to understand the reasons that when a man's money is funny, his relationship gets put on the back burner. For men; we give you strategies to help you adjust when your partner makes more money than you do; something that is happening more and more in relationships today.

We also discuss how a new or old relationship handles money baggage. Many people today have credit card problems. Or maybe it's their second or third marriage and they have other family financial obligations like alimony and child support. You need to know in advance how to deal with it before the relationship becomes permanent.

If you and your partner are already on the brink of a divorce, we hope after reading the book you'll change your mind. But if that isn't the case, we have a chapter just for you; Getting A Divorce: It Doesn't Have To Be Nasty. We show you how it isn't necessary to use money and/or your children as a weapon. And in fact, doing so is extremely detrimental to both partners-financially, emotionally, and spiritually.

And Finally, in the last chapter, Making Love and Money Work 101, we sum it all up and show you the correct way to make it work. We discuss how to manage money when you are living together. If you're already married, we discuss how to design a financial life together. Should you have separate, or joint accounts or both? What about starting a business together? We'll show you how to do that too. We help you create a spending plan, set financial goals, get started building wealth with $50 a month and protect your assets. And last, we end the chapter with the formula: 25 Action Steps to Making Love and Money Work.

It's A Wealth Creation Journey

Making Love and Money Work is a lifelong wealth creation journey for a relationship. And it's a journey so badly needed in the African-American community. Reading this book is not intended to be a passive experience. It's interactive, and you and your partner or potential partner must play an active role. You should also read it more than once.

There are exercises and many questions you will need to answer and write down, so we encourage and highly recommend that you get the companion *What's Money Got To Do With It?* money journal. Or, you can use a spiral notebook as well. This will enable you to do the homework and have it in one central location. Make sure you keep the journal in a safe place. It is highly confidential and for you and partner's "eyes only". This will allow you both to be totally honest with each other.

The money journal will also allow you both to see the progress you will be making as you venture on this financial journey. Remember what we said earlier, it might not be easy. No, let's be honest. It will not be easy. It will take lots of patience, support and understanding from both partners to make it work. At times, some painful issues may come up. Issues we might not want our partner to know about. You will have to get them out and let them go. Secrets are not allowed. And they are too destructive to the relationship anyway.

It's a different financial ballgame today and the rules have changed for the African-American couple that wants financial independence. The goal of *What's Money Got to Do With It?; The Ultimate Guide On How To Make Love and Money Work in your Relationship* is to help you and your partner in become that wealth-building team. You both want to be on the same financial page. Following the steps we have outlined throughout the book will help you to become that awesome financial team.

The book is packed with information so take your time. Don't rush. Be sure to check out the resource pages in the appendix. If you need more financial information we are sure you can find it there.

Have fun when reading, too. Yes, we know money and relationships are serious business, but it can be fun as well. We found the couples that were Making Love and Money Work were having a great time building wealth, traveling all over the world and following their dreams. There is absolutely no reason why you and your partner can't be doing the same.

We wrote this book to get the money dialogue going in the African-American family. We too are on our own creating wealth journey and we want the Black community to come along.

We hope you like what you have read so far, because it gets even better. So let's not delay one more minute. Good luck on your new financial journey!

Cheryl D. Broussard and Michael A. Burns
September 2002

Chapter 1

Love & Money —
What's Wrong With
This Money Picture?

It's All About The Money!

Cheryl: *When I was very young, my parents taught me the importance of setting goals. Most of the goals had to do with acquiring enough money to buy my favorite Barbie dolls. As I got older I continued to set goals every year except that they got bigger. First, I wanted to make $50,000, then $100,000, then $250,000. The reason—freedom! I didn't want to work for anyone. I didn't want a boss to answer to or a time card to punch. I wanted to do what I wanted to do and having lots of money was the only way I could do it.*

> *The highest use of capital is not to make more money but to make money do more for the betterment of life.*
>
> —— Henry Ford

Gradually, pursuing money became the be-all-to-end-all. Being with family and friends dropped by the wayside. I didn't have time to socialize. I needed all my energy to pursue more money. After working as a financial adviser for several years, I started writing books. I decided I needed to sell 100,000 books and have a minimum of 100 paying speaking engagements every year. That way I'd attain the freedom I desperately desired. But after awhile, friends and family began to ask me, "What freedom?" You're probably wondering the same thing. If selling 100,000 books and speaking 100 different times a year doesn't sound much like freedom, you're right!

But I couldn't see that at the time I was chasing money. Then something terribly unexpected happened. I had a major family and health crisis. In 1996, my mother was diagnosed with lung cancer and was gone in ten months after extensive chemo treatments. Right about that same time my marriage fell apart as well. The next two turned out to be just as dramatic with both of my grandparents passing away back to back. So in a three-year time span I had four very emotionally devastating deaths. (According to psychologist, on the stress scale, divorce is considered a death of a relationship). Confusion, uncertainty and guilt began to take over my life. This of course led to major stress, which caused my own health to get of whack. I stopped exercising, gained weight, and couldn't write one word. It was a challenging period.

After surviving that personal catastrophe, I realized something had to change. But what? I hadn't a clue! So instead of slowing down and taking two steps back to figure out what was really going on, I engaged in sabotaging behavior. I began to do the exact opposite of my former goal of accumulating money. I went on an all-out spending spree. New furniture, new hardwood floors, new clothes, new everything! Money became the enemy. I needed to get rid of it as soon as possible before it caused too much more damage. Luckily, I finally came back to my senses before it was too late. I went back to reading spiritual and personal development books. [The Value In The Value; A Black Woman's Guide Through Life's Dilemmas, Iyanla Vanzant, Simon & Schuster, 1995 and You Can Heal Your Life, Louise L. Hay, Hay House, 1984] From them [and through some deep-down soul searching of my own] I realized that having strong life values was more important than piling up the dollar bills. Now that *my life values are established, I've discovered I can manage the money I already make well enough to stop chasing for more all the time.*

Michael: *Get a good job. Those words ring in my head like a childhood nursery rhyme. My parents would say you should be an attorney or a doctor, but most importantly get a good job with some benefits. Sometimes if feel as though I'm the only one in the world that really didn't know what he wanted to do as a child. My only goals as a kid was to play, go on vacation, and to have fun in the sun. But I did like going places. I was an avid reader of the Encyclopedia and National Geographic. They were my way of "exploring new worlds". I was quite capable of entertaining myself, although my brother and two sisters were always there to provide equal amounts of drama and comic relief. Money wasn't something I really thought about unless I wanted more toys or model cars. When I was in high school money was needed to pay for some of the things I wanted to do like fishing or for buying jazz LP's, 45's or 8-track tapes.*

As child I was stubbornly independent and single minded. My father might call it "hardheaded". When I did want things, my mother would always say, "go ask your father". I think it was at this time that I developed a strong disliking for the word "NO". As a result, I've spent a considerable amount of time not wanting to say that word. "NO" to relationships that probably weren't the best idea and "NO" to jobs that weren't a good fit for me because I didn't want to disappoint people or let them down.

Also, I have had a sense of fear since I can remember-fear of the dark, fear of cameras, fear of my father, and later, the fear of rejection. You know, the usual stuff. And I think that this got in the way of me learning the lesson on valuing myself and having confidence and courage. My father has the "C" words. My brother also. But none of that stuff seemed to rub off on me. I can recall only exhibiting any courage if my back was to the wall and tears were streaming down. In such situations the ability to think quickly on my feet has allowed me to escape danger. But the lack of confidence, courage, and goals have made me the "prey" and not the "hunter." Play it safe and don't take risks. In other words, the result is to get caught up in others agendas. To do what other people think is best for me. Accept their decisions.

So in "following the herd", so to speak, there is safety and security to be had. "Get a good job" is safety and security. In some ways it's a survival instinct of so many generations before me that had to "toe the line" or get the spirit beat, stolen, or lynched from them. "Get a good job" doesn't seem to leave any room for a healthy dose of self-worth. You're just happy that you're not unemployed.

It is no surprise that my relationships with money and love for that matter have been based on a valuation problem. In graduate business school we learned that the value of a share of stock is base on a risk/return model. I've been guilty of taking myself for granted and accepting the warm confines of a sure thing. And in not valuing myself more, I also have not been valuing others enough to say "NO" sometimes. When you know what you're worth, you won't be jumping from job to job or relationship to relationship trying to get someone else to tell you what you're worth. They don't know. Only you do. I received a business degree because someone thought it was a good thing to do. I got an MBA because it was a good thing to have. I worked 7 years for IBM because my best friend was going to work for them and it "looked good" on the resume. And although all were great opportunities for personal growth, none of them were early goals of mine. They were more like goals of the moment. Did them just because someone suggested that it would be a good idea.

Money! It's one of the most emotionally charged issues of our lives. And it is the leading cause of conflict and divorce for all American couples. You may try to deal with money by pretending that it doesn't matter. But, in reality, financial pressures affect your relationships every single day of your life. You may make the mistake of thinking that all your money challenges would simply go away if only you just had enough. Nothing could be further from the truth. No matter how well you do — or don't — manage your money, you will at some point struggle with it for an infinite variety of reasons. Your rent may go up, your stocks may plunge, you may lose your job. Fill in the blank.

Even big dough in the bank won't necessarily shelter you from the storm. If you're rich, your greatest concern may be whether Uncle Sam will change the tax laws and bite off a big chunk of your bread. So, regardless of where you are financially, money can unsettle you either way.

Wouldn't it be great if the money issues in our relationships naturally fell into place? You receive an attractive job offer out of state, your beloved agrees to move. You put the house up for sale and it goes for $5,000 more than you asked. Escrow closes, you relocate and your partner finds work with an increase in salary. Sounds great doesn't it? Financial experts call this scenario "being in the flow". It happens, but like Michael Jordan "in the zone", not very often.

Instead, money frequently imperils male-female relationships. You're already tired, overworked and underpaid. Your monthly expenses usually outlast your paycheck. You and your partner argue about whose abusing the credit cards or not putting enough into savings and investments. Your money issues become an obstacle in the road that trip you up. They knock you off the route you are traveling together and force you onto separate paths.

Whether you know it or not you have a relationship with your money just as you have a relationship with your lover. Oftentimes your relationship with your money mirrors how you deal with yourself and other people. For example, Michael and I have found that people who have controlling personalities do not readily discuss finances with their significant other. *Jennifer and Doug are a good example. Married three years, rarely if ever do they discuss money. Doug, a third generation accountant handles all the bills and investments. Not one purchase for the household can be made without his approval. Once when they were newly married, Jennifer made the mistake and purchased a $150 dress for a New Year's Eve party without telling Doug. When the bill arrived he was livid and immediately closed the credit card account. Definitely, Doug's behavior was extreme. But this is what he learned from his dad, and his dad from his dad. The behavior was simply being passed down to each new generation.*

People who are insecure may have a tendency to want to hide money from their partner. *For Terry, it was growing up with a mother who didn't trust men, since her husband emptied their small savings account and walked out on his family of three girls. From that day, Terry continued to hear from her mother, "always have money* *stashed away that no one knows about, keep it secret". So when Terry met and married Larry, those words continued to hunt her and still do today. That's why she has a $10,000 investment account that Larry knows nothing about.*

On the other hand, partners who trust each other will work out their financial goals before they make spending decisions so that they know they're on the same page.

After dating two years and becoming engaged, Janice and Robert agreed that every month they would sit down and plan their money life. They set financial goals for the month and discussed any major purchases needed for the household. There were no financial surprises. Every month they both knew exactly how much money was in the checking and investment account.

No matter which way it goes down, money is always a major source of potential trouble between you and yours. So why is it so often a taboo subject? Shame, guilt, fear of rejection, or delusions of power are among the main reasons. You may harbor some of these feelings but not be consciously aware of them. Yet, you may act them out in your personal life. Recognizing when you're falling prey to these danger signals is the first step toward openly addressing and overcoming them. Take a moment to read the list below. Do any of these situations sound familiar?

Danger Signals Between Couples

- Your discussions about money usually turn into shouting matches in which no sensible decisions are made.

- You and your sweetie compete with each other to see who brings home the biggest salary or picks the best stocks.

- You're both uncomfortable with negotiating for a car, a house loan or a pay increase.

- Just when your money is "In the Flow", a major financial crisis hits and you both feel pressured to file bankruptcy.

- You view spending money on non-basic items as wasteful but your partner thinks you're a tightwad. Your differing "money personalities" create friction.

- No matter how carefully you two manage the money, you don't seem to be getting ahead.

If you and your partner are caught up in any of these costly and disheartening loops, you probably have some misconceptions about how money works. *What's Money Got to Do With It* is your guide to banishing those misconceptions. Read on, and you will see that you have more control over your money and your relationship than you may think.

How Money Challenges Relationships

Sandra and Ray

After dating for a year and a half, and getting married six months ago, the bliss is beginning to fade for Sandra and Ray. It seems every day for the past month they have been fighting about money. Unfortunately, they'd never talked about it before the ceremony. It turns out that Ray, a computer repair technician is a high-tech gadget man. He just spent $5,000 on the latest PC without discussing it with Sandra. Sandra, a human relations specialist has been equally cavalier. She just now got around to mentioning her $15,000 MasterCard balance.

Sandra and Ray's story is not atypical of relationships today. And it leads us right into the first of **10 Money Challenges** we see in personal partnerships these days, any of which can cause financial havoc for you.

Money Challenge 1: Poor Communication

Yes, "money talks" as Susan L. Taylor says in the foreword to this book. Too bad people don't. Money is a silent partner whose presence nonetheless speaks louder than words. One reason you don't like to talk about money could be that the subject is one you associate with pain. Lack of enough cash may cause you anxiety, frustration, fear, insecurity, worry, anger, embarrassment or humiliation. Why discuss something that gives you so much grief?

But why does money exert such a powerful sway over you? Isn't it just strips of papers with funny faces that serves as a medium of exchange? Well, you may link money with buying success and happiness through assets like a bigger house or a better car. Your role models may be movie stars who routinely buy multi-million-dollar mansions in the Hollywood Hills or rap stars who tool around in Rolls Royces and Bentleys. When you aren't able to get these things, or reasonable facsimiles of, you may blame your partner. As far as you're concerned he or she is the reason you can't have those things.

If you are a woman, talking about money is even more difficult. You have to be extra careful when bringing up the subject to your partner since your comments may be interpreted as a challenge to his manhood. For men, money is connected to their masculinity. It is the source of their power, their tour de force. Your man wants you to think he knows more about money than you do. And the chances of him admitting he doesn't are highly unlikely. Later in the book we will show you how to communicate with your partner about money without wounding his ego. If you are a man, we'll show you how including your woman in your financial affairs will help the two of you build a solid financial foundation.

Money Challenge 2: Money History

If you're a woman who grew up with a tightwad, controlling father, you may insist on having a separate account in your relationship because money to you means independence.

If you're a man who grew up with parents who didn't give you much affection but lavished you with lots of gifts instead, you may overspend on "toys". Money to you means love.

Would you be surprised to learn that how you handle money is based on what you learned during childhood? Most of your money habits and attitudes were shaped as you observed your parent's handling of money. You saw how they got excited over money, got depressed over money, even fought over money. From a child's point of view this behavior was quite confusing. But you did learn one thing—money is very important! As a result, the value and the meaning of money became more mystified. It is these early money lessons that stay with us and create our money styles.

If you're African American and you have some sense of history, reflect on the violence that has been visited upon your community as a result of money, and the relationship of the community as a whole to American society regarding money. Sure to be a few intense feelings associated with that reality.

Stop right now and think about how you feel about money. Is there a gnawing undercurrent of anxiety about your future relationship with money? We know the feeling. *We've been through it separately and together.*

You, too have some of these emotions around money, and if you and your partner don't understand where they come from, arguments are likely to follow. In Chapter

2, we'll talk more about your money history. We'll help you and your partner determine how your childhoods have influenced your adult attitudes toward money. We'll also show you how other influences such as your peers, your religion, our society, and especially the media have a continuing impact on your personal money history.

Money Challenge 3: Different Money Styles

As we have seen, there is a link between your unconscious feelings about money and the way in which you earn it, spend it, save it, and invest it. In other words, you have a Money Style. You just may not know what it is

Here are some different Money Styles. See which styles most closely describe you and your partner and we'll discuss them in more depth in Chapter 5.

- **Hoarder**. You like to save money. You have a hard time buying luxury items for yourself or your partner. A new winter coat, a vacation to the Caribbean or tickets to the Prince concert are unjustified as long as the old coat, a vacation within 100 miles of home or a Janet Jackson concert on Showtime are available.

- **Spender**. You enjoy buying goods and services for immediate pleasure. You see a new pair of shoes for an upcoming dinner date or a soothing massage after a workout at the gym as necessities. You don't like to save money for future purchases or long-term financial goals. And you absolutely hate to create and stick to a budget.

- **Binger**. You go without to save money and then turn right around and spend it all on new clothes or a new car. You combine the tight pockets of a Hoarder with the pleasurable financial release of the Spender. Bingers symbolically gain then lose their money.

- **Procrastinator**. You feel anxious about paying bills or managing money. You wait until the last minute to take care of financial matters. You wish they would just go away.

- **Chaser**. You are happiest when you have large amounts of money to save or invest. You equate money with your self-worth and personal power.

- **Worrier**. You spend a lot of time checking and rechecking your financial situation. You are concerned where money will come from and where it will go. You constantly fret about potential financial "catastrophes."

- **Risk Taker.** You have a "Las Vegas" flair to your money management style. You're convinced that 401(K)'s, CD's, and any other savings or financial planning instrument are for wimps.

- **Risk Avoider.** You equate a simple interest bearing checking account with white water rafting. Both are dangerous as far as you're concerned.

Whether we are like our parents or completely their opposite, these Money Styles are a direct result of our money history. A funny Wall Street Journal television commercial alludes to the importance of money styles, and how early development determines future choices and decision-making. In the commercial one child from a set of twins separated at birth is weaned on a fishing magazine and the other on the Wall Street Journal. Of course, the financially weaned child grows up to become rich and the other still lives with his parents. While the ad is fictional, our environment does play an extremely important role in the way we handle money. Exposure to wealth puts you in a wealth mindset. Exposure to financial deprivation or a "just getting by" attitude can put you in a poverty or scarcity mindset. Think of the nicknames your parents and friends have graciously bestowed upon you. Names like "tightwad", "cheapskate", "big spender", "money bags", or "penny-pincher". These tags pro-

vide a clue to how others perceive you and may help

you identify which Money Style you have.

Money Challenge 4: Different Education Levels

> *Save a little money each month and at the end of the year you'll be surprised at how little you have!*
>
> —— Ernest Haskins

We believe your level of formal education plays
a very important role in how you and your partner relate to money. In relationships
where there is a disparity in educational attainment, it becomes easier for one party –
usually the woman — to assume that the other – usually the man — knows more
about money even if he majored in ancient history instead of finance. In other words,
"You're smarter than me because you went to college and I didn't". Knowledge of
finance and numbers still is not something women accept as their God-given right,
although that is changing as more women major in financial subjects or go to business school.

It's true that business schools excel at teaching students financial management
concepts and applied techniques. However very few b-schools, if any, teach individuals how to handle their personal finances. In Chapter 18, Making Love and Money
Work 101, we'll show you money management techniques that will help you and
your partner achieve financial excellence, freedom, and peace of mind, regardless of
your education levels.

Money Challenge 5: Inequality in Income Levels

Even when women attain comparable educational levels, men still make more
money. According to the U.S. Bureau of the Census, the median income for men in
1999 (the latest available data) was $25,212. The median income for women was

$14,500, a difference of $10,712. Such substantial income differences can cause major financial issues in a relationship. The major one is financial dependency of the partner who makes the lesser income – usually, but not always, the woman. As mentioned earlier it takes two incomes to meet the basic needs of most families today. If you are the male partner and feel you are footing all the expenses, resentment and anger can lead to a breakdown in communication and a return to Money Challenge 1. On the other hand, if your female mate earns more than you do, you may feel you've lost your role as primary breadwinner. This is a difficult spot for you. To survive possible ridicule from family and friends you must have a strong ego and a strong sense of self. Strategies to help you adjust when your woman earns more are covered in Chapter 13.

What we do see in relationships where incomes are more equal is "cooperative finance" which is what this book is all about. We see both partners taking equal responsibility for creating financial wealth for the family. They both have declared their dreams and are very clear on where they are going "together". In other words, they are on the same financial page. Hopefully this is the outcome you and your partner are striving to achieve. Being on the same financial page is an achievable goal today. We encourage you to read on and follow all the exercises throughout the book.

Money Challenge 6: Inequality in Career

Inequality in careers goes hand in hand with Money Challenge 5, inequality in income. Generally, if a person is continually hitting the "glass ceiling" and is unable to move up the job ladder, their income is severely affected. Again, this issue impacts women the hardest. If you or your partner have these experiences, you may fight over money. One partner may actually accuse the other of being lazy or not smart enough to "make it" when the real reason could be little or no career advancement due to institutional sexism or racism. We'll talk more about how to stick with your partner during bad times later in the book.

Money Challenge 7: Gender Differences

Men Are From Mars, Women Are From Venus, says bestselling author John Gray. Not only are the genders innately different, we are raised differently, too. These differences carries over into how we each deal with money. With men, making money is a sign of power and is much preferred to spending money, whereas women derive much of their power from spending money.

> Women + Spending Money = POWER
> Men + Making Money = POWER

Men are brought up with a more rigid sense of boundaries, and are more autonomous and separate. They see the world as competitive and hierarchical. Men automatically assume when they grow up they'll be able to deal with money. On the other hand, they don't want to admit they haven't a clue how to manage their money. Men have difficulty seeking help. You know how a man will rarely ask for directions when he's lost while driving? It's the same with money. Instead of asking questions about an investment they don't understand, they'll invest anyway and risk losing their shirts. Or they'll hang on to an under-performing investment long after they should have gotten out of it. We know a doctor who has consistently lost hundreds of thousands of dollars in offshore trusts, yet continues to claim they are great investments. He simply won't admit he's made a mistake.

By contrast, women are willing to merge their boundaries with others. They view the world as cooperative and horizontal. The bad part of that world view occurs when women are taught that because they won't be good at managing money they must go out and snare a financially competent man to do it for them. It's true that women have begun to reject that old-fashioned approach. But, I'm afraid the old model of female dependency is fading but slowly.

Despite all the free financial information available on the Internet, on cable stations such as CNBC or CNN Money, and in numerous magazines, women today still say that managing and investing their money is too complicated to do all by themselves. The gender difference also shows up in the money fears women express. Regardless of a woman's economic resources, she worries about becoming penniless in her old age, pushing the last of her belongings in a shopping cart and living under a freeway overpass. It is this fear of losing her assets that causes the majority of women to place their money in low interest, risk free accounts that are safe while growing at a snail's pace.

Men have more logical fears. They worry about being laid off or dying young. That's why a man who feels responsible for taking care of his family feels he has to make as much money as possible while he can. However, this belief can be financially detrimental if it causes him to take extraordinary risks, like investing in a hot but unsubstantiated tip or even gambling at casinos or racetracks.

Money Challenge 8: Socialized To Spend Money

According to Psychology Today, "good US citizens" are those who go out and spend money. This consumerism gospel leads to a financial death trap for individuals and their partners. For example, you may find it difficult to delay your gratification for things that you want rather than need. Instant messaging, cellular phones, wireless access to the Internet, even that American staple, fast foods restaurants, testify to that fact that we have conditioned ourselves to want it when we want it, without having to wait.

That's fine for those who can afford that lifestyle, but not all of us can. In "Luxury Fever – Why Money Fails to Satisfy in an Era of Excess," Robert H. Frank says that the spending habits of the majority of the people in America regardless of income level have been greatly influenced by the spending habits of the super rich. If you or your partner suffer from "Luxury Fever" it may be your pocketbook that's over-heated, not your forehead. The average cost of a car now exceeds $22,000, up more than 75 percent from a decade ago. In order to send your child to a decent public school, you need to buy a home in a more expensive neighborhood. To make sure the kids look hip, you'll buy the $200 Nikes. If you're having a dinner party, you'll serve the most expensive wine.

But appearances can be and often are deceiving. "Whereas those at the top of the economic totem pole have done spectacularly well," says Frank, "the median Ameri-can family has gained literally no ground at all during the past two decades, and those in the bottom fifth have actually suffered earnings losses of more than 10 percent in real terms".

If those words describe you and your partner, our goal with *"What's Money got to Do With It"* is to bring you back to reality. We want to help you and your special one to reprioritize your money and show you how to have everything you want without selling your soul on the altar of consumerism.

This money challenge rings especially true in the African American community. We spend the bulk of our $580 billion dollars of revenue on non-incoming producing consumable products. The good news is that as we gain more financial education we're changing how we spend money. Instead we are investing in money-making

18

assets such as stocks, real estate and starting a business. Definitely there is more room for improvement and we hope this book will serve as your guide.

Money Challenge 9: Lack of Financial Goals in the Relationship

You can make love and money work when you and your partner have financial goals that are in harmony with each other. You must both be very clear on why and how you will manage money to build financial wealth.

The challenge we see today is that couples are not on the same financial page within the relationship.

For Suzanne and Martin, the problem started when she wanted to buy a $50,000 two-seater sports car for a family of four. No matter how much Martin tried to persuade her that spending $50,000 on a car that didn't hold the entire family wouldn't make financial sense. She wasn't go for it. It had always been her desire to own an European sports car and now that she could afford it, that was her intent. After numerous conversations with each other and an impartial financial advisor, they settled on a $30,000 four-door sporty car. They both got what they wanted and were happy. Suzanne and Martin's story is an example of a couple lacking financial goals and not being on the same financial page. Why?

We found that couples are not on the same page because they don't know how to get there. As individuals, we aren't taught how to set goals, especially financial ones, so the majority of us drift through our financial life directionless, reacting to whatever crisis is thrown our way. These un-strategized reactions make us do dumb and careless things with our money right from the very beginning of our working years. So, of course, we bring this same "no-financial goals" attitude to our love relationships. If you and your partner have no joint financial goals nor plans to define them, you are not on the same financial page and as a result are not jointly building your wealth either.

We believe that setting goals together is an absolute must for relationships today. If you only read one chapter in this book, make sure it is Chapter 18. We will show you exactly how to set financial goals and devise a strategy to obtain them.

Money Challenge 10: Race

Race has a major impact on money and relationships: Much more in African American male-female relationships than in white male-female relationships. Not having adequate money or assets is an unfortunate part of the black culture due to financial illiteracy. Many Black men and women continue to carry around anxiety over not having enough or losing what they do have. This anxiety is well-deserved. African Americans in the United States don't enjoy anything close to financial parity with the average white American. As mentioned earlier, the median wealth of black households is less than 10 percent of white households.

The main reason for this shocking disparity is that white Americans inherit a lot of their wealth, including real estate, and also enjoy a larger percentage of two-parent relationships. In black families there are more "single" woman heads of households. In fact, two out of three black children are born to unmarried women. Their lack of marital partners means that black women struggle economically. Black women are fourth on the income list behind white men, white women, and black men. In many cases there is no way they can really make it financially unless they are part of a household with a second income.

Yet according to relationship expert and Essence magazine columnist, Dr. Gwendolyn Goldsby Grant, black men are so angry at working black women that money has become an explosive issue in the black male-female relationship. Some black men feel that black women have "made it" in the working world at their expense. Where did this patently untrue belief come from? Blame it on the media. The media has given a lot of attention to those few black women who have succeeded in breaking through the concrete ceiling of corporate America. This has lead to an erroneous perception that all black women make six figures, live in mansions and drive luxury cars. Walk down the street of any metropolitan city and ask a black woman if she feels she has broken through the "concrete ceiling". We can pretty much guarantee she'll laugh in your face.

The reality is that the average income for black women in corporate America is $16,000. They are living paycheck to paycheck, are barely investing in their company's 401(K) retirement plan and don't have life insurance. This tragic state of affairs is a far cry from the picture being drawn by the media.

The sad part of this story is that we found several black women looking for a Money Prince Charming to come and financially rescue them. A study conducted in 1990 by the Business Higher Education Forum found that what black women wanted first and foremost in a relationship was a partner with a steady cash flow. A prospective partner's income outranked his physical attractiveness, education and occupation. The typical sister who was polled also wanted "Mr. Right" to live in a two-story house in the suburbs, drive a Lexus or a Range Rover, and carry a slew of credit cards to pay for all her heart's desires. (We'll discuss more on looking for a Money Prince Charming in Chapter Nine).

This unrealistic expectation is one cause of the ongoing rift between black men and women regarding money in a relationship. Dr. Grant calls this miscommunication "the shame and blame reaction".

"There is a feeling of failure that accompanies career underachievement or underemployment," she says. "This causes emotional problems even in middle class families. When you don't have money to buy nice things or go to nice places, you feel a sense of shame. You don't want others to see you not being able to join in with everyone else." So instead of black men and women dealing with the real issue they indulge in cover-ups. One cover-up is to blame their partner for any money troubles. Comments such as, "If you made more money, we wouldn't be in this kind of trouble".

Cheryl: *When I was married I remember making this remark several times throughout the relationship.*

  The other comment is "it's all your fault. If you hadn't wasted that money, we would be okay". Both of these remarks are a no-no in any relationship. It doesn't matter if you are African American, White American, Hispanic American or Asian American. Blaming each other does not make love and money work. We will cover this area much more in depth throughout the book.

Michael: *We're not saying that black men and women shouldn't be angry. They have every right to be angry. This country was founded on the free market principle of capitalism. However, African Americans, especially African American men, were not allowed to participate in this system. From working without pay during slavery times, to the use of lynching against successful business owners to the middle of the 20th century, through the vilifying of minority set asides and affirmative action in the late 20th century, the message has been "you won't earn what you deserve and you don't deserve what you earn".*

The reality is that hundreds of years of internalizing this hurt has been counterproductive to developing a healthy mindset among black men and women with respect to money. It's not hard to see why a people would be defensive and overly protective about earning, keeping, and sharing money with others. Living in an oppressive system that doesn't allow them to fully realize the American dream of building individual wealth frustrates both partners. Because they feel powerless they vent their anger on each another instead of focusing on their joint goals as a way to beat the system. They fight and compete with each other and allow the system to beat them.

Both Dr. Goldsby Grant and Dr. Ronn Elmore, a relationship therapist and author, agree that if a black man feels powerless and insecure he will not be able to handle a successful black woman. He will not be able to be emotionally supportive and will pick fights regarding money, unless he is reassured that his woman neither wants to compete with him, nor does she want to take over the relationship. It is here where all men, regardless of color, but especially black men, must realize that affirming your partner's efforts will help both of you as well as your relationship. The key is to understand how to communicative and be supportive of each other.

As you read through these 10 money challenges in relationships, you may identify with one or more of them. Whatever the case, know that you can make the money in your relationship work. To make love and money work, you and your partner must do one thing starting right now. You each must put dealing with money in your relationship on priority status. This means that you each must consciously decide to purposefully work on improving money in your relationship each and every day. With both partners actively involved, you will not only lessen the money arguments, but you will also build financial wealth as a team.

Discipline yourselves to do the money work. Make the necessary time to sit down together to discuss your financial goals and to do the specific steps that are given throughout this book. Placing dealing with money in your relationship on priority status means that it becomes of great conscious importance to you. It also means that you and your partner are committed to the relationship. It means you are willing to do what it takes, in order for you to have a harmonious relationship with each other and with your money.

Chapter 1: Making Love and Money Work Action Steps

1. Buy the companion " *What's Money Got To Do With It*" Money Journal for the answers to the exercises you will complete throughout the book.

2. Make a decision to make dealing with money in your relationship a priority.

3. Determine which money challenge(s) are affecting your relationship today.

Chapter 2

Discovering Your
Money History

Kathy

Balancing a checkbook is difficult for Kathy who comes from a wealthy family. Her father is a well-known politician, her mother an attorney. As a child of affluence she was driven to school and back every day in a chauffeured limousine. Kathy despised and was embarrassed by this perk. The other kids called her rich and spoiled. It left her with an emotional scar she can't seem to erase.

Today, at 40, Kathy wants nothing to do with money. She cries every time Joseph, her significant other, brings up the subject. They all too often end up arguing about it. Though she has an advanced degree in Marketing, she hasn't been able to work for one company for any length of time because she knows that if she stays long enough they may want to promote her, which means she'll probably get a pay raise. And heaven forbid if that happens. She never again wants to experience the embarrassment she felt as a child growing up with money. As a result, she has no savings nor has she built a retirement fund. When asked about her financial situation, her typical response is, "I don't need money".

The amount of money Kathy's family had and how it was used has had a negative impact on how Kathy handles her own money. Have you ever stopped to think about how your childhood experiences molded your money style today? Believe it or not, your ways of dealing with money most likely started years ago with your parents.

For Louise, 62 it was lack of money that has caused her troubles with paying her bills on time every month. Being the oldest of four girls, at the age of ten she was responsible for turning away the bill collectors when they came to the family home or telephoned. " When the bill collector came to the front door, my mom and dad sent me to do their dirty deed. I had to tell them we didn't have any money. To this

day, I have trouble paying my bills on time. It's so bad I won't even open the enve-
lope until the day the bill is due. I do this every month regardless of whether or not
I have money in my checking account. Money is the biggest source of stress in my
life."

If you're like Kathy and Louise, you aren't alone. The purpose of this chapter is to help you and your partner understand how your money history affects your current lives. Once you are both clear on what is influencing you, arguments can be avoided for which neither of you is to blame.

The exercises in this chapter are designed to trigger some of your childhood memories. They may also awaken a little anxiety. For some of us, thinking about money whether in the past or the present is uncomfortable. Still, getting to know your money history has major benefits that are worth the unease. The exercises will help you and your partner to understand how your money style was formed and why you handle money the way you do. You'll learn the reasons why you habitually pick up the check when you dine out with friends or why you allow credit card bills to pile up unopened on the dining room table.

Making peace with your personal financial history is of the utmost importance to you and your mate. Each must clearly understand what caused you to lose confidence and become doubtful about your ability to obtain financial mastery. Once you come to terms, you can begin to substitute positive messages for the negative beliefs you picked up during childhood. Until you do, you are likely to sabotage your relationship with money – and with your partner.

Cheryl: I consider myself to be quite fortunate since money was never an
issue during my childhood. I lived in an extended family household

with my mother, sister, grandparents and an aunt. My mother took my sister and I shopping at the mall at least once a month. Every Christmas we pretty much got every toy we asked for. Every major holiday such as Easter, we got new clothes and had large family dinners. Financially, life was good. When I did want extra toys, such as Barbie doll clothes, my mother told me I could buy as many as I wanted as long as I saved my money and bought it myself. This was my first lesson in setting goals and saving money. I wanted a lot of Barbie doll clothes so I was highly motivated to get money. I did odd jobs for my grandfather around the house. I learn to knit, and made and sold headband for $1.00 to family, friends and students at my grade school.

When I turned 16, I immediately begin working at Sears & Roebuck after school and on the weekends for $1.70 an hour. Most of this money went into savings since my basic needs were taken care of by my mother. I paid for my Caribbean cruise senior trip and by the time I was a sophomore in college I had saved up over $1,500 to buy my first car.

I firmly believe that my money history afforded me the best of both worlds. Not only did I see the positive effects of money but I also learned about work ethics and how important it is to set goals and to save money toward the things you really want. Today, I still follow these same rules. And it has provided me with the type of lifestyle and freedom that I want.

Is there a drawback to my positive money history? In some relationships, yes. Especially if I team up with someone who has a fear of money or grew up with little money in the family household. They may not be as open to spending money or they may worry about it excessively. This happens to be the case with my relationship with Michael.

Michael: *It's not necessarily based on a fear of money more than a distaste for having to ask others for anything. It probably started with simple child wants but later included advice, financial assistance, wisdom. The positive side is that I've always been able to get any job I really wanted by talking my way in and I was never allergic to hard work. I believe in myself and my abilities. The fear factor comes from feeling that I am all alone in making decisions because I have no one to confide in who wouldn't see my request for assistance as a sign of weakness. So procrastination in decision making has to be constantly monitored because of the tendency to desire absolute certainty before proceeding.*

Your Money History

Now, it's time to consider our questions. Don't answer them from your current perspective as an adult. If you do, your ego will more than likely get in the way. Instead, answer from the perspective you remember as a child. For purposes of this exercise "parents" refers to whatever adults raised you. Don't hold back. Be truthful. The more honest you are with yourself the better you'll be able to deal with your money challenges. You and your partner should complete this exercise in privacy. Once you are finished then come together and share what you have learned about each other.

Exercise: Taking Stock of My Money Past

Turn to the Taking Stock of My Money Past in your " **What's Money Got to Do With It** "Money Journal. Or, if you have bought an empty journal especially to go with this book, write on the first page **"Taking Stock of My Money Past"**. Whichever writing vehicle you are using, answer the following questions:

- At what age did you realize the importance of money in your life?

- Can you recall a specific incident? Write down as much as you remember.

- What city did you live in at the time?

- Describe the house or apartment you lived in.

- What family members did you live with? Were there other children? How old were they in relation to you?

- What are some of the best memories you have of your childhood home? Who treated you special? Why? Was there someone you weren't too fond of? Why? Was there ever a time it was difficult or scary to live there? Do you wish you could change some of the things that went on there? If so, what?

- Do your remember making "when I grow up" statements? Did you ever say, "When I grow up, I will never do…" or "if I am a parent, I will do or have…" What made you make these statements?

- When you needed money or a special item for an event at school, who did you ask first—mother, father, or another family member? What was usually their response?

- If you lost something or broke a household item, who would you tell? What was their response?

- If you wanted a new doll or a new bike, how would you get it? If you asked for it, what was the response? If you were afraid to ask for it, why?

- How many friends did you have? Name a couple of your best friends. Did you get along with them? Did you feel left out or bad about yourself? What are some of the things you did to fit in?

- Did you think you were rich? Why? Were any of your friends or family members rich? Why did you think that? Did you like these people? Were they good or bad? Why? Did you want to be rich? Why? When you reached adulthood, how much money did you think you needed to be rich?

- Did you think you were poor? Why? Were any of your friends and family members poor? Why did you think that? Did you think poor people were good or bad? What did you know about poor people? Why did you think poor people were poor?

- Did you like spending time at your friends' houses more than your own home? Why?

- How much money did your family have? Who told you this? Who made the money in your family? Was it enough? How did you know it was or wasn't enough?

- Who was responsible for paying the bills in your family? Were the bills paid on time? How did you know? Did you see your parents argue about money?

What specifically were the arguments about? How did they make you feel?

- Did your parents try to control you with money? If so, did you rebel or did you conform? How so?

- Did your parents enjoy their money by going on family vacations and buying Christmas and birthday gifts? If yes, how did you feel? If not, how did you feel?

- Who spent the most money? Who made most of the money decisions? Did they spend wisely or waste it on things they didn't need? How did you know?

- Did your parents talk about money? If yes, what did you hear? If no, why do you think they didn't? Remember some of the specific money conversations you heard. What feelings came up?

- Were your parents happy with each other? Why did you think this?

- Did you feel loved and respected by your parents? How did they show it?

- Did any adult ever talk to you about money? Who was this person? What exactly did they say and why? How did you feel? If not, did they talk to any other children in your family about money?

- Did you receive an allowance? If yes, how much? Could you do anything you wanted with it? Did your friends get an allowance? How much? If you didn't receive an allowance, why? Where did you get spending money? Did you like to spend your money or save it in your piggy bank? What did your parents say about how you spent money? Were you always asking for more money?

- When did your parents say you were doing a great job and they were proud of you? How did you feel? When did you want your parents to tell you they are proud of you? What particular person did you want to hear that from? Why that person?

- Did you dream about being married? What did you imagine marriage would be like? Was their someone you knew who had this type of relationship? Who? What were some of the specific things they did?

- Did you always feel safe and protected? Why? Was there a particular place you felt physically the safest? Was there a person you felt safest with? Why? Was there someone you didn't feel safe with? Why? What were some of the things that made you feel safe?

- If you are a woman, name six women who were in your early life. If you are a man, name six men. Which of these adults had a life you wanted to have when you grew up? Were any of those adults married? Did they have good marriages? Why did you think that?

- If you could ask your parents any questions about money what would they be?

- Congratulations. You have just completed your money past. Did these questions and your answers help you to remember why managing your money has been so difficult? Were you able to gain insights about stumbling blocks that trouble you today? Confronting your past money history can help you resolve current conflicts. Read over your answers once again. Were there any questions that hit you hard? If so, did you feel sad, mad, hurt, or happy? Put a star next to those questions. Later when you and your partner exchange your past money histories, pay particular attention to the starred questions. If you both star similar questions, take note. These are the issues you may want to discuss in greater depth.

Chapter 2: Making Love and Money Work Action Steps

1. Explore your past money experiences by completing the Taking Stock of My Money Past exercise. Be truthful and write the answers down in your money journal.

2. Based on the exercise you just completed, write a brief summary of your money past. Once again, focus on the areas that caused you the greatest emotional reaction. This summary should really help you to see where you and your partner are money challenged and why you developed the current beliefs that rule your behavior. With this information you both are now one step closer to becoming true money soulmates. Job well done!

Notes

Chapter 3

What Outdated Money Beliefs Are You Bringing To Your Relationship?

Now that you are more aware of how your money history influences your behavior within your relationship, let's move on to the next step: discarding the out-dated money beliefs that can hurt your ability to work with your partner. Outdated money beliefs fall into two broad categories: those that are based on whether you are a man or a woman and those that you may hold regardless of your gender. Clinging to these beliefs can place an unnecessary burden on your relationship. If you can get rid of them, you will have a stronger and much more prosperous partnership.

Female Money Beliefs

A number of women we surveyed stated they won't give the time of day to a man unless he has money. We firmly believe this attitude stems from a female gender belief that a man who loves a woman

> *Money frees you from doing things you dislike. Since I dislike doing nearly every-thing, money is handy.*
>
> —— Groucho Marx

must take care of her and therefore must have lots of money. This damaging belief puts an inordinate amount of pressure on a man. In fact, we think this is the reason there are so many single men out there. Many men today live in fear that they won't be able to support a family financially. So rather than subject themselves to the em-barrassment of not fulfilling that responsibility, they stay single late into there 40's and 50's. Once married, men who feel overly responsible can have a hard time shar-ing the money decisions, which can lead to frustration on the part of their wives.

Male Money Beliefs

Michael: One of the reasons I've been single for so long is from the belief that I have to "make it" before I can get married. A woman is not going to be attracted to a man that did not have a clearly defined career path.

Many men, on the other hand, consider women to be incompetent money managers. Unfortunately, some women buy into this stereotype as well. Other women, while they may not overspend, will simply refuse to educate themselves on financial matters. Their ignorance puts the bulk of the financial responsibilities on the man, who may eventually resent carrying this burden.

How are a man and woman who subscribe to these gender-based beliefs likely to behave within a partnership?

- He likes to take credit when they have money, but blame others when they don't.

- She gives credit to her partner when they have money, blames herself when they don't.

- If money or investment decisions are pending, he tends to just go and do it, whereas she wants to discuss it beforehand.

Do you see you or your partner in these gender beliefs? Making love and money work involves identifying and changing those beliefs that adversely affect your money behaviors. Once you do that, you're on your way toward a more successful partnership.

Non-gender Beliefs that also Sabotage Success

"Whether you think you can or you think you cannot, you are probably right."

While many of our beliefs are based on gender, others are equal opportunity attitudes. If you and your partner believe you won't have a good relationship, have the money to buy a home, or achieve success in meeting your financial goals, then you probably won't. With limiting beliefs like these, you are defeated before you begin.

Often these beliefs stem from past failures. When we fear failure again, we prevent ourselves from following through on steps to build our financial wealth. Which is why it's essential that you both know what limiting money beliefs you each bring to the table. That way, if one of them rears its ugly head, you will both recognize it, call each other on it and take action steps against it.

Couples who make money and love work move from being pessimistic to being optimistic. No matter how their parents managed their money, they have chosen to manage theirs differently. While recognizing past shortcomings, they move on to picture themselves succeeding financially. They develop a powerful certainty that they will be able to buy their own home or build a six or seven figure investment portfolio. They are a team and together they will make it happen.

Discover Your Limiting Money Beliefs

Limiting money beliefs come in all sizes and shapes. Other couples have listed theirs below. See how many you share.

→ If I have enough money I will always be safe.

→ Money protects me from all danger.

→ Money is the root of all evil.

→ Money doesn't grow on trees.

→ Money can't buy you love.

→ Money talks.

➡ Rich people are arrogant, rude, insensitive, greedy and selfish.

➡ It is easier for a camel to go through the eye of a needle than for a rich man to enter into the Kingdom of God.

➡ If I have enough money, I can buy financial independence.

➡ If I have enough money, more people will love me.

➡ It is easier to love a rich person than a poor person.

➡ If I have enough money nobody will push me around.

➡ If I have lots of money, I will be truly happy.

➡ The person with the most gold makes the rules.

➡ I can't trust people with my money.

➡ I'll never make more than $35,000 a year.

➡ If you want money, you're selfish and you are only thinking of yourself.

➡ I can't afford it!

Did anything on this list cause you to react? The stronger the reaction the stronger the belief. It is these beliefs that prevent many of us from reaching our full financial potential.

Now it's time to pull out your *What's Money Got To Do With It* money journal and create your own list. Record all the money beliefs that hold you back. Later on you and your partner will probably add to the list as you encounter other money challenges. That's good. Facing these limiting money beliefs is the first step in getting rid of them so you your mate can build a solid relationship.

Our Money Beliefs

Michael and I decided to test our theory about limiting money beliefs. This is what we came up with:

Cheryl's Money Beliefs

- My divorce would take all my money and I'll become a bag lady.

- I'll never be able to buy the beach house of my dreams.

- I'll never deserve to be wealthy.

- I'll have to sacrifice fun to become wealthy.

- God will punish me for the times I wasted money.

- If I depend on a man financially I'll be indebted to him forever.

- I can only depend on myself to get what I want.

Michael's Money Beliefs

- I'm not smart enough to make millions.

- The time for becoming wealthy is when you're un your 20's and 30's.

- I won't become rich but won't be poor either—stuck in a mediocre money rut.

- I don't think there is enough money to go around.

- I would have to sacrifice friends, family, or something really important to become wealthy.

- My parents didn't impart the mentality for becoming rich, so I am forced to repeat what they did financially.

- Compared to my colleagues I don't feel I'm doing as well financially.

When we looked at our money belief lists, we understood why we were not managing our money to the best of our ability. We both had made major money mistakes in business before we met each other. I (Cheryl) spent far too much money ($12,000) on stationary and business forms for my money management firm and Michael put over $50,000 on his credit cards for his internet business. Both of these cases were not smart financial decisions. Especially coming from two financially educated individuals. By doing the exercise we discovered we both had major limiting money beliefs that caused us to sabotage the way we handled money.

Yeah? What? You wanna a piece of me? Come on !... I got your budget right here!!!

Since then, we've changed our money behavior. We sit down once a quarter and go over our individual and joint financial goals. If either one of us is exhibiting sabotaging money behavior, we immediately point it out to the other in a loving, nonthreatening way. This is the benefit of being on the same financial page. Regardless of who makes the most money we are a team. And our goal is to support each other in achieving those individual and joint financial goals.

Changing Your Limiting Beliefs

Now that you know what your limiting money beliefs are, the next step is to change or get rid of them in order to develop a positive money consciousness. How do you do that? The most effective way is to realize deep down that if you don't make changes in the way you manage your money you will create massive financial challenges for yourself and your significant other.

According to psychologists, one of the best ways to change negative money beliefs is to raise your new positive money beliefs to the level of conviction. A conviction is a deeply held certainty that gives you the power to overcome negative money messages from the past and to manage your money right from now on. For example, the conviction to get out of debt will force you and your partner to cut up all but one of your maxed-out credit cards, call the banks and stores to cancel them, and resist the urge to order new ones. Or if your conviction is to save $20,000 for a down payment for a home, you and your loved one will make consistently smart choices with your money to do so. Neither will be easily persuaded to buy things you don't need.

To create strength of conviction will require that you two become extremely clear and focused on what you want your money to do for you. If you recall, one of the money challenges couples faced in Chapter 1 was the lack of financial goals. Thus, writing financial goals and a plan to attain them is a key part of your new strategy. Financial self-reliance only comes when you direct all your money actions toward attaining those goals, including putting as much as you can afford into your investments or paying off your one remaining credit card bill every month.

Another way to strengthen your new money beliefs is to educate yourself on everything to do with money. Attend seminars, read "how-to" money books, and talk to financially successful people. Find out what they did to amass their wealth, then do what they do even if on a smaller scale. The main thing is to take steps in the right direction to get better control over your money.

In order for these changes in money beliefs to work in your relationship, you both must have similar convictions regarding money. Otherwise, one partner may sabotage the other. This is why both must complete the exercises in the book. Remember, the reason you are reading this book is to improve money in your relationship and your life. You both need to be involved to attain that goal.

Once you get rid of your negative limiting beliefs, you'll need to replace them with a more positive set. Try these on for size:

New Money Beliefs

- I am financially independent and free.

- All my money is working for me, increasing my abundance, joy, and life force.

- Regardless of my past money mistakes I can attain financial peace of mind.

- When my partner prospers, I also prosper.

- I have enough money to spare and plenty to share.

- I am smart enough to make millions.

- I am worthy of being successful and wealthy.

Chapter 3: Making Love and Money Action Steps

1. Identify the money beliefs that control your money behaviors. In order for you to change your money behavior, you must change your money beliefs.

2. Eliminate your limited money beliefs and replace them with some of the new money beliefs we have listed.

Chapter 4

Personal Money Values — What Really Counts

Money and success don't change people; they merely amplify what is already there. —— Will Smith

We bet you're wondering what your personal values have to do with money. Plenty! Values guide our every decision, especially those dealing with money. Some of us are good at setting lofty financial and life goals. We pride ourselves in doing whatever it takes to achieve them. We sacrifice our health, our family ties and our friendships only to ask when we've arrived at the top, "Is this all there is?" The reason; we really didn't know what we truly valued in life. So many of us are so busy chasing the dollar and being driven by our ego that we make wrong financial decisions that come back to haunt us later in life. The truth is, you will only achieve real financial freedom for yourself and your partner when you decide what your highest values are in life and then commit to live by them every single day.

Basic Life Values

We came up with 14 Basic Life Values that we hold. They include:

Love	Success
Freedom	Making Money
Being with Family and Friends	Power
Adventure	Comfort
Fun	Happiness
Passion	Spirituality
Health	
Security	

We're sure all of these values are also important to you. But you may not rank them equally. You'll do more to follow some than to live by others. In fact, each person who looks at this list will see some values as being more paramount than others.

The hierarchy of your values controls the way you make life decisions. Here's an example. If love is No. 1 on your list but making money is No. 1 on your partner's list, you're at home waiting by the fireplace with your 5 Star romantic dinner while she's at the office working on her latest deal and won't be home until midnight. If this happens enough times it can cause a rift in the relationship. Duh!

To clear up what was going on in our own lives, we decided to list our hierarchies of values. Here's what came up, Cheryl's first. You and your partner will have an opportunity to do this exercise later in the chapter.

<u>Values</u>	<u>Cheryl's Old List of Values</u>
1. Love	Freedom
2. Freedom	Success
3. Being with Family & Friends	Making Money
4. Success	Adventure
5. Adventure	Power
6. Making Money	Love
7. Fun	Passion
8. Power	Spirituality
9. Passion	Happiness
10. Comfort	Fun
11. Health	Comfort
12. Happiness	Being with Family & Friends
13. Security	Health
14. Spirituality	Security

Cheryl: *As I looked at my list, I suddenly understood exactly why my life had turned chaotic. Freedom, success and making money were at the top. Being with friends and family and paying attention to my health were way down at the bottom. Not surprising, since I had set annual goals of selling 100,000 books and speaking at 100 events. True, I was making lots of money. But I felt disconnected from those around me. I was not having fun, nor was I happy. As my chart shows, happiness and fun were also far down on the list. Basically, I had lost perspective of what was really important. I was waking up every morning asking, "Is this all there is?"*

The direction you take with your life and your money is controlled by your values. Their force is what leads you to make decisions. When you are clear on what's really important in your life, making the best money and life decisions becomes a lot easier. You also realize that acquiring "stuff" and more "stuff" will not fulfill you. Setting financial goals without knowing what you truly value in life is the precise reason you begin to question yourself once the goals are achieved.

Cheryl: *Doing this exercise made me reevaluate my hierarchy of values as well as my finances. I began to ask myself what order my values needed to be in to live the life I wanted. I realized that if I wanted to change my life and my money I needed to switch the order of my values. Here is what my new list evolved into:*

Cheryl's New List of Values

1. Spirituality
2. Love
3. Health
4. Happiness
5. Being with Family and Friends
6. Making Money
7. Adventure
8. Fun
9. Passion
10. Success
11. Freedom
12. Power
13. Security
14. Comfort

The Impact of Values in Your Relationships

Knowing your own values helps you to focus on why you do what you do with your money and your life. Knowing your mate's values is equally important to give you insight on why they make certain life and money decisions. Misunderstood perspectives about work, life and money can wreak havoc on a relationship. If your priorities are worlds apart—no shared values or visions—your bond isn't likely to last. By sharing some of the same values, you may be able to overcome the differences that naturally occur between people.

Michael: *To test this theory, I did the exercise as well. Here's the order of the list that I came up with:*

Michael's Value List

1. Love
2. Happiness
3. Health
4. Spirituality
5. Passion
6. Freedom
7. Adventure
8. Success
9. Making Money
10. Being with Family & Friends
11. Power
12. Fun
13. Comfort
14. Security

CB & MB: Now, let's put both lists side by side to see how well we match up:

Michael's Value List	Cheryl's Value List
1. Love	Spirituality
2. Happiness	Love
3. Health	Health
4. Spirituality	Happiness

5. Passion	Being with Family and Friends
6. Freedom	Making Money
7. Adventure	Adventure
8. Success	Fun
9. Making Money	Passion
10. Being with Family & Friends	Success
11. Power	Freedom
12. Fun	Power
13. Comfort	Comfort
14. Security	Security

As you can see our values are somewhat similar. The top four values are the same except arranged in a different order. The major issues we may have a problem with are making money and being with family and friends. We list them at No. 9 (Michael) and No. 6 (Cheryl) respectively. We list Being with Family and Friends as No. 5 (Cheryl) and No. 10 (Michael) respectively. While neither is causing a conflict in our relationship today, it may in the future, so these are the two areas we know we must work on to prevent them from creating a wedge between us.

Steven and Elizabeth

We wanted to further validate this theory, so we tested the exercise on a few more couples whose money is working in their relationship. *Steven and Elizabeth of Orlando, Florida have been married for seven years with no children. Steven is a CPA and controller for a major corporation and Elizabeth is a college professor. Money is plentiful with each earning over $100,000 a year. They own their own home and two pieces of rental property. They both put the maximum into their com-*

pany 401(k) plans and invest $2,500 a month in the stock market. Here are Steven and Elizabeth's values lists:

Steven's Value List	Elizabeth's Value List
1. Health	Health
2. Love	Love
3. Happiness	Happiness
4. Spirituality	Spirituality
5. Passion	Being with Family and Friends
6. Freedom	Making Money
7. Adventure	Fun
8. Success	Adventure
9. Making Money	Passion
10. Being with Family & Friends	Success
11. Power	Freedom
12. Fun	Power
13. Comfort	Comfort
14. Security	Security

Clearly, Steven and Elizabeth's values are closely aligned. The first four are the same and the others aren't too far off. This explains their success at managing money and accumulating wealth. They are in sync.

Knowing you and your partner's values is only one of many steps to making love and money work. Whether you are single or in a relationship, take the time right now to put your values in order. If you have a partner, ask him or her do it as well. We have provided space below. Feel free to add additional values. Remember, this isn't the final word on whether your relationship will last if your values are completely different. It just means you both will need to sit down and discuss the reason there are differences and how you can minimize them for the benefit of the relationship.

For those who are considering marriage, we highly recommend this as a pre-marital exercise. It will open up the discussion on life and money issues before you set the date, allowing you both to work on any weak areas – and there will be weak areas — before you tie the knot. Using this strategy will improve your chances of enjoying a happy and financially blissful relationship.

Personal Values Exercise

	Your Values	Partner's Values
Love	1.	1.
Freedom	2.	2.
Being with Family & Friends	3.	3.
Success	4.	4.
Adventure	5.	5.
Making Money	6.	6.
Fun	7.	7.
Power	8.	8.
Passion	9.	9.
Comfort	10.	10.
Health	11.	11.
Happiness	12.	12.
Spirituality	13.	13.
Security	14.	14.

Chapter 4: Making Love and Money Work Action Steps

1. Your values play a major role in how you spend and save money. Complete the values exercise and compare them to your partner.

Chapter 5

What Is Your Money Style?

While money creates the most dissension in a relationship, the stress doesn't necessarily come from not having enough. Oftentimes it stems from the different money styles couples bring to the partnership.

Carol and Ron

When Carol and Ron first began dating, spending money was never a concern. Exclusive restaurants, getaway weekends, evenings at the theater, flowers, gifts: Ron's spare-no-expense attitude swept Carol off her feet. But now that they are married with a first child on the way, Carol wishes her husband would curtail his spending sprees and save for the future—the way she wants to.

What happened? Sometimes what initially attracted us to our partner becomes less appealing as the relationship progresses. And money is no exception. In fact, it's a potential hot button issue from start to finish. When money is plentiful, the button may stay cool. When money gets tight, the button may warm up. But by understanding how your partner's money style may differ radically from your own, you two can find the middle ground, confront and overcome your conflict.

There is so much emotional meaning attached to money. To one person it means love or security; to another power and control. These attitudes are learned in childhood while watching our parents cooperate — or not cooperate as the case may have been. Then when we become involved in a relationship we reenact what we observed, usually mimicking the same money styles as our parents or going in the opposite direction.

Some people are so angry about their childhoods that they subconsciously fail financially in order to retaliate against their parents. Going bankrupt is a powerful way to prove to your parents they did a lousy job of raising you. Of course, this behavior doesn't benefit you. If anything, it will probably backfire because money or the lack of it will not resolve your emotional problems. Besides, it takes too much energy to keep up the fight against your parents. That energy could be put to better use by developing a money style that works for you.

Partners in relationships where money is working are able to set aside their family money habits. In fact, they resist any outside influences from friends and relatives. They are able to forgive their parents for any perceived slights. If they didn't they'd keep alive the image of an unhappy childhood and preserve their money victim mentality. By not forgiving our parents, we continue to stay hooked into a money style that doesn't serve us well. Going to the other end of the spectrum by having a money style that is totally contrary to your parents doesn't always work either. Oftentimes, the more we try to be different from our parents, the more we unconsciously imitate them. In our relationships we may try to pick someone with a money style that is the direct opposite of our parents, yet the difference may cause a great deal of conflict.

Gail and Martin

Martin, a former client of Cheryl's, married Gail, an extravagant spender, because he was trying to avoid another money-worrying woman like his mother. He wanted someone who had a free and easy style. This difference in money style turned out to be a nightmare. He was so uncomfortable with how Gail was handling their money that, much to his chagrin, he began to take on his mother's style. Every time Gail spent money he wanted to know how much she spent, where she spent it and why she spent it. He tried to put her on a tight budget and got angry when she didn't obtain his approval on any purchase over thirty dollars. As you can see, choosing a wife with a spendthrift money style was indeed an overreaction to his need to avoid his mother's frugal style.

When we have emotional ties with our family money styles, we keep alive a pattern that spills over into our other money relationships. The anger we have against our parents pollutes our love partnerships without our realizing it. Until we resolve that resentment we can't develop our own style of managing money. Instead, we give up our power to be financially savvy adults.

We would love to tell you that we all enter this world with the ability and self-esteem to achieve our financial goals. Unfortunately, that just isn't the case. We aren't given the opportunity to develop our own money style because our money conditioning is far too powerful and one-sided. Our money history is not only filled with the beliefs of our parents but also the other important adults in our lives— grandparents, teachers, even aunts and uncles we emulate.

Sometimes we are lucky and the money messages we receive are positive. *As a child, Dave had an uncle he admired. "Uncle Leonard was an entrepreneur," Dave recalls. "He owned a gas station as well as rental property." When Dave helped out at the gas station or tagged along when Uncle Leonard went to collect the rent, he unconsciously absorbed his uncle's business practices. As an adult, Dave, too, bought income property. As with Uncle Leonard, Dave's investments in property were financially successful.*

Sometimes we aren't so lucky. *When Sybil was a child, her father would take her with him to the race track. For him, money was for betting, winning, and betting again until you lost it. Now in her 30s, Sybil tends to spend her money as soon as she gets it, a compulsion that keeps her from advancing herself and her family financially.*

If you are like Sybil, you need to get past the negative money messages and habits you were exposed to. That's why you and your partner must spend time understanding your money histories, beliefs and values before you both can move forward and develop a true financial partnership.

Money Styles

In Chapter One we listed different money styles as one of the major challenges in a relationship. We asked you to answer a series of questions to help you determine your money style. Let's talk more about each of those styles. There is also a short exercise your and your partner can do to discover your money style. We'll tell you which styles tend to click and which ones are like oil and water in a relationship.

Most of us fit into one or more of eight money styles: **Hoarders**, **Spenders**, **Bingers**, **Chasers**, **Worriers**, **Risk Takers**, **Risk Avoiders**, and **Procrastinators**.

If you are a Hoarder Money Equals Security. You:

- Take personal charge of your money.

- Believe that because life is a struggle you must hold on tightly to your money.

- Doubt that people and /or financial institutions can be trusted with your money.

- Show little interest in stocks and mutual fund investments.

You have a difficult time spending money. You live by the motto "saving for a rainy day". "Budgeting" is another one of your favorite words. You love the process of putting a spending plan together and have no problem sticking to it. In fact, reconciling it every day is part of your normal routine. Spending "Benjamins" on vacations, entertainment and gifts for your lover, family or friends is pretty much out of the question. Investing tends to be a challenge for you as well. You don't want to take any risks and need an ironclad guarantee the money will always be there. If you are an extreme Hoarder, you would rather put your money in a coffee can under the bed than in a savings account backed by "the full faith and credit of the United States government"!

Now, we are all for partners saving money. We highly recommend it. But not to the degree that you are so worried you can't enjoy life. Being frugal is smart today, but to get the most out of your relationship, you may need to loosen the purse strings just a little.

Money Hoarder's Action Plan

1. Start changing your money beliefs. As you read earlier, beliefs that there will never be enough money to go around or that financial advisors and institutions aren't trustworthy cause money-hoarding behavior. Reread Chapter 3 on money beliefs and really examine how and when your beliefs were formed. If your parents or grandparents lived through the Great Depression of the 1930s, you may have learned to be a Hoarder from them. Or you just may be naturally tight with your money.

2. Begin to enjoy you money. But don't splurge. We don't want you to leap from being a Money Hoarder to a Money Spender in one bound. Instead, start small. Buy an inexpensive gift for a friend or relative even if you think it's a waste of money.

3. Schedule an appointment to meet with a financial advisor who has been referred to you by a trusted friend or relative. Invest a minimum of $1,000 in a stock mutual fund. One to consider is an index fund. More on index funds in chapter 18.

If you are a Spender Money Equals Pleasure. You:

- Have a "Gotta have it right now" and "Live for today" attitude.

- Spend money impulsively, based on your emotions.

- Lack discipline in saving money.

- Tend to live "paycheck to paycheck".

- Seek validation from external sources like designer clothes and luxury cars.

- Lack confidence in your money management skills.

You don't think twice about buying whatever you want. The words "savings", "budget", and "investments" are just not in your vocabulary. Spending money makes you feel good, especially when you are depressed or frustrated. It's a reward you feel you are entitled to. As quickly as you make money you spend it—short-term pleasure, no long-term accumulation of capital. Managing money by creating and maintaining a budget is a challenge, so you live paycheck to paycheck. You shop at Nordstrom's with a J.C. Penney income. You may be at the top in your career and income, but because of your spending habits and lack of investments you don't have the assets to prove your worth. Instead, you buy products reflecting your desired social status—expensive clothes and cars. Your co-workers, family and friends think you're doing well. Only you know you're not. What's missing are the internal building blocks that support and encourage you to achieve genuine financial success. But armed with the right money knowledge and skills, you can turn your wasteful behavior around. You need to master your emotions to master your money.

Money Spender's Action Plan:

1. Track your spending for the next four weeks. (Worksheets are available in chapter 18). Knowing where your dollars are going every month is a sound and successful money management strategy and may even inspire you to control your impulse spending.

2. Set goals and create a realistic time-line. When you aren't clear on what you want to do with your money, it slips right through your fingers. Later on we will show you step by step how to set goals and to develop a realistic plan to achieve them.

3. Learn how to play the money game. Financial education is the key. Attend financial seminars. If time permits, enroll in an adult education class. Read money books, magazines, and newspapers. Go on the Internet; It's full of financial information. (See the top financial websites in the Appendix). Money management is nowhere near as complicated as you may think.

4. Step out of your money comfort box. You will not feel comfortable about money until you begin working with it—not just earning it but saving and investing it too. Work on your fear of money by opening a basic savings account at your local bank or credit union. Once the balance is $500-$1,000, consider moving part of it to a mutual fund. Check out **www.morningstar.com** for a listing of the top mutual funds and they're past returns.

5. Get financial help from an expert. Just because you're a spender now doesn't mean you have to be one forever. Everybody can change negative spending habits as long as they have a big enough reason to do it. This is where your financial goals come into play. If you aren't sure how to set financial goals and create a

Please return the items by the
due date(s) listed below, to
any Memphis Public Library
location.   For renewals:
Automated line: 452-2047
Randolph Branch: 415-2779
Online: www.memphislibrary.org

Date due: 9/29/2022,23:59
Item ID: 0115232188348
Title: What's money got to do with it? : the ult
imate gu
Author: Broussard, Cheryl D.

By using the Memphis Public Libraries, you saved
: $27.95

NO RENEWALS FOR:
Audio-visual materials.

strategy, a financial advisor can assist you. How do you find one? Talk to money savvy friends and relatives and ask for a referral.

6.   Don't allow yourself to fritter your money away. Make your new objective to save and invest your money to build real, long-term wealth.

If you are a Binger Money Equals Pain and Pleasure. You:

- Save and save, and then have a spending attack.

- You'll either blow the money all at once on an expensive item you didn't plan to

- Buy something because it's a bargain whether you need it or not.

You combine two money styles. You're both a Money Spender and a Money Chaser. You'll diligently save for a rainy day but at the first sign of an emotional problem spend it all on a shopping binge. Your erratic save-spend pattern leads you into serious debt. You also suffer from the "It Was on Sale!" syndrome. You'll buy a marked-down ski jacket in July. Trouble is you *don't* ski.

Money Binger Action Plan:

Follow the six steps in the Money Spender's action plan as well as the following:

1.   If you sense a spending attack coming on, immediately pull out your journal and write down what you are feeling emotionally. Ask yourself, "Why do I need to spend this money?" Write out a list of five to 10 reasons. Next, ask yourself, "How will NOT spending this money improve my life?" Again, write out a list of

five to 10 reasons. This process is a way of talking yourself out of spending your money and talking yourself into saving and investing it.

2. As with any type of addiction, changing your habits takes time. If you find you aren't able to go cold turkey on a "shop attack", go ahead and shop, but just be conscious of what you are spending your money on. Instead of going to a discount outlet mall, go to a bookstore instead. You'll only be able to carry so many books to the register and at least you are buying something you can learn from.

To a Money Chaser Money Equals Self-Worth. You:

*   Like to talk about how much money you have.

*   Think that all that money makes you important.

*   Believe that showering money on your partner shows how much you love them.

*   Are comfortable, perhaps too comfortable, with taking risks.

Your reason for living is to pile up vast sums of money. You look for investments that have a high rate of return and you equate your self-worth or personal power with those large sums of cash. Lack of money leads to feelings of inadequacy, failure, or in severe cases, depression. You have difficulty giving up control of your money so find financial advice from others unacceptable. Or, if you do have an advisor and are also have a worrier co-style you may constantly bug your advisor to put your money into long-shot investments with high risk-return potential. You may work like a demon, driven tirelessly by the need to fatten your bank account. An overtime, moonlighting, no-time-for-family kind of person, you may think there is no problem in your relationship that can't be solved by a liberal application of dollars. You don't hide the fact that you equate money with happiness, freedom, achievement and personal power. In addition, you are good at making it. But however confident you are in your financial abilities, whether real or imagined, you are probably challenged in other aspects of personal life including long-term relationships or marriage.

Money Chaser's Action Plan

1. Try to think less each day about making money. See if you can work up from one less hour a week to one less day per month. You might explore a new hobby (other than the dollar bill) that you can put your energies into, like painting or music. Imagine that your "money ship" is on cruise control and you needn't make a course correction for one full hour, day, or week. Realize that you are managing your money well enough to take a brief "money vacation".

2. If you're brave enough, have your partner role-play with you regarding your money obsession. See how he or she perceives your preoccupation with accumulating cash. Have some fun with it as they show you another side of your relationship with money — and them.

3. Take action on a goal that doesn't involve a great deal of money. Realize that a balanced life is important and that the time away from thinking about money makes you sharper when you return your focus to it.

Cheryl—The Money Chaser

As I mentioned earlier, this is the category I fall more into. Although today I'm not as obsessed about money and prefer more balance in my life. Being a money chaser definitely has had its benefits.

I have achieved many of my short and long term goals of owning my own home, starting and running a business and building an investment portfolio.

Now that I understand the need for more balance, I've included more noncash and nonmaterial goals. Basically, I have overhauled my priorities.

To a Money Worrier Money Equals Anxiety. You:

- Lose sleep over money.

- Are dogged by a nagging sense of impending financial doom.

- Are very pessimistic about money in their life.

- Would probably be right at home in the Great Depression era.

You are always thinking, "How can I lose less money?" Your obsession with money rivals the Chaser but for very different reasons. You are overly pessimistic about money, probably to the point that if you had more, you would only worry more. Even with a decent income, you believe you are "one paycheck away from being homeless". By your very nature, you are controlled by money and are helpless to defend yourself against the negative financial forces you fear. "Murphy's Law" may be the guiding principle in financial matters for you, as in "Whatever bad can happen, will happen." Unlike the Chaser, you avoid talking about money because it upsets your nerves.

Money Worrier Action Plan

1. If you are a spiritual individual, adopt the "Let go and let God" affirmation. Say to yourself, "Okay, I've done all I can up to this point and I'm not going to give it any more energy because I know things ARE going to be all right."

2. Find a close friend who knows you very well. Have them act out your worrying about money for 10 minutes in a kind of soap opera parody. Money Worriers suffer from a serious case of taking things too seriously.

3. Declare a "Worry Free Money Zone" in your household. Anyone moving into that zone is prohibited from bringing a worrisome attitude about money with them.

4. Try to figure out when you worry most about money. Answer the question "has my worrying changed the situation any?" Go back to your money beliefs in Chapter 3 and find out when you started down the Money Worry path. Then take a different direction down a no-worry path. Just like "Talking don't cook no rice", worrying does not change your money situation. However, if you must worry about your money, schedule a daily worry time, but begin to shorten it each day.

Michael—The Money Worrier

I used to worry that my salary wasn't at the level it should have been compared to what my professional friends were making. More recently I have worried that my client base would dry up leaving me no means to support myself or pay off the considerable debt I accrued from the dot com start-up.

I finally got to the point that I felt all this worrying was affecting my health. I focus more on the positive aspects of my situation and the fact that, compared to a lot of people in this world, I'm actually pretty blessed. Bring it on!

To Money Risk Takers Money Equals Adrenaline. You:

- Enjoy the thrill of taking risks with your money.

- Think you "know it all" on how to manage and invest your money.

- Are easily frustrated with basic savings and investment accounts.

- Invest in stock options (puts and calls), hedge funds and futures.

You are like a Chaser in your financial aggressiveness. However, you lack the financial acumen or determination of the Chaser and probably have a higher assessment of your skills than actually exists. You see diversification in investing as needless running around, and planning as excess paperwork. Whereas a Chaser wants to accumulate money and may take great risks to do so, your goal is taking risks with your money and the adrenaline rush that results. You may actually be surprised or even severely depressed if your investment doesn't pay off. You don't have time for slow growth CD's or mutual funds.

Money Risk Taker Action Plan

1. Set priorities. Financial success requires clear goals and a strategy to achieve them. Establish a commitment of financial excellence and continually evaluate your progress against your commitment.

2. Question your risk-taking. If you are going to gamble, understand the rules of the game. Realize that you may not always win. Learn to take educated, calculated risks.

3. Set limits. Get real about your money. Know where you stand financially and don't risk more than you can lose.

4. Reevaluate your drive for the adrenaline rush. What belief do you have about money that it is fulfilling? Find another safe and legal outlet to fulfill this desire. Take up hang-gliding or bungie jumping. Better still, volunteer at the Boys and Girls Club and get a thrill from helping disadvantaged youngsters.

5. Remove emotion from your money dealings. Taking extraordinary risks out of fear, hurt or anger damages you financially.

To a Money Risk Avoider Money Equals Pain. You:

- Have little desire to be highly involved in your money management.

- Do not need money to increase your self-esteem or self-worth.

- Are usually content with your money situation.

- Think investing in stocks and mutual funds is crazy.

In the old story, if the Risk Taker were the hare racing ahead, the Risk Avoider would be the tortoise, plodding along. Both styles may be low on financial savvy, however, which could generally end them up in the same place. And while as a Risk Avoider you might not stash your holdings under your mattress, your idea of a thrill ride is a low-risk municipal bond or CD. You'd rather be safe than sorry and can't imagine yourself investing in the stock market. You may be happiest when you are planning for financial security sometime in the distant future.

Money Risk Avoider Action Plan

1. Join an investment club. Investing $25 to $50 a month with a group of people is a lot less risky than investing on your own. It's also a great way to learn how to play the stock market game.

2. Invest in a 401(K) or tax-deferred plan with your company. If you already have a 401(K) or tax-deferred plan, invest a minimum of 25 percent in your 401(K)'s higher growth stock mutual fund options.

3. Go online, if available, and use our resource list of online brokerage firms to buy 10 shares of a stock in your company or a company whose products you are familiar with or use around the house.

4. In your Money Journal, write out these affirmations several times:

    -   It is okay to take some risks with my money.
    -   I deserve to have a much higher return on my money.
    -   If my money doesn't work hard for me, I will continue to have to work hard for my money.

To the Money Procrastinator Money Equals Fear. You:

-   Are afraid of money.

-   Put off balancing your checkbook and paying your bills.

- Are passive when it comes to money management, hoping your money will just "take care of itself".

- Lack confidence in your money management skills

While the Money Worrier fears that some financial catastrophe will pop up and bite her in the butt, you, the money-phobic Procrastinator, simply fear money itself. You hope the financial necessities of life will just take care of themselves. You tend toward last minute bill paying or income tax filing, fearing you lack the appropriate skills to take care of those chores. If you are an Extreme Money Procrastinator, you may develop feelings of anxiety or panic when tackling financial matters.

Money Procrastinator Action Plan

1. Take one bill you are constantly late on and pay it as soon as it arrives. Feel good that it is now paid and you no longer need to think about it.

2. Develop a spending plan and commit to sticking to it for at least three months.

3. Dedicate two hours, one day a week as your money time. During this time you'll balance your checkbook, pay bills that are due, and review your spending plan. The more you perform these activities, the more they become natural money management habits.

4. Go back to Chapter 3 and recheck your money beliefs. Look specifically for the reasons why money causes you so much fear and pain. Acknowledging your fears is the first step toward controlling them. Also, keep in mind that it's okay to feel fear. Fear can teach you a lot about yourself.

So You've Discovered Your Style. So What?

Now that you've pinpointed your money style, here's something else to consider. In relationships, just as differing personalities often attract each other, so do differing money styles. While relationships generally work better when the two partners are more similar than different, mix-and-match money styles don't have to spell doom.

In the most common combination, a Spender is attracted to a Chaser and vice versa. What generally happens in this case is that the two partners eventually balance themselves out as one takes on the money style of the other. While the Spender/Chaser relationship is the most typical merger of money styles, it isn't the only one. Another favorite is the Risk Taker and the Risk Avoider. In this relationship, one partner who likes to gamble, maybe in the stock market or on real estate, teams up with one who wants complete financial security. Putting most of the money in the bank in a low-interest-earning passbook savings account suits them just fine. In another popular combo, a Money Worrier pairs up with a Money Avoider. The Worrier is forever fretting about not having enough money while the Avoider doesn't even want to talk about it.

Of course, any time people with similar money styles join forces, they've given themselves a head start toward success. If two Chasers get together, for example, one may become less obsessed with earning money knowing that the other is watching his or her back. If two Spenders commit to each other, one may become more of a tightwad in reaction to the other's excessive spending.

How Do We Match Up?

With Michael being the Money Worrier and I (Cheryl) the Money Chaser (according to the chart) we are actually good money mates. While I (Cheryl) am busy chasing and making money, Michael would be taking great care of it. While it may sound like a money match made in heaven that definitely isn't the case. We wish it were that easy. But as you know in any relationship there are always other factors to consider and that's why we want you to look at individual money styles as only one of several components to look at when considering a partner.

The differences in our money styles are challenging in our relationship because of one reason—the male ego. In fact, it's very rare that any man will sit back and allow their woman to make all the money. It just isn't written in the male psyche. (We talk more about this in chapter 13, When She Earns More). If it were the other way around—the female as the worrier and the male as the chaser, it may work very well since he would have the most money which also means he would have the most power. So to keep the peace in our case we both play an active role in making and managing money.

Who Could Be Your Money Soul-Mate?

Find your ideal money style match on the Money Compatibility Partner Chart 5-1. Don't worry if you're already in a relationship with someone we recommend you avoid. These are only guidelines. Communication is the key to making money work in your present relationship, regardless of your differing money styles. A partnership will work with any two money styles as long as you both talk about it and agree on what you both want to accomplish financially.

	Chaser	Procrastinator	Worrier	Risk Avoider	Risk Taker	Hoarder	Spender	Binger
Chaser	Creates competition, no relationship	One-sided, Procrastinator would turn over money responsibility to chaser	The more money made the more the worry	Conflict, but can learn from each other ②	Can work	Chaser would help maximize money, Hoarder would help keep it ①	Major conflict ③	Chaser would see Binger as financially irresponsible, won't work
Procrastinator	① Will work if Chaser involved with money	Someone will need to take control or you are both in trouble ③	Might force Worrier to become Hoarder	Will not help each other financially, stay stagnant	May lead to more financial trouble	Stable match but no money ②	No budgeting, ①	Is that a light at the end of the tunnel or an oncoming train?
Worrier	Will manage the money①	Someone will become a Hoarder	Invest in antacids, both will need them	Stable but no wealth	Depends who is in control of money; (W) maybe, (RT) no	Stable but no wealth generation ②	Increased worrying for the Worrier ③	Too much worry and not enough money ③
Risk Avoider	Possible initial conflict, but each can learn from the other ①	Financially stagnant	Money will be safe but not growing and working for them	No way, at retirement you both will regret it	Force Risk Taker to think more carefully about $$ decisions; good communication = good match ②	Stable but no wealth generation	Fall prey to cost of living increases, no investments, no money	Little savings and no investments ③
Risk Taker	Both want to make money, Chaser will not allow Risk Taker to make foolish investments	Be careful. The Risk Taker may be irresponsible and worsen fear of money mgmt	Might think Worrier is holding them back from making money, could be good	Force Risk Taker to think more carefully about $$ decisions; good communication = good match ②	A wild ride into financial ruin ③	Opposites, Risk Taker help Hoarder loosen up, Hoarder may be more financially savvy ②	No financial controls, no checks and balances	May make risk taker slow down risky activities
Hoarder	Hoarder helps keep money, Chaser helps money grow①	Can you live on love alone? There might not be much money	Stable but no money①	Possible financial security issues, not much money to work with	If Hoarder can teach Risk Taker to save money	Plenty of money hidden in the mattress, but no fun	Might help Hoarder to live a little ①	Help Binger with spending attacks
Spender	Spender will spend all the money a Chaser makes②	A sinking ship, no money, no bill paying, no financial controls③	Lots of arguments over control of money, short-term relationship	One day you'll wake up and find you have no money, plan on working 3 jobs	Out of control, flashy lifestyle, and eventually the poor house ③	Hoarder helps Spender with budgeting and curtailing of spending ①	Polarize or financially die	½ the time you'll be okay, the other ½ watch out!
Binger	Will work as long as there are separate accounts ①	Nope, Binger needs someone with financial control, procrastinator has no backbone①	Binger would cause worrier to go over the edge①	Money will not "work" for them, no investments, maybe no savings	Not a good role model for Binger	Will have money and make Binger aware of binge/purge, but no wealth ②	½ The time you'll be okay, the other ½ watch out!	It will work if both aren't having a spending attack at the same time

1 = Best
2 = Might Work
3 = Avoid

Chart 5-1: Money Compatible Partner Chart

Chapter 5: Making Love and Money Work Action Steps

1. Read through the list of money styles and determine which style or styles describe you.

2. Determine your partner's as well. Compare your money styles on the money compatibility chart and see if you're relationship is a 1, 2 or 3. Remember these are only guidelines. Don't take the chart too seriously!

Notes

Chapter 6

Fighting Over Money...
What's That All About?

Jill's husband, Herman, was called into his bank to discuss his accounts. "Your finances are in terrible shape," the banker stated. "Your loan is overdue." "Yes, I know," said Herman. "It's my wife Jill; she's out of control." "Why do you allow your wife to spend more money than you have?" asked the banker. "Frankly", replied Herman with a deep sign, "because I'd rather argue with you than with her."

Source: the Internet

Demystifying Money Fights

For most couples, the question isn't "Have you ever fought about money?" Rather, it's "When was the last time?" A month ago? Last week? This morning? Maybe it was a disagreement over something simple: You forgot to write down the last three ATM withdrawals and as a result he bounced a check. Or maybe he splurged on a new DVD player that you considered outrageously expensive.

We already know that money causes the most contention in a relationship. Sex comes in second. Even more surprising, the amount of income earned by the partners doesn't matter as much as how that income is managed and spent. Couples fight whether they jointly make $50,000 or $500,000. Why? One reason is that money management has become more complicated. We have do-it-yourself 401(K)'s, umpteen versions of the IRA and thousands of investment choices. More options mean more decisions, which means increased potential for disagreements.

We've also seen that arguments about money also boil down to issues of control, values, meanings and beliefs. When the fight is over power and control, each partner wants to decide where the money will go. When it's about values, it's related to their different money histories and styles. When it's about meanings, it's usually related to gender differences. When it's about beliefs, one partner may believe if they don't save...save...save, they won't be able to make it through the coming rainy day, while the other may believe the exact opposite, that they better live for today, since tomorrow is not promised.

What's The Underlying or Hidden Agenda?

That's why the real fights about money are not about the almighty dollar. They go much deeper. Author and relationship therapist Dr. Ronn Elmore agrees with us that feelings around money include power, control, security, fear, doubt, independence, and levels of commitment. We call these Hidden Agendas. Why? Because hidden agendas are beliefs. And if we hold a certain belief we will find additional information to support that belief. For example, if a man believes his partner is financially incompetent or untrustworthy with money, he'll interpret many of her small mistakes as proof of mismanagement.

She: "I forgot to record that ATM withdrawal."

He: "See, I knew you couldn't handle your money."

If these hidden agendas are left unspoken, they build hurt and frustration. Partners end up arguing over small mistakes or things that really don't matter.

What's Behind the Hidden Agendas

There are three main issues associated with hidden agendas:

1. **TRUST.** Does my partner trust me? Love me? Care about me?

2. **INTIMACY.** Is my partner inter-
    ested in me? My thoughts? Feelings?
    Dreams and goals? Does he or she
    value my opinions? Is he or she open
    and willing to listen to my ideas?

> *All married couples should learn the
> art of battle as they learn the art of
> making love. Good battle is objective
> and honest — never vicious or cruel.
> Good battle is healthy and construc-
> tive, and brings to a marriage the
> principle of equal partnerships.*
>
> —— Ann Landers

3. **SELF-WORTH.** Where do I fit in
    this relationship? As an equal? One
    step below? Does what I want matter? Am I included in the important deci-
    sion-making?

These three issues reflect the basic needs in life: the need for love, self-esteem
and control over one's life. Being respectful of each partner's hidden agendas will
lessen the heated debates over money.

The Financial Battleground

At the end of Chapter Five, we discussed eight common money style attractions.
While any combination can cause problems, there are three incompatible money styles
in particular we want to point out here that can lead a relationship into a financial
battleground. They are:

1. The Spender and the Hoarder.

2. The Money Chaser and the Money Chaser.

3. The Procrastinator and the Hoarder

Money Styles Conflict 1: A Spender Teams Up With A Hoarder

This is the opposite money style attraction most likely to lead to conflict in a relationship. It's common for a partner who rarely spends a dollar on themselves to team up with someone who has no trouble buying lavish, expensive gifts. The trouble is that the same characteristics that draw you to your partner can later pit you against them.

Spenders, who usually haven't a care in the world about money, are okay with having a mere $10 in the bank, while their Hoarder partner can't sleep at night without a $10,000 balance. The more the Spender splurges on clothes and luxury items, the more anxious the Hoarder becomes. Soon the financial sniping begins.

Achieving Financial Stability and Equilibrium

If you're in this particular relationship, don't despair: there is a way to achieve some stability. First, establish joint checking and savings accounts to cover household expenses and shared goals like retirement and investments. Second, set up separate checking accounts for money that can be spent, no questions asked. Each partner can decide how much goes into their separate account, based on what their individual income allows. What matters most is that joint short and long-term goals are being taken care of first. The Spender needs to continue to keep those shared goals in mind when they are out spending. The existence of those goals should curtail some of the impulse spending.

If you're in a Spender-Hoarder relationship, you can strengthen your financial stability even further by using software programs such as MS Money or Quicken to make your savings goals more concrete. The programs will allow you to set up a plan for meeting a short-term goal, such as paying off all your credit card debts, or a long-term goal like saving $25,000 for a down payment on a new home.

Trade Places

Another way for you to really understand your partner's money style is to trade money styles for a month. Hoarders should go on a onetime shopping spree and Spenders should take over the bill paying and investment management. After the month is over, talk about how it felt to trade places. This will help each of you to be better in tune with your own attitudes toward money. You each will probably see the benefit of having two different money styles.

Money Styles Conflict 2: The Money Chaser and the Money Chaser

That's right: Two of a kind. The money relationship between two Money Chasers can turn into a royal battle over power, competition and control, especially if one partner is bringing in slightly more than the other. If it's the man with the bigger paycheck, he feels he should have more to say about money in the relationship. This sets up the power struggle because although the woman is contributing with her substantial income, she still feels less valued. This power struggle tends to be less of a problem when the woman earns the slightly higher income. (See Chapter 13, When She Earns More.)

The other challenge is that two Money Chasers don't have time for a relationship. They are both working 24/7 to earn more than enough money to put in all of their various accounts. Neither is at home nurturing the relationship.

Finding Common Ground

Someone will need to step back from the effort to make money in this relationship to make it work. An easy way is to take turns. One year one partner will be responsible for making the bulk of the money and the next year it's the other partner's turn. The partner who is taking the year off will still work and contribute to the household finances, just not to the same extent. Instead of putting in overtime hours they'll work a normal 9-5. It will be this partner's responsibility to support the other's efforts and to concentrate on reestablishing balance and connection in the relationship. For example, the partner "on sabbatical" could plan a vacation for the two of them, then help the fellow Chaser carve out the time off to go. A dinner date, a Sunday afternoon hike, a visit with family or friends: these kinds of simple activities will help both Chasers remember what the really important things in life are.

Money Style Conflict 3: The Procrastinator and the Hoarder

In this relationship, one partner color-codes and sorts the monthly bills neatly in a file cabinet, while the other tosses them into a shoebox. Maintaining joint accounts usually adds to the problem—especially when keeping track of check writing and ATM withdrawals. Procrastinators do everything in their power to avoid dealing with money. Paying their bills on time and balancing their checkbooks is like having a tooth removed without novocaine. Meanwhile, the Hoarder goes nuts if a checkbook reconciliation is off by a penny. What usually happens in this relationship is that to avoid conflict, the Hoarder takes on all the financial responsibilities. Unfortunately, this tends to lead to resentment by the partner who is doing all the work.

Making It Work

If you are a hoarder don't think that you're the only one who can pay the bills or that your partner can't handle it. Try sharing financial duties for one quarter or one half of the year. If one partner pays the bills, the other should do the record keeping. This method allows both partners to understand where the money is going.

Using a computer is the other way to go. By automating bill paying, the cable, mortgage, and car loans are paid directly out of your checking account every month. This allows both partners to keep accurate tabs on where they stand financially. Either partner can check to see which checks have cleared and what the balance is. If your bank doesn't offer online services, we have included in the appendix, resources to locate a bank that does.

Whatever Your Money Style

While the three style combinations just listed usually cause the most problems in relationships, don't think that if you're in a different mix you're out of the woods. Regardless of your styles, there are going to be conflicts about money in your relationship. What really matters is how well you communicate to resolve them. You can start by kicking to the curb the "talking about money is taboo" belief. For most of us, talking about money is more forbidden than talking about sex. There are partners today that don't know what each other makes. The reason: they either feel ashamed they don't make as much as they think they should or guilty for making too much. These are extremely damaging beliefs that will definitely block making money work in your relationship. The question you both must ask is, "Do we want to bask in financial bliss or sing the financial blues?"

The best way to avoid singing the financial blues is to talk about money openly. When you do that, you're saying you don't want money to be a struggle. You're also demonstrating how you both value and respect each other. Will talking about money be easy? Absolutely not! Can two people in an intimate relationship talk about money in an effective and nonthreatening way? Absolutely! In the next chapter you will learn how, when and what to say about money to your partner. We go one step further and provide specific advice on when women should not talk to their men about money. This information alone is worth the price of the book. By the end of the chapter you'll know the specific communication techniques to create *Ujamma (cooperative economics—4th Principle of Kwanzaa) i*n your relationship.

Notes

Chapter 7

Viva La Difference — Communication Styles Of Men And Women

Women's English Lesson

Yes=No

No=Yes

Maybe=No

We need=I want

I'm sorry=You'll be sorry

We need to talk=I need to complain

Sure, go ahead=I don't want you to

Do what you want=You'll pay for this later

I'm not upset=Of course I'm upset

You have to learn to communicate=Just agree with me

Source: Internet

While the quote on the previous page is comical, there is some truth in it. No doubt about it, men and women do communicate differently. That's why it's impossible to discuss communicating about money in a relationship without first delving into why and how men and women are different in the first place. And only by understanding the differ-

> *Relationships sometimes fail when a man can't understand why his woman isn't more like a man, and a woman expects her man to act the same way she does. Under pressure, men drink alcohol and invade other countries; women eat chocolate and go shopping..*

ences between men and women can we start building on our collective strengths rather than our individual weaknesses.

Relationships sometimes fail when a man can't understand why his woman isn't more like a man, and a woman expects her man to act the same way she does. Under pressure, men drink alcohol and invade other countries; women eat chocolate and go shopping.

The sexes simply process information differently, think differently, believe different things, and have different perceptions, priorities, and behavior. No wonder we communicate differently! Women, you know how a man will not stop and ask for directions when he is lost while driving. He considers such a move a sign of weakness. Well, he does the same thing with his money.

Why is this? In prehistoric times, a man's success was measured by his ability to make a kill and bring it home. His self-worth was measured by his woman's appreciation for his struggle and effort. His duties were to get food, be a protector, and procreate —nothing else. He wasn't expected to change the diapers or put out the garbage.

His woman had her defining role as well. She was the child bearer. She was also responsible for caring for the children, cleaning the cave, and gathering edible plants, fruits and nuts. No need for her to worry about the major food supply or fight the enemy. She measured her self-worth by how well she did her domestic duties. And she was happy when her partner appreciated her nurturing and homemaking skills.

> *A great relationship is not when the "Perfect" couple comes together. It is when an imperfect couple learns to enjoy their differences.*
>
> —— Dave Meurer

That's when life was simple. Each partner clearly understood the other's purpose. They didn't get caught up in relationship issues. They were too concerned about surviving in an environment that included all kinds of dangers, including being attacked by wild animals or incurable diseases. These patterns still exist among some isolated peoples around the world.

Compare those cultures to American society and you will find the rules are quite different. In fact, the rules have been thrown out. In their place we find a lot of confused and unhappy relationships and a 50 percent divorce rate among those bold enough to attempt marriage.

In mainstream America, gone are the days when a family was solely dependent on the man to survive. Nor are women expected to stay at home and spend all their time taking care of the kids – when there are kids. Today, gender roles are changing dramatically. In many relationships, both genders are demanding love, passion, and personal fulfillment. They can concentrate on these emotional luxuries because being eaten alive is no longer a threat. At least not by wild animals, although there are plenty of man-made beasts out there one needs to be aware of.

All of this is to say that our history and genetics are what have conspired to make men and women different. These differences impact how we communicate with each other on all subject matters. If we don't take these differences into consideration, we will have a very frustrating relationship. When the differences are understood, we will be able to handle them – and even celebrate them.

Men Aren't Into Talking!

When it comes to communicating, men are not great conversationalists when compared to women. Men evolved from hunters not talkers. Have you noticed how men aren't able to watch television and talk at the same time? They need to focus on

What a woman Says...   What a man hears...

one activity at a time. Women are the exact opposite; they can talk on the phone, feed the baby, and type on the computer all at the same time.

In a relationship, partners need to discuss the different ways they work through problems. Let's take a mythical couple: Rob and Robin. When Robin has a problem she needs to talk about it. She doesn't expect Rob to respond with solutions. She just wants him to listen. Conversely, when Rob has a problem he talks silently to himself.

The fact that he doesn't talk to Robin doesn't mean there's something wrong with their relationship.

When To Talk Money

Most couples know they need to talk about money. But money can be uncomfortable to discuss. The best way to approach it is to start talking about it in the beginning of the relationship. After the third or fourth date is a good time. By then most couples are more relaxed and more willing to discuss important topics. This is also the time when a person's true financial colors begin to emerge. A partner with a "take-charge attitude" who demands to pay for everything or flashes money around may also try to take charge of everything else in the relationship. The nonverbal cues are important to look out for too! For example, if he or she spends money haphazardly and yet lives paycheck to paycheck, they may have a problem with money management.

In the dating stages of a relationship, couples always put on their best behavior. In many cases a man will wine and dine and buy lavish gifts for the first few dates to reel the woman in. (Remember, men are hunters; They love the thrill of the chase). Once she's caught, there goes the special treatment. Not always,

but often enough. A woman may find that her mate actually dislikes spending money and only spent to impress her. Unfortunately, by the time the woman finds out the real deal, she's deeply entrenched in the relationship. The way to avoid this financial heartache is to immediately start talking about money *histories, values, beliefs and styles* if it looks like the relationship will last more than three or four months.

If you are already married or in a permanent relationship, our advice is the same. Start talking about money today and continue by scheduling a money talk date every month. Set up a specific time and a private place that both partners agree on where you can discuss money matters comfortably and without interruption. Don't do it late at night when you both are exhausted from working all day. Don't do it at a dinner party in front of friends. Don't try to cover all your money issues on every money talk date; it may be too overwhelming. Select one specific topic to cover in depth. For example, if paying off credit card debt is a priority, focus solely on that issue. Map out a detailed step-by-step strategy to pay them off in 12 to 14 months and write the plan down in your money journal. Now you have created a system for both partners to follow. In Chapter 18 we provide more tips on having a money talk.

Be honest, truthful, and sensitive toward each other when talking about money. Anything either of you say that makes your partner feel bad will damage the talk because it will communicate an unintended thought and trigger a defensive and retaliatory posture. This is the time you want to share your opinion openly and ask for what you want. If a specific action needs to be taken, both must agree on it. Once the money talk has begun, neither partner should interrupt, leave the room, or make disparaging remarks or faces. No personal or verbal attacks. This isn't the time to play the blame game. And focus only on the money issue not on your partner. Don't bring up other relationship issues during this time either. This talk is reserved for money only.

Making money work for both of you starts when you share financial information equally. You must also bring your fears and insecurities into the open. It is at this time that you learn more about each other and put money into its proper perspective. Money loses some of its destructive power when you both become less reactionary and more communicative about what money means. This will help alleviate money conflicts and help bring you closer.

What Exactly to Say

When you two have your money talk, lay everything out on the table. Really explore what money means to each of you. Talk about the beliefs you identified in Chapter 3. Are there certain stereotypes you each have internalized? Women are financially incompetent. Men are money-hungry. Does one partner feel he or she needs to compete with the other for money and power? Why? What past issues regarding money does this bring up? This discussion is healthy for the relationship and brings you much closer together financially as well as emotionally.

The whole idea behind making love and money work is to develop a financial team within the relationship. Here are the money questions you both must discuss and answer in the beginning stages as well as throughout the relationship when additional financial challenges come up:

- How much did each of you earn last year? This year?
- What are you personal assets? What are your personal debts?
- Do you want to open joint checking, savings, and investment accounts? Or do you want separate accounts?

- Will you split joint debts evenly?
- Do you want joint credit card accounts? If yes, will you both be responsible for payment and will you pay the entire balance off in 30 days or less?
- What savings and investment methods will you use for large purchases—home, car, vacation, and retirement?
- What are your individual financial goals?

- If the relationship ends through separation, divorce or death, how will each of your assets and debts be divided?
- Who will be responsible for money matters on a day-to-day basis?
- What do you want to achieve financially in the next five years? In this lifetime?
- Are there any past or present credit problems?

These questions are only a beginning of the many more you will discuss throughout your relationship. As you can see, you are really getting everything out in the open; even if it is financially negative. Hiding negative money secrets within your relationship will not work because they <u>will</u> come back to haunt you. Your objective is to create a financial team within your relationship. Answering these questions will help you make money decisions that will keep you two in sync.

For Women Only: How to Talk About Money With Your Man

Men tend to use short, structured sentences when they speak. They usually have an opening, a point, and a conclusion. It's generally easy to follow what they mean or want. If you begin speaking about several different subject areas with a man, he will probably get lost. So when talking to your partner about money, don't talk about credit cards, investments and retirement planning all at the same time. Focus on one area, conclude the conversation and move on to the next subject area. To be convincing or persuasive with your partner, present only one clear thought or idea at a time. Adopt the motto, "Keep it simple".

Interrupting your partner is something else you don't want to do. When men interrupt each other, it is because they are beginning to feel competitive or aggressive. Because men are problem solvers, their sentences are solution oriented. In order for him to get his solution across you must allow him to complete his sentence.

You've heard this before, "men aren't mind readers". That's true. But they are direct. Women, you have to say exactly what you mean. Tell your man specifically what you want in your relationship and with your money. And if you really want him to listen, tell him way in advance you want to talk and provide an outline of exactly what you want to discuss.

When Not *To Talk to Your Man About Money*

If your partner is having trouble at work, hold off talking to him about any money challenges. Bringing up the subject will probably only make things worse. A stressed out man tends to clam up and stop talking. The reason: he is focusing all his energy on trying to solve his problem. Unlike you, he doesn't always want to tell what's going on in his life. He would rather read the newspaper or surf the Internet while coming up with his own solutions. This is the major reason why men so often refuse professional counseling. As with directions when they're out driving, they consider asking for help a sign of weakness.

When you give your man the space and the time to deal with his challenges his way, he will love you for it. And once he has figured out what he needs to do to solve his problem, he'll return to normal and respect you even more. So, if your partner is in a deep funk, say, "I can see that you are concerned about your situation at work. Let me know when and if you want to talk about it. I'm here to listen." Then leave him alone.

If he comes home from work, grunts out a few words and plops down in front of the TV with remote control glued to hand, head in the other direction. In fact, call you girlfriend and get out of the house. If you return and he is still there looking like a rerun from the Twilight Zone, kiss him on the cheek and go about your business. This behavior may go on for several days. That's okay. It just means he hasn't solved the problem yet. Once it is solved, he'll return to his happy self again.

Here are other times to be a silent money partner:

- As soon as he walks in the door. Bad timing. Men need transition time before reaching talk mode. Allow him to shower, change clothes, relax a little. If you bring up money troubles before then, he'll probably ignore you or respond in a crabby way.

- When he's watching "the game". Don't waste your words; they'll only fall on deaf ears.

- On your way to a party. Pre-party money talk means trouble. If you're only halfway through the argument by the time you arrive, it will carry over into the festivities. Add drinking to the mix and before the night is over you will end up having a knock-down-drag-out fight.

- When he just screwed up big time. Never bring up the subject of money when he is feeling embarrassed or inadequate. He will not be thinking rationally just then and may say something that he really doesn't mean.

Rusty's remote confirms the suspicions of most women in America on the close relationship between men and their remote controllers...

Yeah baby, touch me like that again,
Oooooo, you know you like it,
Yeah, you turn me ON/OFF,
Yessss!
Say my name, say my name,
Oooo, I love it when you MUTE me !!

What A Man May Do When Stressed Out Over Money

Now that you know men don't talk when they are dealing with a financial or any other challenge, let us share what they may do. Remember the famous sculpture by Rodin called The Thinker? It portrays a man sitting on a rock, chin-on-fist, thinking. That's what men do. They find a proverbial rock and just sit there all by themselves and think until they have figured out what they need to do. When he is on this "rock" he doesn't want to be disturbed, not even by his male friends. And especially not by his woman. If you do try to climb up there and help him you may be deeply hurt by his reactions or words, so stay off the rock.

Here are some modern day versions of the rock:

<u>Reading a Newspaper or Magazine.</u> Don't ever tell your partner anything that is important when he is involved in this activity. He probably won't remember a thing.

<u>Playing Golf or Tennis.</u> When playing sports, particularly tennis and golf, there is very little conversation going on. This allows him to focus on his challenge and to work out a solution. These activities speed up his problem solving process.

<u>Watching Television and Surfing the Channels.</u> Many women find it extremely irritating when their partner sits staring at the TV, remote in hand, flipping through the channels. What's up with that? The TV allows him to forget about his money, career, and personal problems. Surfing the channels is a clear signal he's on his rock—stay away!

<u>Playing Video games</u>. A mindless yet challenging activity, especially the war games. The games provide fantasy solution-solving to work and life problems. *(Michael's favorite)*

When There Isn't Enough Money

It's hard enough for partners to talk to each other when there is a specific financial problem at hand. But what about when there is not enough money in the first place? And no matter how financially astute you and your partner are, in today's environment there is a high possibility you will experience a period of financial scarcity at some point in your relationship. Coping with the setback will not be easy, especially if it is severe (such as a disabling injury or major job loss). Coping over an extended period of time can be exhausting as well. But when you can count on each other for support and, just as important, communicate that support to one another, the tough times can be made more bearable.

If you're a man, don't be afraid to admit that you have a hard time asking for help, especially from your partner. You don't want to appear weak, or burden your loved one, so you try to deal with your challenges alone. While it's okay for you to do this for a short while — a couple of weeks or so — if it goes on for a long time she may begin to feel disconnected from you. Better you should go to her for sympathy and understanding as she would to you. If you and your partner allow it, working together to overcome a financial crisis can actually strengthen your relationship. Knowing that you survived the hard times increases your confidence in being able to cope with not only money challenges but other life challenges as well. This enables you and your partner to develop a strong bond that time cannot weaken.

Financial challenges help to make your life more meaningful (although it may not seem like it when you're going through them). They force you and your partner to look deeply inside your souls to assess what is <u>really</u> important. They force you to reprioritize your values. And you learn to appreciate the importance of your relationship.

What <u>Not</u> To Do When The Money Is Funny

When money isn't working it is very easy to play the "blame game". But in reality, neither one of you is more at fault for your money life than the other. When you don't play the blame game, it means that you both are sharing responsibilities equally for whatever money situation you are presently in. Forget about who ran up the VISA bill. The point is to come together on the issue to create a better money future; one based on mutual respect. You both will need to let go of what happened in the past. Let go of how each of you played a part in where you are financially today.

To avoid playing the money blame game:

- Don't allow money to interfere with your intimate relationships. Don't with-hold sex to punish your partner over disagreements about money.

- Don't use money to manipulate or control your partner. Never use earning power as a weapon in an argument.

- Don't demean each other because of low cash flow.

- Don't allow your self-esteem to deflate because of insufficient money.

- Don't max out on your credit cards to make yourself "feel better."

- Don't pressure each other to spend money on things you don't need.

- Do accept mutual responsibility for bills paid late.

- Do accept mutual responsibility for insufficient money to pay the bills.

- Do accept mutual responsibility for mismanaged checking accounts and bounced checks.

- Do accept mutual responsibility for insufficient money going toward a retirement account.

In a nutshell, anything dealing with money in the relationship is the responsibility of both partners, regardless of what money styles you each have. Until this concept is thoroughly understood, you will have difficulty grasping the other recommendations in this book.

What To Do When Your Money Is Funny

Number one, take a deep breath and relax. Work together to keep your spirits up. You don't want to be down and depressed at the same time. Realize that you can get through this just like millions of other people have. If you get irrational and panicky, you'll probably do something stupid and make matters worse. Whatever you do, don't borrow money from a paycheck advance loan company that charges an exorbitant 30 percent finance charge or that you have to pay back with your next paycheck, plus a huge service fee. Both are designed to get you into a financial hole and keep you there.

Here are some ways to eliminate money stress in your relationship:

- Rather than bringing up the money issue at the wrong time (See When *Not* to Talk about Money above) make an appointment with your partner for a scheduled, time-limited discussion. This gives your lover time to mentally and emotionally prepare.

- Depersonalize the topic. Say "the" money, not "my" or "your" money.

- Practice "working together" economics. If the money setback is due to a partner's sudden unemployment, it is a <u>family</u> problem.

- Make a special effort to be loving and affectionate to each other.

- Reset your family money goals so that buying "stuff" is less important.

- Prepare for the unexpected. Increase your savings with a "rainy day" plan to weather the next financial crisis

Though you don't want to play the blame game with your partner, you also don't want to hold back any feelings from him or her, either. Holding back feelings will only add to your stress. The key is to state how you feel without being critical or accusing of each other. Suppressed feelings add a ton of emotional distance between the two of you at a time when you need to be a closely working team.

Talk To Your Children

During any stressful times, children worry and absorb their parent's nervousness. Don't be afraid to share with them some (not necessarily all) of the financial challenges the family is facing. By holding back you may inadvertently damage how they will handle money later in their own adult lives. Instead, explain to them how they can help by making fewer requests for money, new clothes or new toys. Ask for their help and show your appreciation.

Cheryl: *Once when I experienced a lull in my income, I called a family meeting with my son, who was in grade school at the time. I explained the problem and the financial changes we needed to make to solve it. He understood perfectly and while he would sometimes forget and ask for things, gradually he stopped. I firmly believe he learned some valuable money lessons that he will carry over into his adult life.*

Once you and your partner have conquered the financial demons, take some time for the two of you to be alone together. Don't run out and plan a trip to Tahiti. Remember, no more financial debt. Your new focus is on wealth building. Instead, go to the beach, or a park or just relax together in the backyard. Sometimes the best things in life really are free. This is the time to make your relationship and your finances a priority. Also remember this: financial challenges don't make or break you. It's how you and your partner respond to the challenge that determines your success or failure.

We're In This Together

Let's review what we've learned in these first seven chapters. Money conflicts in your relationship began with you and your partner's money histories. They continued as your beliefs, values and styles clashed. Remember that before the relationship began, each of you made your financial decisions independently of the other. Each assumed your way was the best way.

The ideal money relationship evolves out of that history when you put your two methods together to create a strong and dynamic partnership that honors both of you. There is no reason to fight and compete with each other. If this is happening in your relationship, it is usually because one of you feels powerless in regard to money and is venting your frustration on the other. The issue of powerlessness must be dealt with first before money matters enter into the picture. At this point, you both should be ready to create a new financial team to improve your financial lives. You can start by embodying into your relationship the four money cornerstones that will lay the foundation for making love and money work.

Chapter 8

How To Lay The Four Money Cornerstones And

How To Have The Win-Win Money Fight

Now that you and your partner have uncovered the underlying causes of the conflicts in your money relationship and taken steps to ban them from your lives, you

> *Never go to bed angry, stay up and fight.*
> —— Phyllis Diller

are ready to move on toward building a strong and enduring financial partnership. It's time to talk about making love and money work! First of all, we have identified four cornerstones that you can lay to create a solid financial foundation for a strong money relationship structure. Those cornerstones are Commitment, Trust, Respect, and Compromise.

Money Cornerstone 1: Commitment

Making money work in your relationship is impossible without a firm commitment from both partners. You need to make sure this money cornerstone is in place, because changing your money beliefs, your money behavior, and how you communicate about money takes time. The commitment to make your money relationship better is what will keep you going when the financial going gets rough.

Are you both willing to commit to making the necessary changes in your money life? Complete this exercise to get the answer.

Exercise: Commitment To Wealth Building Statement

On a blank page in your money journal, write at the top "Commitment to Wealth Building Statement". Now write the following statement and fill in the blanks:

"We, _____, are committed to turning our money life around. We are committed to building wealth together to create financial freedom and peace of mind. We are committed to saving and investing our money and stopping all impulse purchases and excessive use of our credit cards. We are committed to making our money work for us, even when it gets difficult."

Both must sign this commitment. Then read it aloud to each other.

This becomes a binding contract between you and your partner. This commitment, based on honesty and a strong desire, will give you both the motivation to stay on track to achieve financial success.

The first step toward fulfilling this commitment is to follow through on the monthly money talk we mentioned earlier. You need a time and a place to consistently work together on your money. If your memories of dealing with money together are painful, causing you to avoid the issue, make every effort to let that go. Today is a new day. What happened in the past stays in the past. Don't allow it to affect your future outcomes. Agree right now to make your monthly money talks a must. In fact, to get control of your money even faster, you may want to consider meeting weekly until you have your money plan and strategy in place, then revert to monthly meetings.

Why are these meetings so essential? They are a way to show each other that you <u>are</u> in this together and that you want a better life evolving around your money. They show you are now willing to move beyond your past money history and beliefs. You're tired of struggling financially and you're committed to making changes.

Keeping this commitment, week after week and month after month, will prepare you to lay the second money cornerstone of making love and money work—Trust.

Money Cornerstone 2: Trust

Trust is the mainstay of a happy relationship. Without trust you hold back on intimacy and are always on guard. When there isn't trust you can't commit heart and soul to the relationship. Without intimacy, without commitment, what's left to hold your relationship together? And then to add money challenges on top of that? Forget it.

We firmly believe lack of trust is the primary reason couples fight over money. Does one of you have little say over financial decisions? Is one of you keeping your income a secret? Can one of you buy whatever you want while the other has to ask for permission? Does one of you feel controlled by the other? If so, one of you is very dependent on the other for money or love and will not risk challenging the status quo. This type of relationship has very little trust.

Trust isn't something that comes automatically with love. It also doesn't come because you have been together for a long time. In fact, among many couples, the trust that usually prevails in other areas of the relationship seems to fly right out the window when the money arguments begin.

> *Honesty is the best policy—*
> *when there's money in it.*
>
> —Mark Twain

Trust is formed, day by day, week after week by staying focused and keeping your commitments to each other. Keeping the money dialogue going every week and month, no matter what, builds trust.

But some behaviors work just the opposite. Keeping money secrets, hiding money and assets, and covertly shopping and hiding purchases in the garage or closet are the three Trust Busters guaranteed to kill any sense of trust.

Trust Buster 1: Keeping Financial Secrets

Renee, a marketing manager, and Brian, an entrepreneur who had started and run two small businesses, had been together for five years before she found out he was paying down $30,000 in credit card debt. He had never offered to divulge his debt and she had never asked him. Once she knew, she regretted not having brought up the financial factor earlier. She didn't because she knew money was a sensitive issue with Brian and she didn't want to make him feel worse. This is where the weekly or monthly money talks would have come in handy. Together they could have devised a plan to pay off the debt much sooner. Yet, because there was fear and mistrust in the relationship that didn't happen.

Fortunately, things went differently for *Gina, an administrative assistant, and Martin, a municipal bus driver. Gina had declared bankruptcy several years before she met Martin. After eight months of dating, Gina was afraid that if she told Martin about the BK, he might think she was irresponsible with money and end the relationship. But once she explained that she had run into financial trouble after losing her job he understood and wasn't scared off.* The fact that she cleared the decks while they were dating says a lot about building trust and means there will be no unpleasant surprises if they do decide to get married. Money secrets left untold will backfire and hurt a relationship.

Trust Buster 2: Hiding Cash or Assets

In an early scene in the movie "Waiting To Exhale", based on the blockbuster novel by Terry McMillan, Bernadette, played by Angela Bassett, finds out that her soon to be ex-husband, played by Michael Beach, owns property and accounts in his own name. She promptly sets his car on fire. While we don't recommend that harsh a reaction, the scene dramatizes what happens in a relationship when trust is betrayed.

Hiding money and assets is quite easy if one spouse or partner owns his or her own business. There are a number of ways to relocate money; offshore trust, bank accounts, and new businesses to name a few. In the movie, the divorce judge hands over a large part of the undisclosed assets to Bernadette. Luckily for her, the assets were discovered before the divorce became final. But even if that weren't the case, and the assets were somehow discovered after the divorce, the untrustworthy partner can still be taken back to court and hit with stiff fines and penalties.

When we say you shouldn't hide money or assets from your partner, we're not talking about wives who maintain an emergency fund in their own name. We encourage women to save money on the side in case the marriage or relationship falls apart. In fact, having a rainy day fund is fine for both partners – as long as each knows about it.

Trust Buster 3: Covert Shopping and Secret Purchases

Secret shopping can be trouble in a relationship. It's a sign of lack of trust. It also signals that one partner has more power over the other and the weaker, childlike partner is afraid to be scolded by the "parent", or dominant partner.

While both men and women hide purchases, this behavior is more prevalent among women. Especially women who don't feel they are an equal partner in handling the family finances. Instead of openly discussing their concerns over money with their partner, they take their fight for power underground. They hide or lie about the amount of money they have spent and on what. It's their way of usurping their money-controlling partner.

If this is going on in your relationship, it must immediately stop. Lying, cheating and deceiving about money can do irreparable harm. Sometimes as much harm as finding out your partner has had an affair. Trust and money are intimate partners just like you and your loved one. So keep the following trust facts in mind. They will prepare you for the third money cornerstone to making love and money work – Respect.

Trust Facts

- If you can't be open and truthful with your partner, you can't develop trust.

- You cannot wait until you feel trusting before you start trusting.

- No matter what your justification is, keeping financial secrets, hiding money, and secretly shopping sow distrust in your relationship.

- If there is distrust over money in your relationship, say something immediately. Avoiding the issue will not make it go away.

- There are no guarantees with money. Trusting in each other is taking a leap of faith.

Money Cornerstone 3: Respect

Your kisses, sweeter than honey,
Guess what, so is my money,
All I'm asking is for a little respect when you come home
—Aretha Franklin

Aretha's lyrics say it all. People want respect —especially in their relationships. Being disrespectful of your partner may stem from your outdated money beliefs. Go back and see if any of them include the language of disrespect. Is one of your beliefs that you don't value each other? This belief is far too common in personal relationships. It may have to do with couples taking each other for granted.

Here's a way to test that. Imagine you and your partner are in a business together. You've both invested time, money and energy into making the business successful. You each come with different skills. The strong skills of one partner complement the weak skills of the other partner and vice versa. Therefore you bring a balanced set of skills to the business.

What would happen to the business if you treated each other with disrespect? What if you both spent time tearing down each other's money-making ideas, or ways to improve the company? Needless to say, you wouldn't be in business very long. Neither of you would tolerate the criticisms, judgment calls, and second-guessing of the other. Well, this is exactly what many of us do in our intimate money relationships. We blame, judge, and berate each other for money mistakes that may or may not have been avoided.

In fact, your relationship is a business partnership consisting of two teammates with different skills who are building a firm foundation of financial freedom and wealth. The business won't last long if the team players don't treat each other with respect. When you show respect it doesn't mean you

> *Don't hold to anger, hurt or pain. They steal your energy and keep you from love.*
>
> — Leo Buscaglia

have to agree on everything. It does means you accept your partner for who he or she is. It also means you see your partner as being competent and making smart money and other basic decisions.

There are two other areas, Resentment and Revenge, that fall within the category of respect and that also need to be discussed in dealing with money.

Resentment and Money

Harboring any type of resentment toward past or present partners will turn your money "funny". When you allow resentment to hold you back, you surrender your power to create meaningful change in your financial life. Resentment in relationships comes from unrealistically high expectations. To get rid of it, stop being overly dependent on your partner to make you happy. He or she can't make you happy unless you are already happy. If money challenges were a reason for the breakup of previous relationships, forgive past partners right now for the hurts they caused. If you don't, you will repeat the same old money challenges in the future rather than opening your heart to abundance and prosperity.

Writing a Setting Free Letter

Forgiving and releasing resentment isn't easy but it can — and must — be done in order for you and your partner to take your financial relationship to the next level. An excellent way to let go of negative feelings is to write a letter to the person you are angry with or resentful toward. Make believe they are right there listening to you and let it all hang out. Here's a format to follow:

Dear _____

I am angry or frustrated that...

I resent that...

I am worried or scared that...

I am embarrassed or ashamed that...

I forgive and thank you for...

I love you,

When you write I Love You at the end of the letter, it is very cleansing. By the way, don't mail the letter. Its contents are really meant for *you*.

The next time you are upset and angry with your partner assess your feelings before you say anything. If you have the "we-got-to-talk" attitude, or you feel the need to tell someone off or teach him or her a lesson, then you need to hold back. Instead, try writing a *Setting Free* Letter.

It may only take 10 to 15 minutes, time enough for you to cool down. Once your feelings have returned to being more loving and you still want to have a heart-to-heart conversation, then go for it. Calmly approach your partner with an overview of your concerns or discuss what you would like to see happen with the family finances in the future. When one or both of you begin to express what you want

> *Forgiveness does not change the past, but it does enlarge the future.*
>
> — Paul Boese

or need financially, you immediately begin to release the block of resentment and anger. The key to making love and money work is to focus on the positive, how you want your relationship and money to work, rather than the negative, what isn't working.

Remember, your partner is different from you. Don't be hurt by his or her mistakes. Indeed, don't take them personally at all. Forgiving others for their mistakes as well as forgiving yourself is the key to abolishing resentment, so that love and money can flow freely again. By practicing forgiveness, getting clear, and asking for what you want, your relationship can last a lifetime.

Revenge and Money

Carolyn and Bill

When Bill, Carolyn's husband of 19 years, didn't qualify for his company's bonus for three quarters in a row, she attributed this failure to his not working hard enough. Carolyn made $50,000 a year as a human resource manager for an up-and-coming Silicon Valley company. Bill's nearly $35,000 salary as fast food restaurant manager brought their total income to about $80,000 yet, it barely covered the cost of living in that expensive region, so his extra bonus was badly needed. But talking about money proved far too difficult for Carolyn. Instead she sought revenge through shopping. Her rationale? Since Bill wasn't making an extra effort to earn the company bonus, why should she bust her butt working 12-hour days? She felt she was the only one really making the money in the household. She began to see her money as hers and his money as his. The marriage was headed for financial doom until they sat down and saw what the problem really was.

Revenge is one of the hidden agendas we spoke about in Chapter 6. The hidden agenda in this situation was Carolyn's belief that Bill was lazy. After the couple talked several times with a financial planner, Carolyn realized that her complaining and criticizing made Bill feel totally inadequate. He didn't say anything. He just didn't put in the overtime hours required to earn the bonus. By the time the truth came out, the family finances were already so far in arrears that Bill agreed to let Carolyn cover the losses in exchange for assenting to an uncontested divorce. End of story.

> *Compromise: An amiable arrangement between husband and wife whereby they argee to let her have her own way.*
>
> —— Anonymous

The lesson: Just like resentment, revenge damages relationships. If you are currently in the revenge mode in your relationship, schedule a money talk as soon as possible. If there is too much anger, write the *Setting Free* letter first. Let go of the rage before you have the money talk. Otherwise it will be a waste of time because neither of you will be able to really hear what the other is saying. There is no power in revenge. When you release it and instead give honor and respect to your partner, you are ready for the fourth cornerstone toward making love and money work: Compromise.

Money Cornerstone 4: Compromise

A Time to Cooperate

If you are serious about building your money life together, create an alliance and form a synergistic relationship. Act in a way that says, "The money belongs to both of us". Abolish all "what's yours is yours and what's mine is mine" money messages. This divisive message leads couples to stand guard over each other's expenses, hide assets, and debate who is in control of the checkbook. This is fine if you're the comptroller for your company, but it's a poor way to negotiate money in your personal relationship.

The new money message is "cooperative finance". It says you will share work and wealth to strengthen your relationship. When practicing cooperative finance, depersonalize money and convey a "this is ours" sentiment. Sit down and develop mutual goals and talk about your present life together and your future aspirations.

For example, we annually sit down and write out the goals and dreams we want to accomplish for the year. By sharing where we want to go and what we want to do, we are able to see how we can assist each other in realizing those objectives. This in turn strengthens our relationship.

Besides creating a big financial plan together, be creative and energetic about showing your willingness to share the little things. When you pick up your dry cleaning, pick up and pay for your partner's too. Resist asking him how much he paid for tickets to that NBA game or what her hairdresser charged for those new braids. Ask him if he is satisfied with how you two are handling the savings and investments. Let her know you don't mind not buying a new computer this year, given the unexpected cost of plumbing repairs for the kitchen. When he tells you he wants to quit his job to start a new business, don't automatically cry out, "But what about the money!" This is the time to cooperate and show support for each other including your differences. Do not allow your money fears to discourage you from saying, "I love you" by sharing your money. Don't judge your self-worth by society's economic standards. Your value and your worth come from within, and so do your partner's.

If you want to build a life together, build it. Don't let anything get in the way. Learn to cooperate and compromise. It's a way for both of you to get what you need. It truly is a win-win way of making love and money work.

The Win-Win Money Fight

Once you've learned to compromise, however, there are still bound to be some money disagreements. Don't forget, you each bring different money backgrounds into the relationship. Money disagreements are okay. They are a part of every good partnership. The trick is learning *how* to disagree by having a Win-Win money fight, in which the money issues are resolved and both partners fully understand why the conflict was necessary in the first place.

How do you go about learning to handle money differences in a win-win way? First, if either of you is in a "fight to the death" mode, calm down. Nothing is accomplished in that frame of mind. Come back to the discussion later when you both can hear what the other is saying and you won't run the risk of saying something you really don't mean.

One of the challenges of any fight within a relationship is that the initial issue gets lost and issues that were raised previously or that one partner has never even heard before take center stage. The toughest fighting skill is sticking to the point. It is important that both partners are able to express their concerns and opinions. We didn't say this would be easy. However, you don't want hurt and anger to build up. As we said earlier, resentment will begin to set in and destroy the intimacy of the relationship.

Win-Win Money Fight Rules

- Money confrontation must be by invitation only. You need to process your own anger before including your mate and not when one partner feels like having a shouting match. Both partners need to agree to an appointment to discuss the issue. It can be done during your weekly money talk, or a special date can be made to discuss that specific issue.

- Gather up all necessary financial papers before you sit down to discuss money. When each of you knows the other's full income, what your spending needs are, and how much savings and investments you want to build, you will understand how to stay on track. Men and women tend to process information differently. This can lead to money disagreements simply because each person heard the same information differently. Having a piece of paper directly in front of you guarantees that both partners are seeing the same thing.

☑ *I, Cheryl, like to see data in writing; it's how I process information.*

☑ *I, Michael, can hear the data and understand immediately in my head what is being said. I don't need to see it written down.*

■ To make it easier to gather your information, all financial documents should be stored in a file drawer to which you both have access. This enables each to locate information on your investment accounts, insurance and other important financial or legal documents.

■ Listen one at a time. If one of you is voicing your concerns, the other must do everything in your power to keep your mouth shut. You should both be able to get your perspectives on the table without interruption.

■ If one partner feels overwhelmed, there's less chance for resolution. So either of you can call a time-out at any time. The one who calls the break needs to also suggest a time to reconvene – say in 20 to 30 minutes. If the discussion is full of anger and adrenaline is running high, take a longer time out. Say something like, "Let's talk about this in an hour when we're both less upset!"

■ Don't dig up the money past. If it happened years ago and you have already argued over it, or even if you never argued about it at the time, let it go. Past issues will only dig both of you deeper into your negative rut.

■ Keep your feelings about money separate from other issues. Don't allow the topic of discussion to become a weapon for future fights.

- Share fears about money, such as not having enough to send the kids to college or to retire in a lifestyle of your choice. Next, talk about your money hopes and dreams.

- Spell out to each other how your money handling style makes each of you feel. Describe it, don't critique it. This isn't the time to be judgmental or critical.

- Don't just agree to end the fight. Take the time to negotiate financial decisions based on what you've just discussed. The partner who always agrees may later feel they weren't able to express how they really felt. This only leads to suppressed frustration and anger.

- Make sure you are fighting over the right thing. Don't fight about bounced checks when the real issue is that you don't feel loved and respected. Search for what is really going on here. What is the hidden agenda? Feeling hurt because you don't think your partner is taking an interest in you? Feeling powerless and out of control in the relationship? If so, these are the issues that must be dealt with first. Allow each other the time and freedom to express openly and honestly without contradicting. Responding with anger, impatience, or insensitivity will only stir up fears of being unloved, uncared for, or controlled. Once hidden agendas are revealed, agree that when any behavior that ignites your hidden fear comes up, you will let your partner know immediately. It's these little things that chip away at the spirit of the relationship and, often, partners don't say anything until it's too late. Remember how Carolyn, the human resources manager, dogged Bill, the fast food restaurant manager, but he didn't say anything? Knowing what sets these hidden agendas off in advance will help the two of you work them out.

- Aim for a Win-Win solution. Reject the "winner take all" approach which will only result in both partners losing because the loser will always resent the defeat. These defeats cause resentment and revenge that will awaken the ego's desire to get even – the way Bill got even with Carolyn — which will put severe strains on the financial harmony of the relationship.

Why Win-Win Is Important

The purpose behind the money fight rules is to find solutions to the money challenges that will satisfy you both. Begin by acknowledging that the money isn't working in the relationship. When both partners take ownership of the money challenges real change can take place. Once that acknowledgment is made, come up with a plan of action and an agreement to review the plan after a set period of time. When that time comes determine if the plan meets the needs of both of you. The major point here is that both partners must emerge from the money argument feeling good about your way of resolving your money issues as a couple.

The Win-Win money fight ensures that each person feels heard and understood on matters related to the family money. You've arrived at a decision after thoughtful consideration of each other's money feelings, histories, and habits. In fact, win-win money fights are actually good for relationships. They clear the air, get money issues out of the back closet and into the open, and create a sense of camaraderie. By working out the money conflicts you feel closer to each other and realize that you really are in this together.

Chapters 6, 7 and 8: Making Love and Money Work Action Steps

1. Talk about money after the 3rd or 4th date. Look out for the nonverbal cues, there's a lot of meaning to them.

2. If you are already in a relationship, schedule monthly money talks. Map out your strategies to get out of debt and build wealth. Get all the money concerns out on the table.

3. Depersonalize money. Use the words "the" money, not "my" or "your" money.

4. Practice cooperative economics. Decide that you are both in this together.

5. Lay the foundation for making love and money work with the four money cornerstones—commitment, trust, respect and compromise.

6. Follow the Win-Win Money Fight rules when having a money disagreement. It will save your relationship.

Chapter 9

For Women Only — Searching For A Money Prince Charming? Get Real!

Prince Charmings ᴙ Us

"You never have to worry about money again!"

Regina

Regina, an editor for a leading New York fashion magazine, never thought in a million years she would still be single at 35. But for the last 15 years, none of the men she dated had lived up to her expectations. They didn't have high status careers or high incomes. Most drove old cars. She, on the other hand, is looking for a professional brother making a minimum of $100,000 and driving a new model Mercedes or Lexus. Furthermore, Regina has no intentions of working after the wedding. She expects her future hubby to work while she goes to lunch and shopping with the girls.

> *I'd marry again if I found a man who had $15 million and would sign over half of it to me before the marriage and guarantee he'd be dead within a year.*
>
> —— Bette Davis

Oh, well. She figures the man of her dreams will come along eventually.

Regina's story is not uncommon, just usually unspoken. A small, deeply hidden part of our female psyche still wants a Money Prince Charming to take care of us so we don't have to take care of ourselves. This statement may be hard for many of us to swallow, but it's true. Denying it only makes it worse. In this chapter we invite you to admit it, get past it, and get on with what you really need to do with your financial life.

You wouldn't think twice about returning that $300 dress you bought last week at Macy's if it didn't fit. If your cell phone bill had charges on it you didn't make, you'd be the first to call AT&T and give them a piece of your mind. But pretending that you need a man to protect you from making truly life-altering financial decisions allows you to play the victim when it comes to your money. It lets you off the hook for your own financial responsibilities. You can tell yourself, "My money ain't right because I ain't found Mr. Right." Or you can claim you haven't bought your own home or invested in the stock market because you don't have a partner to do those things with yet.

But these are excuses we give ourselves so that we don't have to take charge of our money. Despite what we have achieved in our careers, we chose not to control our destiny. Then we worry about growing old and poor. Go figure!

Bag Lady-To-Be?

Fear of growing old and poor is not entirely unreasonable, mind you. According to a Working Woman magazine survey, one of every two of its readers actually worry about becoming bag ladies, those piti-ful street persons we see pushing shopping carts and sleeping in shel-ters. This dread of destitution is a re-sult of conflict between "the man as

> *A successful man is one who makes more money than his wife can spend. A successful woman is one who can find such a man.*
>
> — Lana Turner

breadwinner" traditional ethic versus the "I am woman, hear me roar" feminist move-ment that says women must become self-sufficient. The real issue is that women now know that, not only do they need to earn money, they also need to manage and invest it. But they are afraid if they do well with their money what will they need a man for?

Do you feel internal conflict with part of you wanting financial self-sufficiency while the other part wants to be Daddy's little girl? These thought patterns truly undermine your ability and confidence to make it on your own. Couple this with the disparity in income between men and women and it's no wonder you have trouble taking yourself to the next financial level.

Don't get us wrong, we know it's not easy. In spite of the Equal Pay Act passed over 30 years ago, women still suffer from economic discrimination. Today, the median pay of a full-time working woman remains at 75 percent of a man's, yet women contribute 50 percent or more to households that in many cases are struggling to match high costs of education, food, housing, and taxes. After 40 years of uninterrupted full-time work, a woman earning the national median income for women and retiring at age 65 will have earned $818,840 pretax income. A man earning the national median income for men for the same length of time and retiring at age 65 will have earned $1,289,840 pretax income. A difference of close to $500,000! This is economic discrimination at its best.

This huge earning difference carries over into Social Security, with women receiving 60 percent of the benefits men get since benefits are based on a person's earnings. Women on average receive $4,226 annually in Social Security payments compared to a man's average annual benefit of $7,342. To make matters worse, Money Magazine reports that 61 percent of working women today do not have pension plans. Neither are they investing in employer sponsored 401(K) plans or IRA's. The magazine also reports that, *other than Social Security* (our emphasis), 76 percent of retired women today receive no pension benefits at all. No wonder women have "bag lady" nightmares. With these numbers, we are right to be concerned about growing old alone and with dwindling incomes.

But How Serious Are We About Managing Our Money?

Last year in an effort to help women overcome those fears, we created the Ms. Money Millionaire Financial Boot Camp workshop. We advertised a four-hour seminar with refreshments to help women change their mindset about money, manage their cash, invest in the stock market, and plan for retirement. The message was "let's get down and dirty and get our money straight." The cost was $49.95 or $45 with a free gift if you registered in advance. The result was a standing-room-only session filled with more than 60 women eager to take charge of their money.

Afterward, everyone said we should hold a second workshop, an all-day one this time, with even more information on stocks, bonds and retirement planning. Our team walked away feeling elated. We were really making a difference in the lives of these women! We immediately began planning the second Financial Boot Camp – an all-day affair. We were going to roll up everyone's sleeves and get to the core of their financial challenges. We would cover such topics as How to Invest in the Stock Market, How to Build a Million-Dollar Nest Egg – just what our attendees said they wanted.

We wrote up a flyer with all the new information. We also raised the price to reflect the fact that the seminar would be all day and would incorporate lots of additional information. We would provide light snacks and beverages but the attendees would be responsible for their own lunches. We mailed the flyers to all the women who attended the first Boot Camp and, of course, to thousands of other potential attendees. After a couple of weeks without any significant registrations from the first boot campers, we polled them to see what was wrong. We were extremely disappointed in what we heard. Women said they didn't sign up because A) they didn't like the idea of paying more money and not getting lunch, and B) there would be no free gifts. We were shocked. "What about the topics?" we asked our would-be attendees. "Isn't this what you wanted? You said you wanted an all-day sessions. Here it is! You said you said you wanted to learn about how to invest and build a retirement nest egg…what about that?"

None of that seemed to matter.

Cheryl: *Let me give you more proof of women not really wanting to take financial responsibility. I once spoke at an all-women, weekend conference in the Caribbean. The seminar was titled Millionaire Mania: Smart Women Finish Rich. Some 125 professional women attended by invitation only. My talk on Friday afternoon emphasized not spending money on things we really don't need, but instead on investing in assets to accumulate long-term wealth. Humorously, but with a serious undertone, I discouraged the women from going crazy on the all-day shopping spree planned for Saturday.*

Needless to say, my words fell on deaf ears. On Saturday night at the seminar's closing ceremony, the hostess of the event proudly stated that attendees had dropped over $400,000 at one of the jewelry stores on the island. Had anyone heard what I'd said the day before? Maybe they misunderstood and thought gold jewelry and diamond baubles were the long-term assets I was talking about.

Let's see: $400,000 divided by 125 women. That equals $3,200 per person. Imagine if they had all come together and bought a house on the island and turned it into a luxury, six-room bed and breakfast open 365 days a year and charging $500 a night. In case you don't want to do the math, that would come to an annual total of $1,095,000. It was at that point that I realized that many of us really just don't get it! We don't really want to know about money. We'd rather live paycheck to paycheck and deep in debt and, if we are single, hope and pray some man will come and whisk all the bad money stuff away! Well sisters, I'm here to tell you it doesn't work that way. If you are waiting to be rescued, you might as well close this book. This infor-

mation is not for you and we hope you still have the receipt for the purchase. For those of you who want the money and the relationship to be right, keep reading. In this chapter we'll show you how you can have both.

(As for the Financial Boot Camp? That was the last time we offered an all-day session and it was the last time we provided refreshments. But we do continue to give away free gifts.)

Get Rid Of the Money Prince Charming Myth

Whether you are single, in a relationship, or married, eliminating the myth that your M*oney Prince Charming* will – or has — come along to sweep you off your feet is the most important financial decision you will ever make. Giving up that fantasy will be difficult since it is tightly woven into most of our psyches. If you don't believe that, ask yourself the following questions:

- Do you believe that managing money is the man's job or that men are privy to money secrets that women don't know?

- Do you shut down mentally when you start to deal with your money?

- Do you believe you just weren't born with money smarts?

If you answered yes to any of these questions, the Money Prince Charming myth undermines your ability to learn to take care of you. It encourages you to think that managing your money is someone else's job. But life is not about losing who you really are and what you stand for in life. Life is about controlling your financial future yourself.

If you are married and already think your husband is your Money Prince Charming, don't believe for a minute that you no longer need to manage money. As a spouse, you are just as vulnerable to financial disaster as a single woman, especially if you and your Money Prince Charming decide to divorce.

Divorce is a financial disaster for most married women. Their income almost always goes down. In 1994 (the latest national data available) the median household income for married couples with children was $47,000, but for families headed by single mothers less than $16,000. Today, 59 percent of single mothers are the sole support of their children and nearly half live below the poverty line. Worse still, single black mothers are at the bottom of the ladder with median incomes of only $10,000.

And don't think society will take care of you and your children if you divorce. It will not. A research report by Namkee C. Ghoi in the Journal of Family Issues states that despite an average 23-year work history, over a third of divorced women are poor or near poor after retirement.

Jan, a homemaker we know, found this out the hard way. She had been married for 21 years to David, a businessman and local elected official, when one day David decided he wanted a divorce. In complete charge of the family finances, David left home and stopped making the mortgage payments. Jan lost the house when it went into foreclosure. The divorce was extremely nasty and many secrets were revealed. It turned out that for the previous five years, David had kept a mistress on the side and was paying the mortgage on a new house three blocks from Jan's home. When one of David's businesses went belly up he could no longer maintain two mortgage payments and keep up the facade. At the time we interviewed Jan, five years had gone by and they were still in court.

Today, Jan is a brand new woman. She reads financial books and attends seminars every chance she gets. "It feels goods to pay my own bills and write out my own checks," she says. "My goal is to never again be financially dependent on a man — or anyone else for that matter."

Married security may not last forever. Stop abdicating total financial responsibility to the man in your life. If you don't, you are taking great financial risks. In the event your Love Boat springs a leak, neither the government nor anyone else will bail you out.

Why Do You Believe the Money Prince Charming Myth, Anyway?

Here are four major beliefs of the Money Prince Charming fantasy that we found among women in our research group. To make sure that love and money is working in your relationship, make sure you don't believe any of them:

Myth 1: The man is supposed to pay for everything

This tradition is left over from the days of Ozzie and Harriet that no longer exist. These days, it usually takes two incomes just to survive. And in today's world of working women, men are less willing to shoulder the entire bulk of the financial burden. Besides, when your man to pay for everything, it places you in a subordinate position with little power in the relationship. That's not a position you want to be in.

Even if you're not in a relationship right now, you need to think the same way. When you start dating a new man, graciously accept his paying for the first two or three dates. Then, offer to pay for the next one or two. Most men will appreciate the gesture and will see you as someone who at least has some financial moxie. Offering to pay also lets him know you have a sense of independence. It also eliminates the assumption that you are saying, "In order to get to know me, (read, intimately), you have to pay for it." Neither party wants to feel exploited or unfairly treated, which could occur — especially if you both have comparable incomes and resources. When both parties begin to view each other as being fair, it brings a healthy sense of respect to the relationship. If you're a married working couple, same goes. Change up on dinner out and divvy up the monthly bills as well. We'll discuss more on bill paying in Chapter 14.

Myth 2: The man should make more money than the woman

Even though this is an outdated belief, we are sad to report there are women who still subscribe to it. True, men on average still out-earn women — $1 to 75 cents. Even among male and female millionaires, the men earned on average $2.41 million, according to the Internal Revenue Service, while the women earned on average $2.27 million, or roughly 94 cents for each dollar the men earned.

But that gap is closing. In many fields heavily populated by females in upper management, such as banking and advertising, women out-earn men. And this trend is expected to cross over into other industries as well, based on statistics showing women outpacing men in obtaining college and advanced degrees which should push them further up the ladder into higher paying positions. Among men and women earning between $500,000 and $1 million, for example, men still outnumbered women 10 to 1, according to the IRS. But women in that category earned on average $670,000 compared to men in that category at $668,000, or about $2,000 more.

Myth 3: Only the man should work.

With very few exceptions, two incomes are needed these days for the average black middle-class couple to pay rent for a livable place or to buy a home, educate their children, and take vacations. In fact, in certain high-cost regions, such as the

San Francisco Bay Area where we live, one partner almost needs to have a full *and* a part-time job while the other holds down at least a full-time job if expenses are to be met.

Myth 4: What my man spends on me tells me how much he loves me

Yeah right! The amount of money a man spends on you doesn't indicate how much he loves or cares for you. Any man who spends lavishly on you, especially in the beginning of the relationship, usually wants something in return, namely sex. Even more wicked, it could be his way of trying to control you .The old saying, "There is no such thing as a free lunch" rings true in relationships, too.

Sharing Is the Key

Forget those myths about what a man is supposed to pony up. To paraphrase President John F. Kennedy, "Ask not what your relationship can do for you, but what you can do for your relationship". To establish such a constructive dialogue, couples must bring money out from under the mattress and onto the dining room table.

One of the first truths to realize is that money won't bring you love and happiness. Neither will select someone by how much income they have, what status their job holds, what brand of threads they wear or what kind of wheels they drive. If you are thinking along those lines, a viable long-term relationship may be next to impossible. Nor can you expect your mate to buy you a home, a car and clothes. That's your responsibility. Instead, you must come together on financial issues to make love and money work. Together you will communicate and decide how to save, invest and spend money to get what you both want. By sharing, you strengthen the relationship because now each partner has a stake in its direction and preservation.

Don't Play the Financial Waiting Game

Once you begin untangling the Money Prince Charming myth, love and money will no longer be co-dependent. We realize this won't happen overnight but it will happen if you have faith in your ability to take charge of your financial life. Surround yourself with friends who think the same way. Join an all-female investment club. At the beauty salon or spa, change the conversation from men, celebrities, and cooking to stocks, index mutual funds or real estate. Make your financial well-being your first, not your last priority. When you're financial straight, you'll look for a partner who also has his head together – and settle for nothing less. As Susan L. Taylor of Essence magazine says, "Not everyone deserves a front row seat in your life."

Make sure you reserve that seat for the right person to come into your life, not someone who is only there for you to lean on financially. Instead, you should be the

one with the six or seven-figure investment portfolio or the new house on the corner lot with a view of the water. To get to that point, you'll have to stop waiting for that mythical Money Prince Charming to come along. You'll have to be your own knight in shining armor. In the next chapter, again geared toward the female half of the partnership (guys, you'll be next), we'll help you start that process by healing your own money wounds. We'll show you how to be the best that you can be financially.

Notes

Chapter 10

More For Women Only — Take Charge Of Your Money Life

Now that you are no longer looking for a Money Prince Charming, it's time to take over your own financial life. We start by identifying the four money wounds we believe may cause you to avoid taking full responsibility for your financial fate. They are:

1. **Lack of self-love**
2. **Not feeling worthy of having money**
3. **Living a life out of harmony**
4. **Shopping to fill the love void**

Money Wound 1: Lack of Self Love

When you don't love yourself, you handle your money in an unloving and wasteful way. Women who don't love themselves tend to get involved with men they also don't love either for reasons of financial security or to get something they don't believe they can get for themselves.

Do you ever hear a little voice in your head that says you are inadequate and unworthy of affection? That little voice says you should be doing better and even be looking better. It tells you other people are smarter, prettier, and luckier than you. That whatever you accomplish isn't good enough. That you don't have what it takes to succeed financially. That if you make one wrong move you'll be considered a failure.

Like all us women, your internal nag makes you feel unsure or just plain bad about yourself. When that tape starts to roll you immediately feel unworthy. Even though you are an intelligent woman, you deny yourself self-love and instead focus on your deficiencies.

Well, get over it! Self-punishment is damaging emotionally, spiritually and financially. Quit telling yourself, "I'll love myself when I find the man of my dreams, move up in my career, or hit the Lotto." You are the most lovable person in your life right now. Adopt the late Lucille Ball's motto: "Love yourself first, and everything else falls into line – you really have to love yourself to get anything done in this world."

Money Wound 2: Not Feeling Worthy of Having Money

The not-feeling-worthy-of-having-money wound plays a close second to the lack-of-self-love-money wound. When you don't love <u>you</u>, you don't feel deserving of having money to live the lifestyle of your dreams. The bad news is that you project these feel-

> *I will realize my own worth when I accept I have the power and the ability to create my ideal life.*
>
> — Iyanla Vanzant

ing into the workplace and into your relationships. You don't ask for what you want – more money, career promotions, a loving partner – and, sure enough, you don't get it.

Don't believe us? Do you find you are constantly asking yourself the following questions?

- Why don't I ask for a raise?

- How come I'm not earning what I think I'm worth?

- Why can't I save money?

- Why do I waste money on things I don't need?

- Why am I looking for a man to take care of me?

If you are asking these questions, chances are you don't believe you are worthy of having money.

The good news is that it's time to strip off that self-imposed label of unworthiness and learn to establish high expectations for yourself.

> *You are the architect of your life and you decide your destiny.*
>
> — Swami Rama

In other words, take care of you first. In the beginning it may be difficult to believe in yourself if you have never been taught that you are worth believing in. Start by accepting you just the way you are – flaws and all. Affirm that there is nothing wrong with you. Understand that you are a special person put here to fulfill a special mission. Do you love children and find teaching a fulfilling occupation? Do you feel a higher power working through you as you care for the sick at the hospital where you are employed? Do you believe you are uniquely suited to market products that help people live healthier? Whatever it is, when you find your mission you'll feel worthy, as Mr. Rogers used to say, "Just because you're you."

When you feel worthy of yourself you will bring an abundance of love and respect to your relationship. You will value your partner and see no reason to compete with or try to change him. You won't need to win every money argument nor always prove your point. When you do feel compelled to have the last word, you will realize that reaction is not your partner's problem, it's yours. Heal yourself and become the type of financial partner you so desperately want your partner to be.

Money Wound 3: Life Out Of Harmony

When life throws you major challenges – divorce, death, unwanted career changes or business losses, it is easy to fall into the victim role with your money and look to someone else to take over. As a victim you become helpless, hopeless, and unwilling to do what you need to do to get through the challenge.

No doubt about it, life's challenges are difficult. There is no way to escape its ebbs and flows. And if you struggle against or resist a financial challenge it zooms completely out of control. Instead, you must work in partnership with life challenges and look for the lesson or blessing that lies hidden within them.

Cheryl: *The divorce was my wake-up call. It was the first time I had financial challenges. So it was definitely a growth period for me. Now I was totally responsible for my financial life. If I wanted my money and life to be better, it was up to me. I no longer had excuses. As a result, I took the bull by the horn and turned my financial life around. I wrote more books and lectured around the country. Soon money was no longer an issue. The blessing was that I could do it on my own if necessary. And with that belief came self-confidence that would not allow me to accept mediocrity in a relationship. It also deepened my faith, and has helped me to understand that there is a higher spirit guiding us.*

Oftentimes, a financial crisis offers a chance to start over and direct your life in the manner that is best for you. So when you deal with a major financial challenge, here's what you should NOT do. Don't:

1. Hold yourself responsible for the bad thing that happened. A job layoff may be due to a merger or a slowdown in the economy. A death in the family that impacts you financially may be due to illness. Both of these circumstances are out of your control.

2. Criticize yourself. Telling yourself you screwed up or you're awful and a failure is self-destructive. You make a bad situation worse by kicking yourself when you are down.

3. Start a new relationship. This is not a good time. Rather, focus on healing yourself. Write in your journal, take long walks in the park, enroll in a class, light a candle, read a book. Find nurturing activities that are low cost. Going to the outlet mall or to the club every night do not count as low-cost nurturing activities. You're likely to wind up with a shopping bag of items you don't need or a pickup partner who is a one-night stand. Spend time enjoying your own company or that of close friends until you are able to get through a major part of the challenge.

If you are already in a relationship, on the other hand, let your partner know you need his support during this difficult time. Don't try to be Superwoman and handle it all by yourself. Earlier we talked about the importance of communication when a relationship is bucking financial challenges. Go back and reread that section again.

> *Given a choice between chocolate and shopping, women choose—both!*
> — J.C. Penney's TV commercial

Money Wound 4: Shopping To Fill The Love Void

Nina, single and 35, is an account representative for a pharmaceutical company. She makes over $60,000 a year but has nothing to show for it, except four closets packed with designer clothes and shoes. "I've been in so many relationships lately, and I can't believe I haven't found that right person yet," She laments. "Since I'm not seeing anyone, I spend my weekends shopping at the outlet malls. When I'm at the mall I don't feel so lonely."

If you're a single woman wishing for a mate you can probably relate to Nina's story. When we don't feel loved or appreciated our scarred over money wounds open up. We feel angry, depressed, and sad from the empty feeling in our heart. To fill the void we shop.

Some of us shop to be ready when our Prince Charming arrives. The trappings – clothes, make up, fragrances, candles, and luxury bed linen – all feed that fantasy. We feel comforted with our things around us while we wait.

But shopping can become an addiction just like drugs. When we make a purchase our hormonal system releases a class of chemicals called endorphins that flood our nervous systems and make us feel pleasurably excited. As with other chemicals, however, the "high" wears off in 20 or 30 minutes and we find ourselves wanting another fix. So we buy again to get another shot of endorphin. By the time we get home with all our bags, the high has worn off and we feel guilty and depressed, which starts the cycle all over again.

Still, some women, like Lydia, 42, a corporate lawyer we know, spend freely because, yep, you guessed it, they expect a Money Prince Charming to take care of the serious, long-term issues like investments and retirement. Lydia thinks, "I'll buy what I need for now and when he comes along, he'll take over."

When Lydia finally "gets it" and sees that she may have to support herself until the end, it may be too late. Even though she rents a well-appointed apartment in a fashionable high rise, dresses beautifully, and drives a nice car, her best years to amass long-term wealth will soon slip by. Without a substantial financial cushion to get her through her retirement years, she may have to continue working past the age of 65.

If this sounds like you, regardless of your age, stop for a moment and think how your life would be if you applied the same drive, energy, and vision you use in shopping to managing your money and reducing your debt. Instead of bargain hunting for the latest designer handbag, if you shopped around for a lower rate on your credit card. Instead of having a rack full of shoes you rarely wear, if you had a portfolio of investments earning from 10 percent to 35 percent a year. And all that *before* you met the man of your dreams.

Today you can't afford to enter into a relationship with a "money blindfold" on because at some point in your life — whether you find a Money Prince Charming or not — you may end up completely responsible for your financial survival. Some statistics from the National Center for Women and Retirement Research prove our point even further:

- 70 percent of married baby boomer women (those born between 1946 and 1962) will outlive their husbands.

- The average life expectancy for women is 79 years, compared with 72 for men.

- Elderly women are twice as likely than men to live their retirement years in poverty.

- 58 percent of baby boomer women have less than $10,000 saved in a pension or 401(K) plan. Baby boomer men have saved three times that amount.

It's No Longer A Option!

Building financial security for yourself for the long term is no longer an option. There are no quick fixes. It's time to create a new value system that will guide you to make smart money decisions. To rid yourself of a lifetime of money denial attitudes, habits, and techniques. By having money and knowing how to manage and grow it, you will be free to live your life with whom you wish, to go after the dreams you really want, and to worry less about becoming poor during your last years.

So, the next time you feel the urge to shop kick in, do one or all of the following to overcome the desire:

- Put on your favorite fast-paced CD and dance around the house. You'll get the same endorphin high and be in better shape as well.

- Call a friend for moral support.

- Look at your written goals, they'll keep you inspired

- Ask yourself. "Will buying _____ get me closer to my goal of _____?

Heal Those Money Wounds and Move On

Whichever money wounds are crippling you and whether you are in or out of a relationship, raise your spirits by ceasing all attacks on your self-esteem. Tell your inner critic "adios", and begin to focus on positive solutions to alleviate your financial challenges. We aren't going to claim it will happen overnight. It can be a slow and difficult process. Your inner critic may continue to taunt you for while. But stand up to her and tell her where to get off. You're going to get your life back in harmony. Here are 13 steps to take:

1. **Be compassionate towards yourself.** Be as caring as you would be toward a friend who was going through the same problems. Tell yourself these challenges are only temporary. Pray for guidance to make life peaceful again.

2. **Face your challenge head on.** Living in denial will make your money challenges seem more difficult than they really are. Don't play the victim by asking yourself why this happened to you. It did and now you must fix it and move on.

3. **Trust yourself.** Remember how you've successfully dealt with other life challenges, like graduating from college or having a baby. You got through those so surely you can get through this.

4. **Encourage yourself.** Think about what you would say to a friend whose life is out of harmony:

    -   "You've been through bad times before, and you can get through this one too."

    -   "For every problem there's a solution. Let's figure out what we can do."

    -   "Stop focusing on what you haven't done. Look at what you have done, and done well."

5. **Take Care of Yourself First.** Making money work in your relationship begins with taking care of you first, not your partner. Strive to better your own life in all ways, especially financially. Instead of looking to a man to provide for you, provide for yourself. Fuel your own dreams and kindle your own passions. The man you team up with will be lucky to find you, not the other way around. The finan-

cial values a man brings to your relationship should complement your values not compete with them. A woman friend of ours always counsels single sisters looking for a relationship to remember that "a man should simplify your life, not complicate it."

When you make yourself the best that you can be, your relationships will benefit. If you want a successful, emotionally stable, healthy and well-rounded man in your life, you must develop those qualities yourself. Because if you don't value yourself enough to provide all the things you want, why should anyone else?

6. **Get to Know and Love the Real You.** Begin to take time out to pamper yourself and get involved in activities that you enjoy. Spend time in solitude. Take long baths sometimes instead of a shower. Get a massage once or twice a month. Read books that soothe your soul. Get adequate rest. Replace the negative messages with positive ones on the tape that continuously runs through your mind. While you cannot change what happened in the past, you can change the way you talk to yourself. You don't have to stay stuck being unhappy and unfulfilled. The choice is up to you. Become your own success coach. Every day write down something positive in your money journal.

7. **Focus on the one thing you like to do better than anything else**. What natural talent lies hidden within your soul? What small thing do you do better than anyone else? Doing what you enjoy and doing it to the best of your ability raises your self-esteem and makes you feel worthy and valuable. Cook from scratch, play tennis, plant flowers, knit or crochet, train for marathons, sing in the church choir, mentor a young girl, visit patients in nursing homes. If you aren't sure what you do best, think about the one thing you do when time goes by way too fast or you're having so much fun you don't want to stop and find yourself saying "I

wish I could do this all the time". If that still doesn't help, talk to friends and family. Sometimes they are able to recognize talents in your that your are unable to see. Whatever it is, make sure you spend time every single day doing it.

8. **Don't be so hard on yourself**. When you experience a setback, give yourself a break. No one is perfect. If you mess up, don't call yourself dumb or stupid. These seemingly innocent reprimands are devastating to your psyche. Mistakes are just that – mistakes! If you screw up, acknowledge it, take full responsibility for it, and find a way to fix it. Worrying about it wastes a ton of your energy.

9. **Eliminate "I can't" from your vocabulary.** When you say, "I can't find a good man" or "I can't manage my money", guess what? You're right! Replace "I can't" with "I can" and "I will". Put some conviction behind those words. Tell yourself: "I deserve the best! I can achieve whatever I put my mind to it!"

10. **Surround yourself with positive people.** Look closely at your friendships. Spending time with positive people enhances your self-image, inspires and uplifts you. When you surround yourself with negative people you have a tendency to take on their personas. Be leery of advice you receive from these people. Misery DOES love company

11. **Be worthy of respect**. Respect is something you must give in order to receive. Manage your life in such a way that others respect you because they can see that you respect yourself.

12. **Be true to your word.** If you tell someone you are going to do something be sure to follow through. Your word is your bond. Do all you can to be as trust-worthy as possible. Don't worry about being taken for granted – that isn't likely

to happen. You want to develop a reputation for being a woman of her word, a wonderful trait to have in your life and relationships.

13. **Be kind and go the extra mile**. Kindness is what makes the world go around. When you are kind to others, they will be kind to you in return. When you go the extra mile and do something wonderful for others, a good thing will come back to you. When it does, it will kick up your self-esteem to the next level. Starting today, apply this golden rule to every area of your life. It will improve you and all your relationships.

The bottom line is that you are a powerful woman in control of your own destiny. Always give yourself priority treatment. Never allow anyone to prevent you from being the best that you can be, even your partner. Learn how to manage your own money and take responsibility for doing the things that will empower you to live a better life. If you are psychologically, emotionally, and financially independent, you'll never become a prisoner of love. Picture your life as beautiful and exciting – with or without a partner. The more independent you become, the better your chances of attracting and experiencing a special love affair. When you become the kind of woman that both you and the man you choose to be with can respect, you will have a relationship where love and money work.

Chapters 9 and 10 Making Love and Money Work Action Steps:

1. Take responsibility for your own life and don't expect a man to make you happy.

2. Make sure you are the best person you can be.

---

3. Learn to manage, save, and invest your own money. Attend financial classes and workshops. Read money, personal empowerment and starting your own business books. *The Black Woman's Guide To Financial Independence; Smart Ways to Take Charge Of Your Money, Build Wealth, And Achieve Financial Security (Penguin) and Sister CEO; The Black Woman's Guide To Starting Your Own Business (Viking)* is a good place to start.

4. Enjoy your life and be open and ready for opportunities.

5. Love and respect yourself. When you do, you will draw good people to you.

6. Never act financially desperate for a man. Good men will run the other way.

7. Begin to ask yourself, "What do I want out of life?"

8. Stay on top of your finances. Start investing and growing your money. Start or become a member of an investment club.

9. Pay off all your debt as quickly as possible. The pressure of two many bills can be stressful and may contribute to a need to be rescued.

Chapter 11

Work, Money, and Power — How Men View Money

You know my late husband, bless his soul, was such a miserly person...he loved money more than just about anything...

He even asked me to bury him with all his money when he died...made me promise!...

Girl, I know you weren't fool enough to put all that money in there with that man!...

Listen girl, I'm a Christian woman and I can't lie...

You didn't...you put all that money in the casket???

I sure did, I wrote that man a check!

OK, guys, it's your turn. Picture an early morning on the Kalahari plain. The air is fresh and full of the promise of a successful day of hunting. The tribesmen are doing all the preparations as the younger children, especially the 8 to 10-year-old boys, watch and learn the skills they will need one day. These skills have been passed down through countless generations from father to son and warrior to warrior. The elder of the tribe, old, lean, and fit, discusses the plans with the other men in the hunting party. Shareef, 17, listens attentively to every detail. This is his first hunt and he is eager to prove his worthiness. Soon he will bid goodbye to his mate, Sharmaine, 16, and set out on the journey to unfold. (They married young in those days.)

> *Shareef:* Honey, I think I'm going to be home pretty late from the hunt. We've killed everything in the neighborhood, so we'll probably have to go farther away. Since this is my first real hunt, I am assigned to flush the game out into the open. Not qualified to use my spear yet. Maybe next time. Either way, please have my dinner ready when I get back.
>
> *Sharmaine:* Boy, that sure was a long meeting. Are you sure they know what they're doing?
>
> *Shareef:* Yes, I'm sure.
>
> *Sharmaine:* You're the flusher? Doesn't the flusher get the last pick of the animal skins? Not only that, Azizi next door said that it's usually the smallest hide. Aw, baby, you know I already made room in our hut for a large skin. Why can't Frank be the flusher? You're smarter than he is.

Shareef: But, Sweetie, Frank has been on two hunts before, and besides, why do you need such a big skin?

Sharmaine: I'm just tired of hearing Azizi brag about the one Armand brought back for her. She gets on my last nerve. Maybe you could do a little side hunting on the weekend? You really don't have to participate in the ceremonial male bonding dances, which would give you the extra time.

———

Work, money, and power. Is there anything that occupies a man's mind more than this trio? Sex? Yes, we think about sex a lot. But we men can't obtain a continuing supply of sex without money and power. What's the saying? Women use sex to get money, and men use money to get sex. Sports? Not a chance. Sports are a rest stop we use to keep the brotherly bond between us strong. But they're a diversion on the way to work, money, and power. What about professional sports? Most men, especially black men, go into professional sports because they see it as the quickest and best avenue available to obtain money and power. Few would be willing to suffer the major injuries and massive abuse to their bodies if it were not for the big bucks.

Men are conditioned to focus on work, money, and power in order to feel good about themselves as men. Work, money, and power are the carrots dangling on the stick we believe we must grab to achieve "manhood."

Take Michael's story, for example.

Michael: *When I was growing up in the 1960's, money wasn't always a part of my life or the lives of my parents or grandparents. One income per family was by far the norm, and divorces weren't as "fast food" as they are today. So the perception of money's importance in my household was minimal. My parents didn't have a lot of it, yet they got married, had children, made sure their children were educated, and formed businesses when they were able.*

But since the post-World War II economic expansion money has grown in importance as black folks have gained more freedom of movement and access to higher income streams. The rise of the mass media has been another factor contributing to the perceived importance of money in today's social discourse. Every day the media tell us how much better our lives would be if only we had more money.

So when I speak of my money troubles, they comprise a complex tapestry of old, hand-me-down beliefs, my own ego, the competing definitions of manhood, the discovery of my passion, and the desire to be responsible. As a man, raised in the environment I was raised in, I have this attitude that I don't want anyone to help me financially with anything. I hate with a passion having to ask for money. I believe it's a sign of weakness and I'm not sure where that belief started. It's like this voice in my head is saying, "You're how old and you still don't know how to hunt for yourself?"

So when my funds are low and the bills start to pile up, I have to fight the urge to go out and buy lottery tickets, especially when the payoffs balloon into the millions. It's that eternal hope that someone or something will rescue me financially and I won't have to worry about money for the rest of my life. But every time I do succumb to the seduction of the pot-of-gold at the end of the rainbow, I feel cheap and used. Lottery mentality says, "I deserve something for nothing". Sucker! Credit cards breed a similar mentality: "I just charged a new car on my credit card and I don't have to make a payment on it for three months." *Sucker!*

When I decided to join the "dot-com" gold rush in early 2000, I had planned on using a new career as a recruiter as a springboard to success within the high-tech industry. After resigning my job as a technical trainer in Southern California, I moved 400 miles to the San Francisco Bay Area in Northern California, set up a temporary living arrangement, and started learning the ropes. Six months later, the new job folded. And because of the hours I had to put in, on the new job I had no time to pursue a fallback plan. To top it off, money I had saved for emergencies was tied up in the stock market, heavily weighted in high-tech, some in stocks I invested in based on "tips" no less. When the dot-com sector collapsed, I felt as if fate were doing everything in its power to see that NOTHING went right.

In situations like this one, a man often has a "fight or flight" response. If he feels he cannot be an economic force, he experiences a corresponding loss of self-respect. He feels like he should remove himself from the situation if he doesn't see it changing anytime soon. My choices were to stick it out or go back to L.A. and possibly "beg" for my old job back. But like in the movie "The Matrix", I had already been down that "old job" path and I knew where it lead-- nowhere! So I decided to take the risk and forsake safety and security with the realization that in today's corporate environment, it really doesn't exist anyway. I was firmly committed to this new direction.

As I look back on my dilemma, part of my frustration comes from knowing that I used outdated money models, passed on to me by the

generations before me. I was programmed for safety and security—
the "go to school, get a god job, get married, raise children, and
retire" formula. Just leave it to the corporation to take care of you.
Unfortunately, that model was based partially on the economic boom
of my parents generation. These days, large corporations can't com-
mit to keeping employees for 25 years because of mismanagement,
downsizing, mergers, or other strategies to up the stock price. I had
to turn adversity into opportunity. I wasn't going to work for a cor-
poration from the inside, I would work with corporations from the
outside. I would develop a new type of employment based on a free
agent model.

What Motivates Men?

Most of us men are dreamers. We probably lead the league in "harebrained" schemes that we feel will change our lives, our partnerships, and the world around us. Sometimes we have to sift through a lot of rock to find that gold nugget. Who was the guy just before the guy who finally mastered fire? He's somewhere either frozen solid or burned to a crisp. How many men died on Mt. Everest before Tenzing Norgay and Sir Edmund Hillary reached the summit? Were their dreams any less valid than those of Norgay and Hillary?

Men are also competitors. We compete for just about everything. And competition brings on comparisons: Who has the larger house, bigger penis, finer woman, newer television, latest gadget, or most purebred dog. Take that tag line in a recent car commercial that says, "...but secretly you're feeling I'm better than you". The "winner" feels a sense of power over the "loser".

In America, especially, it's about winning even more than competing. You never hear much about the runner-ups. Who lost the last Super Bowl? Who cares, though they were the second best team in the NFL? Who were the Bronze medalists in the last Olympics? Third best in the world, they got branded with the big "L" across the forehead – Losers! Reminds us of a joke about two friends chancing upon a grizzly bear in the woods. One guy starts putting on running shoes and his buddy says, "Are you crazy? Do you really think you can outrun a grizzly bear?" To which the first fellow replies, "Of course not. I just have to outrun you".

So what do work, money, and power have to do with your developing a workable partnership with your significant other, which is what this book is all about? Let's take work, money and power, in inverse order.

The Meaning of Power

Boundaries, territories, conquests, accomplishments. You know how a dog rarely walks by a fire hydrant without "leaving his mark"? Well, you instinctively mark where you've been too so that other men, and just as important, all women, know you were there. Before you descend the mountain, you have to stand on the summit and post a flag that says, "I was here first." You need to conquer, to master, to possess, to overcome – whether it be the environment, the weather, your physical limitations, the other guy, animals, machines, and, oh, by the way, women.

Most graffiti artists are men. Besides their attempts at artistic expression, the power to claim territory, alter the landscape, and let others know they were there is why they do it. Power is the ability to secure our boundaries, hold on to our "marked" territories or conquests, and accumulate and possess our "things". The longer we can do these things, the greater our measure of power. The Guinness Book of Records means more to us men than it does to women, we guarantee you. For men, life is a never-ending contest.

If you have the choice of being considered "handsome", "strong" or "powerful", which one will you take? If you're like most men, you'll chose "powerful" hands down. The catch phrase "You da man!" doesn't mean you're handsome or strong. It means you're calling the shots. 'Nuf said.

To be sure, the pursuit of power isn't confined entirely to men. Women are attracted to power like moths to light. Sure, Monica Lewinsky thought Bill Clinton was handsome. But if ole' Bill had been a handsome gas station attendant down in Arkansas, do you think Monica would have flashed her thong underwear at him? No way. It was being intimate with a powerful man, not a cute man, that Monica lusted after. As for strong, Mike Tyson is strong. But women don't visit him in hotel rooms or even marry him because he's strong. The millions he earns as a prizefighter are what give him the power to command the continuing presence of female companionship in his life.

Today women are also going after power on their own accord. They are asserting themselves in such "male" sports as boxing, soccer, and football. They are making inroads into other previously male-dominated areas like mountain climbing, even politics, in an attempt to be recognized as physical peers of men, or even as having "male" tendencies, therefore hoping to be more respected or justly rewarded economically. Because of continuing disparities in income levels, women believe the only way to be compensated like men is to act like men. That is, to wield power.

In 2002, Hewlett-Packard CEO Carly Fiorina battled ruthlessly to win shareholder approval to merge HP with Compaq. She embraced the seduction of power and made the "tough decision" — sometimes a euphemism for feeling no guilt – knowing the merger will mean "downsizing" thousands of employees out of their jobs. Point is, men and women are rewarded more for exercising the analytical and competitive judgments that typify the masculine working style than for a feminine working style that involves nurturing, healing, and cooperation.

But in a personal relationship, it can be just the other way around. Chances are your partner wields enormous power over you by exercising her so-called feminine "wiles." When Sharmaine coyly tried to persuade Shareef to maneuver Frank into being the flusher, she told Shareef he was smarter than Frank. Shareef may have been flattered, but he also reminded Sharmaine that he was the flusher this time around, no questions asked, and she could take that or leave it. She took it – this time. So, while men seek to display power in their relationships, they must recognize that women wield power, too, albeit in different ways.

The Meaning of Money

The old Aphorism, "money is power" is absolutely true. There is no question that the more money you have the more power you have.

Paul T., Cardiologist

For men, the power in their personal partnership is almost always about the money. Your chances of attracting a desirable mate go up exponentially with the number of zeros behind the balances in your checking account. Your dollar bills are the equivalent of Shareef's animal skin. A large percentage of men feel that if they have lots of "Benjamins" they can enjoy the company of women who wouldn't give them the time of day otherwise. And for the most part, they are absolutely correct.

There once was a athlete whose name we won't say
Who was strong as an ox but with a brain made of clay.
He wasn't good looking, nor behaved as he should
But dollars he had and, soon after, a fine actress in Hollywood.

As a man you are acculturated to believe that the accumulation of money is a status symbol. Even people who despise wealthy individuals (think Hugh Hefner) still respect them simply because they have money. Cash will sugar coat any physical or personal shortcomings and provide you with your "props". How many news stories have you read about white-collar executives getting minor slaps on the wrist for fraud and corruption because they can buy clever legal representation? Everybody is using the phrase "gotta get paid" these days.

Money is intimately woven into the fabric of your self-esteem, in many cases from birth. Societal roles define you as the designated "breadwinner" in a family unit. If you struggle with this role you can suffer at least two consequences:

- An already low self-esteem that descends further if you feel your earnings do not qualify you for the title of warrior in the eyes of potential mates.

- A belief that you must take a job that will destroy your spirit but enable you to prove that you can "win bread".

Not that there aren't many enlightened individuals who, early in life, know what they want to do and pursue their dreams with focus. You may be one of them. However, for most of us, it's go to school and then find a career. And the pressure is on us because until recently women have been spared the cultural responsibility of defining themselves by their occupations. Your job is, by definition, the essence of you. Work is one of the only places you can exercise what you perceive it means to be truly a man.

Let's look at some of the comments from the men we interviewed on the importance of money in their work and personal lives:

What Does Money Represent?

Ben – married, personal advisor, over 50

> *[Money] is a source of protection. It gives you a certain capability of being able to basically get things done.*

Gary– separated, city services, over 40

> *Being employed or making a certain amount of money does give you a certain amount of power, empowers you in some way.*

What Is Your Greatest Fear Regarding Money?

Ben – Married, personal advisor, over 50

> *That I'm in a situation where I have a tremendous need that could be filled through some sort of monetary payment and I don't have that payment. Like some major health problem or some major difficulty, some family member has some sort of problem and usually it comes down to the bottom line – dollars and cents.*

Gary – Separated, city services, over 40

> *Not being able to sustain myself or sustain my family, pay the bills or have the funds to send my kids to school. Truly, a lack of money would be my greatest fear.*

J.R. – Married, entrepreneur, over 30

> *Not having it. I was broke before when I was in college and early on when I first got out of college, and I hate with a passion not having money. Money isn't everything, but like [motivational speaker] Les Brown says, 'It's right up there with air'.*

Think about your attitudes toward having money and wielding power in your personal relationships. Are the two intimately connected? Can you have one without the other?

The Meaning of Work - But Can He Hunt?

Young boys raised in an average family setting are instilled at a relatively early age with the idea that work is a way to develop responsibility and generate money to support whatever hobbies they may have. All of the men in our personal interviews recalled working for money in their preteens. Delivering newspapers, mowing lawns, shoveling snow, washing cars, the list is endless, but the point is the same. If you are a boy, you will be expected to work at something to make money. Sometimes, depending on the family situation, young boys will even work to help support the family.

For a young man, work also means power through a sense of control of one's destiny. "If I have some spending change I have the power to buy the things I want," he learns. "I don't have to ask anyone for an allowance. If I'm a teenage boy, I am a legitimate player in the dating game because I have the one commodity that gives me access to the girls — the money to go out and have fun."

Not that young girls don't work to bring in some money for themselves or the family, particularly in the case of very large families where every able body tries to help out. In general, however, there isn't the same expectation on their heads. Although young women are increasingly raised to be more independent and self-sufficient these days, they aren't usually told to look for a "house husband" to support.

Unfortunately for those of us men who are half of a couple, work is often the best way of keeping our heads above water in their relationship. Work, says John Gray, author of "Men Are From Mars, Women Are From Venus," "is a way to repair the tear in the male energy or ego. His work can become a way for him to feel independent and not so dependent on an intimate loving relationship."

In other words, if Shareef brings back a skin and gives it to Sharmaine, she has a choice. If it's too small for her taste she can fold it up and put it away. If it's big enough to satisfy her competitive feelings toward Azizi, she can put it on her wall. Either way, Shareef has done his job and Sharmaine still has to have his dinner ready when he returns.

What Does Work Mean to You?

If you are a man, work is intimately linked to your self-image. It provides a way for you to compete, mark your territory, exercise your male energy or ego to reach your objectives, and acquire possessions (including a woman). "A man's sense of self-worth is deeply connected to his ability to persist or carry through with a goal," notes David Dieda in "It's a Guy Thing". "And this can be even more important than an intimate relationship," Diedra continues, "because it gets to the heart of the very definition of what a man believes he is".

For a man, work is like that mountain we mentioned earlier. You can see the top and it's measurable, although you may not know how you're going to get there. One way to think about conquering that mountain is to take it in three stages. What stage do you think you are in and what can your partner do to help you advance to the next level?

Chapter 12

The Three Stages
Of A Man's Career

"If a woman is unhappy in her relationship, she can't concentrate on her work. If a man is unhappy at work, he can't focus on his relationship"

— Barbara

Men go through three stages in their careers: The **Not Quite There/Starting Over Stage**, the **Male Passage Stage**, and the **I've Arrived Stage**. At each stage, men have different needs and desires. Let's see where you fit in.

Not Quite There/Starting Over Stage

If you are at the **Not Quite There** stage, you are searching to establish

> *He believes that marriage and a career don't mix. So after the wedding he plans to quit his job.*
>
> — Anonymous

yourself on a competitive career track. You are focusing all your efforts on building your career. You may feel uncertain about your future and have major insecurities about your ability to succeed in life. If you are in the similar **Starting Over** stage, you are changing careers, have been fired or let go, or are having a hard time finding a job or career path. Your finances are shaky, plus all your energy is going into finding employment – or the right employment. Work is a major priority and your relationship comes second. This is when you hope your companion will be patient, listen to you, provide positive reinforcement, comfort you, and give you space to overcome your fears and doubts until you feel confident again. By allowing you to work through your "stuff", your partner will benefit when you come out of your slump.

Michael: When my father was a young man, he took a job with a major aerospace company that changed his life because he made five times more money working for someone else than he did running his own flying business. It turned out to be a nice "career" that enabled him to raise a family of four and eventually retire. But was working for the aerospace company his passion? No. My father was a Tuskegee Airman whose passion was flying airplanes, a passion he sacrificed because he didn't think it was possible to fly airplanes and fulfill his familial responsibilities at the same time. No one had ever told him that if you are good at something you can find a way to generate income from it. So, given a choice between making money now or following his passion and eventually reaping the rewards, there was no way he wasn't going for the money.

Like my father, African American parents, grandparents, and farther-back ancestors sacrificed much to gain access to steady, well-paying jobs. Making more money was the "right" answer for my dad. It was the most responsible thing he could do. As a result, all four of his kids have college degrees but none of us can fly. Think deeply on that one. Sometimes I wonder if my father secretly needs confirmation from his offspring that he made the right choice. Maybe if we all have successful "9-5" careers he will feel justified in his decision to sacrifice his passion.

With that family history, it was not easy for me to pull up "stable" stakes in Southern California and move to the Bay Area. All my life I have been unwilling to take any great risks to achieve anything. Childhood experiences had saddled me with a basic distaste for situations that might embarrass, subject me to ridicule, or showcase my weaknesses. I had developed a sense of cynicism about the way things are in the world — not totally unfounded but, nevertheless, not a healthy outlook. I had settled for the easy and comfortable, while sometimes being an observer rather than a participant. But easy and comfortable doesn't always bring out the best in a person.

Truth of the matter was that my life wasn't going well because I was trying to shoehorn myself into a number of different "careers". These workplaces weren't for me. They were better suited for friends, peers, and others whom I admired. True, I gained a broad array of skills and honed parts of my personality, especially in presenting ideas before an audience, that I would otherwise not have developed. However, I'd never thoughtfully considered what I really wanted to do, so in a sense these careers picked me. Oh, there are lots of jobs I can do, but in the end I'd be unhappy, bored, or both.

I came to realize that a "career" was a legacy of my parent's generation—people who struggled and sometimes died to open doors to "jobs" and "careers" for succeeding generations of African Americans. Parents always want their kids to have more than they had. New socks but old shoes for me and I kept finding myself between a rock and a "9-to-5". I took jobs for the prestige, the money, or the potential for money.

With so much emphasis on settling into a regular occupation, I had become a clock-watcher. I did just enough to get me through the day so I could go home and enjoy life. My motto was, "Live for the weekend." I have a feeling a lot of men do this on the job. Rarely do they rebel. Remember the attorney played by Michael Beach in the movie, "Soul Food"? His wife, played by Vanessa Williams, was also an attorney and couldn't understand why her husband wanted to give up his lucrative law practice for his real passion, music, a profession with no guarantees. The resulting conflict tore up their marriage.

If, like the lawyer in the movie, you're in a career that has you counting the hours, minutes, and seconds until you're free each day to do what you really want to do, it might be a good idea to reevaluate what you are doing. But don't forget to consult with your partner in the process. Unfortunately the trap we sometimes fall into begins with not discovering what we really want to do — our true calling— until it's too late.

Now, as a son of a pilot, I have decided to determine if I can "fly". I've decided to start a technology training firm that would service Northern and Southern California clients. I know that in rejecting a "good job" and a steady paycheck in Los Angeles, I am taking a great risk. Still, one of my new goals is financial independence and I am not going to achieve that by getting a good job with benefits.

Cheryl: *Five months after Michael left L.A. for Oakland, he realized that the job he moved here to take wasn't the right one for him. This realization started to adversely affect his mood and overall well being, which, in turn, adversely affected our relationship. This was happening while we were collaborating on this book. At the time, my personal coach told me we were actually living the book. He was so right. Because I understood that Michael was going through the Starting Over Stage, I realized he needed my backup. If I hadn't known better, I might have ended the relationship. Instead, I suggested he go away for a weekend alone to focus on what he wanted to do about his career. I wanted him to know that he had the freedom and space to work it out and if he needed me, I would be there to support him. Taking that time alone proved to be beneficial.*

Women: How to Help Your Man Through This Stage

If your partner is going through the Not Quite There or Starting Over stage, the first thing you can do is offer positive reinforcement. It's reassuring for him to know you have confidence in him no matter what. This is also the time to show interest in his quest for a second career, the new job he just started, or the small business he's trying to start. Sincere comments like, "I understand why you are spending extra time at the job, is there anything I can do to help you relax?" or "How's the new business going?" are music to his ears. Try saying, "Whatever decision you make, just know that I'm here to support you". Last but not least, say, "Thank you, I really appreciate all the effort you are making toward building our financial future". An understanding partner is a blessing during a time when he needs all the moral support he can get.

All Work and No Play – No Way

Though he's preoccupied with work, your man also needs a little fun in his life. Don't wait for him to suggest it. Take charge and plan outings such as:

- Going to a matinee (they're cheaper than the same movie at night)

- Eating at a new, exotic and inexpensive restaurant

- Browsing at the bookstore

- Working out together at the gym

- Going wine tasting

- Walking to a neighborhood coffee shop

- Spending an afternoon at an outdoor jazz concert

- Attending a worship service or spiritual retreat

- Going hiking or bike riding

These activities will get him away from work for a few hours and lighten the pressure he's feeling which, in turn, will lower his stress-levels, and increase the chances of making love and money work for both of you! A word of caution: Don't plan outings that entail spending a lot of money, even if you offer to foot the bill. Knowing he can't afford to pay may make him feel less of a man at a time when he's already vulnerable to self doubt.

The Male Passage Stage

As a man, the **Male Passage** stage embodies a powerful time of change, as you take your career to the next level. It's powerful because you have a lot more confidence than you did during the Not Quite There/Starting Over stage. You now know that no matter what hurdles you encounter, you'll be able to vault over them and land on your feet.

The boosted sense of self you have at this stage typically leads to an increase in income. And in your mind, more money is equivalent to more power. If you are married, you may not see your spouse as much as you'd like because you're spending most of your time at work. Once your career is firmly established, you'll come back to the relationship much stronger. If you are single, you may hold off getting seriously involved in a relationship until you feel you can simultaneously handle both a career and a home life. When you are ready, however, you will look for a partner with her own career and talents to share your success and accomplishments. Together you will build a financially prosperous life.

There are risks to couples when you are in the Male Passage stage. If your partner doesn't understand what you are doing, you and she may end up like Bill and Karen.

Bill and Karen

Bill, a hard working entrepreneur, has been struggling for the last five years to get his telecommunications business off the ground. He has been in a committed relationship with Karen for three of those years. But Karen doesn't understand what Bill needs. She constantly calls him at the office to ask what time he'll be home and gives him a hard time about working late or being on the road. Karen's behavior has caused tremendous stress in the relationship, which has led to several arguments over work and money. The fact that Karen isn't supportive of his business is the main reason Bill hasn't asked her to marry him. And at this point, he probably never will.

According to several men in our study, this scenario is all too typical. They all said they wished their partners could be more patient and understanding. After all, the reason they were working so hard was to benefit the relationship. If their partners can stick it out as they build their future, the men said, there may be rewards to reap later on.

Women: How to Help Your Man Through This Stage

Do all the things we listed above for women who want to maintain and strengthen their relationship through the Not Quite There/Starting Over stage. One More Suggestion: If you are in a non-married relationship, this isn't the time to pressure your partner into tying the knot. Although he is clearly succeeding on the job or in running his own business, he still needs to concentrate on working and making money. He may respond to pressure to wed by backing away from the relationship, instead.

The I've Arrived Stage — When It Works

As a man in the **I've Arrived** stage, you are successful and comfortable in your career. You are financially stable and socially respected. You know what your goals are and are confident of achieving them. Because you're at the top, you have more time for family and friends. This is a wonderful time for you. You're at the top of your game, pulling in thousands, hundreds of thousands, or even millions. You own your own home, can buy any car you want, and have a handsome investment portfolio watched over by a topflight financial advisor. If you are already in a relationship, it is most likely financially smooth at this point.

Denzel Washington is at the I've Arrived Stage. The night he won the 2002 Academy Award for Best Actor, he thanked those who had worked with him on the movie, "Training Day," and paid homage to Sidney Poitier, the pioneering black movie star who was in the audience. Then Denzel recounted to a worldwide television audience what he had said to his four children earlier that evening. "I told them whether I won or didn't win, we'd be home to celebrate with them. So, kids," he said into the camera, Oscar raised high in his fist, "We're on our way home!" Comfortable with himself and his accomplishments, Denzel was beyond the need to impress others in the after-Oscar party crowd.

As an actor herself, Denzel's wife, Pauletta Pearson, knew how tough it had been for him to establish himself in the cutthroat world of Hollywood. She stuck with him through the rough years early in his career. Now she's enjoying the fruits of their labor – his as an actor, hers as a homemaker, wife and mother. Not only that, they have a family to enjoy together.

When a woman understands the career stage her partner is in, she can get a better feel for her relationship with him. If she knows what a man is looking for and what he is able to give to the relationship based on the stage of his career, it will be easier for her to decide whether or not she wants to get involved – or stay involved — with him. Along with this knowledge, a woman can complement her man as he grows his career. Together they will build a happy, financially prosperous relationship.

That's what Camille Cosby did. Many years ago, when young Bill Cosby asked an even younger Camille to marry him, he was just another poor stand-up comedian. The rest is history. We all know how Cosby developed himself into a global household name. Camille carved out a complementary career, earning advanced degrees, raising five children, and developing charitable, feminist, and educational endeavors under her own name. Today, by virtue of the fortune they have amassed, the Cosbys work together to help black colleges and other worthy institutions and individuals to achieve higher goals.

The I've Arrived Stage — When It Doesn't Work

If you are a single man at the I've Arrived stage, rather than a husband like Denzel or Bill, you may be looking to share life with a woman who already has her career and finances together. You are ripe for a relationship where love and money works. But though you may think you are ready for a woman who wields her own financial clout, you may be surprised at how the real thing scares you off. Here's Jenny's story.

Jenny

Four years ago Jenny dated a very successful businessman who turned out to be scared of commitment. He had been alone for over 17 years and not long before she met him, had left his fiancee at the "altar" one week before the wedding date. This was obviously a red flag, but she didn't pay attention. This guy was in the I've Arrived Stage materially, but not emotionally. He was controlling and always wanted things to go his way. After a few months of dealing with his self-centered behavior, she realized he was bad news and quickly got out of the relationship. As she looks back on it now, the relationship might have worked because they had several interests in common. But she was at a point where she was unwilling to put up with BS from any man. So she couldn't give him what he needed – a woman who did not mind being controlled. He was unable to see her as an independent person used to making her own decisions who, even so, might have been a suitable companion for him at that time in his life.

Sharing the Stage—For Women

While it may seem that we are placing more emphasis on the three stages of the male career than those of the female, we're not. We're merely sharing with you how men think and the types of cultural pressures a man feels to succeed in the workplace. Many readers who are women may say, "I'm not willing to play second fiddle in my relationship because my career is just as important". That's true, and you have every right to feel that way. We <u>have</u> come a long way baby. But based on the conversations we had with couples who are making love and money work, the women didn't have a problem with complementing their partner's careers and were happy and fulfilled in their relationships. These women were not subservient, they were equals. They benefitted from building wealth, traveling, and retiring together with their partners. Making love and money work is all about sharing the fruits of labor in your relationship, not competing against each other.

Chapter 11 and 12 Making Love and Money Work Action Steps

1. Women, no matter what you think always be supportive of your man's career. Don't try to compete. Develop your own complementary career.

2. Men, understand the three different stages you go through in your career. Adjust how you and your partner manage your money and your relationship based on your career stage.

3. Women, if your partner is in the Not Quite There/Starting Over stage of his career, provide him with your vote of confidence. Let him know you appreciate the fact that he is working hard or starting his own business for the benefit of the family and the relationship. Allow him the space to put in the extra time at the office until he is able to get past the challenges of this difficult stage. Your loving support will enhance the relationship.

4. Men, when you are making a major change in your career, money is generally a sore subject to discuss. It is usually tight during the transition. This is the time to suggest that your woman focus on her own money goals. Learn more about investing. Talk to a financial advisor. Figure out ways to make her and your money grow. The less financial pressure she places on you, the less stress on the relationship.

5. Men and women, when you and your partner are going through challenging financial times, don't bail out of the relationship. Money troubles are hard on everyone but particularly for a man who still today believes he must be the primary breadwinner, even if his partner is bringing in six-figures. He must believe he can get out of his financial slump. Sometimes his partner's belief in him is all that is needed.

Notes

Chapter 13

When She Earns More — Helping Couples Adjust When Her Wallet Is Thicker Than His

Sabrina and Andre

Sabrina, 38 and an entertainment attorney, was deeply surprised and disturbed by Andre's reaction when she told him with excitement that she was finally being made a partner at her law firm with an increase in pay to more than $250,000 a year. Andre, [whose job as a marketing executive brought in $80,000 per year] had simply looked at her, said "Uh-huh", and gone back to reading the sports page.

Sabrina was crushed. She had thought he'd be happy to hear her good news and want to celebrate with a bottle of champagne. Didn't he understand that her higher income meant they could buy a larger home and extra vacations? Or that he could now start the consulting business he had been talking about for the last five years? Couldn't he see all the benefits the extra money will bring?

Unfortunately, Andre couldn't. All he could think about was that his partner would now be bringing home bigger paychecks than he. "Now," he muttered to himself, "she'll start trying to tell me what to do." Well, he definitely wasn't going for that! He was still the man no matter how much money she made.

Andre's response actually wasn't all that surprising. In Chapter 11, Work, Power and Money – How Men View Relationships, we learned that men believe money buys them power over women and that they lose that power once their partner's income equals or surpasses theirs. That's exactly how Andre reacted. And Andre is not alone.

> *He, early on, let her know who is the boss. He looked her right in the eye and clearly said "you're the boss!"*
>
> —— Anonymous

Women Are Catching Up

According to one study, about 29 percent of working women earn more than their male partners. Author Randi Minetor, ("Breadwinner Wives and the Men They Marry") ups that figure to 33 percent. Forty-eight percent of working women provide more than 50 percent of their families' incomes. Married female executives at major corporations earn a whopping 75 percent more than their husbands.

The trend is gathering steam. In 1981, the U.S. Census Bureau found that only 16 percent of wives earned more than their husbands. By 1998, that number had grown to 23 percent. Such changing statistics create uncertainty among women as well as men. In a National Marriage and Money Survey conducted by Prudential Securities in 1998, 53 percent of women felt it would be a problem if a wife earned more than her husband, but only 34 percent of men felt that way. On the other hand, while only 48 percent of higher-income women thought they should pay alimony to their former husbands if they divorced, a full 58 percent of men were quite willing to accept alimony if they and their high income wife parted ways. Sounds like we Americans can't decide which way we want to have it.

Black Women, Especially, Are Catching Up

Higher-earning women are particularly prevalent in the African American community. According to the latest U.S. Census Bureau data, 1.7 million black women have a bachelor's degree compared to 1.2 million black men. This means that statistically speaking a black woman has a 30 percent chance of teaming up with a partner who earns less money. And, of course, that means a black man has a 30 percent chance of teaming up with a partner who earns more.

Historically speaking, we all know that black men and women have long had to deal with disparate incomes. Ever since slavery and right down through Reconstruction, Jim Crow, and legalized segregation and discrimination, African American men have been oppressed and disrespected by white society in myriad ways. African American women have also been oppressed but were seen by white people as being less threatening to have around. In many black households, the woman may have made more money as a housemaid, school teacher or social worker than her handyman, truck driver or laborer husband.

Black Men, Especially, Are Feeling Threatened

So though conditions for black men are substantially better in the 21st Century than ever before, our men are still extremely sensitive to appearing weak or dominated, especially by their own women. They are looking for a woman who will build them up, not tear them down merely because they don't have a prestigious job title or a high income. Black men are struggling to become more assertive and to deal effectively with the impact of centuries of continuing racism. They need positive, not negative, support.

Alvis Davis, psychologist and author of "Black Men Not Looking For Sex", emphatically agrees that black men are threatened when their black women partners make more money. Not only because it bruises their ego and makes them doubt their manhood, but because of what we talked about in Chapter 9, Women Looking For A Money Prince Charming. "While black women are improving their economic situation, many still carry around a lot of fairy tale notions," says Davis. "The biggest one is that a smart, smiling, handsome prince with shining black muscles will show up in his Mercedes and sweep them off their feet to happiness forever."

It also doesn't help matters when society, parents, girlfriends, and the media continue to perpetuate this fantasy for black women to the point that when they do meet a man they expect him to measure up to those mythical standards. The men, on the other hand, are well aware of the black woman's fantasy and feel extremely pressured to live up to these high expectations. So being in a relationship with a woman who makes more money is a reminder that he isn't man enough or smart enough to have a job or career that will allow him to be the main breadwinner.

Dr. Larry Davis, author of the book, "Black and Single: Meeting and Choosing a Partner Who is Right for You," adds that black men and women's expectations of themselves and their partners have not kept pace with the employment and economic realities of today. Right now, for example, there are more black women in the workforce. Because of higher education levels, some manage their own businesses or hold down well-paying professional jobs. At the same time, fewer black men are employed due to major losses in manufacturing and heavy industry jobs. In addition, not enough black men are obtaining advanced degrees to keep up with the worldwide shift to information technology.

What You Do When You Feel Threatened

If, like Andre, you suddenly find yourself in a relationship with a woman who earns more money, many questions may pop into your mind. Will her career be more important than our relationship? Why does she need me when she can get everything she wants herself? Will people see her success as an indication of my failure? And finally, the major challenge, will she be willing and able to leave the "I'm-in-charge" attitude at the office or will she bring it home? It's hard enough to deal with your boss at work. You don't want to come home and deal with a competitive and domineering partner as well.

So while you may claim to be supportive of your higher income partner, you may belie that claim by subtly undermining her efforts. You may try to control other aspects of the relationship such as how she dresses, wears her hair, or spends her money. You may try to bring her down by nagging, "Do you have to work late again tonight?" or, "When's the last time I had a home-cooked meal?" You may try to belittle her success by saying "No big deal" or "So what" when she comes home excited about a new accomplishment. Or you may retaliate by insisting that she do all the housework, sympathize with your stressful day, and still be dy-no-mite in bed at night. If she complains, you have the answer: She needs to cut back on time spent at work and devote more time to the family. These remarks will weigh heavily on your partner, causing her to feel so guilty for being a successful career woman that the conflict only serves to drive a wedge into the relationship.

What's Behind Your Unfair Behavior

The biggest fear you may have when your loved one starts earning more than you do is that she won't need you anymore. "In order for a man to stay committed to his relationship," says Dr. Ronn Elmore, a psychotherapist and author of two bestselling relationship books, "he must feel he is bringing something she needs to the table. Knowing she can do just fine without him is a hard pill for him to swallow. The couples who come to me over this issue are fighting over the distribution of money not the lack of it." As Helen, a friend of ours, found out, this conflict can occur even between two high-income earners who ostensibly have no money problems whatsoever.

Helen

Helen's relationship with William, a six-figure marketing executive she met at a marketing conference three years ago, verifies Dr. Elmore's point. They didn't actually meet at the conference; it was at the airport on her way home to Denver and on his to Kansas City. A handsome, distinguished looking man, William spoke with Helen briefly and they exchanged cards. Later, on the plane, Helen read the card and learned that William was a marketing manager for a top beverage corporation. Two questions immediately came to her mind: 1) is he married and 2) could his company sponsor her motivational training seminars. She saw this as an opportunity not to pass up and after a week sent an "it was nice to meet you" note. Okay, so she did make the first move. Hey, that's what networking is all about, right?

Anyway, he took the bait and called a week later. Turns out he was 53, not married, and hadn't been for 16 years. After a lengthy telephone conversation William and Helen agreed to meet for dinner in Chicago, the location of her next speaking engagement. They had dinner and a great conversation. They seemed pretty compatible. The only problem was that she lived in Colorado and he in Missouri. They continued their whirlwind rendezvous' in New York, New Orleans, Kansas City and Denver.

Two months into the relationship, while having dinner, the subject of money came up. They began talking about income and she knew William was "fishing" for information because he mentioned his salary first: $125,000. When she mentioned that her income was $250,000, he was floored. He tried to laugh and joke about it and said it didn't matter to him, but she could tell the information did not sit pretty with him. She realized it was the beginning of the end of their relationship. The next few times they met became a tug of war over who was in "control". William was suddenly determined to tell her how to dress and what exercises to do. He wanted to *order her food and drinks. Needless to say the relationship fell apart. Later, when Helen looked back, she realized William had signaled his discomfort early on by recounting a broken engagement to a woman who made close to $900,000 a year. When she had asked him why, he had said, "We just weren't compatible". This was truly a red flag, yet Helen had refused to see it.*

What Was Going On?

According to Dr. Elmore, William lost power in his own eyes when he discovered Helen made more than he. He tried to regain the power by telling her how to dress, what to eat and drink, and what exercises to do. When Helen didn't go for it, the romantic relationship ended though they kept in touch. Two years later, William married an unemployed woman with a young son whose father had died in an automobile accident. William told Helen that he planned to help raise the young boy and to help his fiancee get her life back in order. It was the classic rescue relationship. William would be in total control: exactly what he needed to feed his ego.

We hope Helen's story doesn't taint your perspective regarding women earning more money then their partner. There are many instances where it does work. Take Lauren and Kurt, a high- powered Los Angeles couple. During their 12-year marriage they have amassed more than $4 million in assets working as a team despite the fact that Lauren way out-earns Kurt.

Lauren and Kurt

Although Lauren, a record producer for a major record label, makes ten times the amount of Kurt's actor income, it has never been an issue. They agreed from the very beginning of their relationship to work together to build wealth and it didn't matter who brought home the most bacon. Today their goal is to accumulate enough income to retire in five more years and travel around the world.

Managing The Money

Lauren and Kurt manage their money with both joint checking and investment accounts as well as separate personal checking and investment accounts. While each is responsible for certain household bills all money-making decisions are made jointly. Their assets include four homes in the United States and the Caribbean and an investment portfolio worth over $1 million.

Lauren and Kurt's Advice on Making Love and Money Work

- *Do something you love. When you are passionate about your work the money will come.*

- *Take your ego out of it. Don't sweat who is bringing in more. Men who have trouble with their partner making more money usually have deeper issues of low self-esteem.*

- *Pay your credit cards off in total every month.*

- *Building wealth takes discipline. In the beginning, don't buy everything you want.*

As you can see, Lauren and Kurt are secure within themselves. They don't follow the old traditional financial script. Instead, they have developed a new code: Any money brought into the relationship is not yours or mine but "ours." It doesn't matter who puts the most in the family pot. Dr. Gwendolyn Goldsby Grant, noted author of "The Best Kind Of Loving—a Black Woman's Guide To Finding Intimacy" and columnist for Essence magazine, says that couples must depersonalize the money. It cannot be <u>her</u> money or <u>his</u> money – it's <u>our</u> money to fund our dreams and to build wealth. That's real love and commitment.

It's Not About The Money

As Lauren and Kurt have done, we black couples must adjust our expectations to reflect changing times. Men, remember that you are equal in your relationship even if your partner brings home a bigger paycheck. Otherwise, you will continue to fear that your higher-earning mate will try to use her power to tell you what to do. Women, stop feeling guilty when you earn more, and don't let your man retaliate by making unreasonable demands in other areas of your life. Keep the vision of the family in mind and don't hesitate to support your man no matter how much less money he is bringing home than you.

A man's worth is **not** defined by the size of his paycheck. Rather than measuring our partners by dollar signs, black women must form an opinion of a man based on intangible assets like how closely our money values and styles jibe, how we get along together and how we treat each other. A successful relationship is based not on money but on love and trust. Positive relationships develop because partners complement each other. They fulfill each others' needs. A man is not less of a man because of the money.

All That Matters Is That There Is More Money In The Bank

The old relationship model is outdated. Black men and women must now give each other the freedom to pursue a more balanced life. Material things aren't the most important part of a relationship. You can have all the money in the world, but if the love and respect isn't there, the relationship is going nowhere. Dr. Elmore cautions black men to remember that every black woman who earns more money isn't down on you because you aren't equally financially successful. Yes, she will want to see that you know how to handle the money, but she doesn't require that you "break the bank" before she gives you the time of day.

To be sure, there are issues that can block a relationship when traditional roles are reversed and the woman earns more. But there are great positive benefits as well. The first one is that a woman's higher income makes for a larger family total that allows everyone to live more comfortably. Second, a woman's higher income takes a huge amount of pressure off her partner to be the major provider. Men are now free to pursue unmet goals like going back to school and getting a law degree or starting a new business, which may actually improve the relationship down the line.

How To Make It Work

We will not say that making this type of relationship work is easy, but it can be done. Changing a thousand-year-old tradition is no small feat for either of you. It entails changing your entire belief system. Here are some suggestions to speed that process.

For Women

- Reveal before you enter into an exclusive relationship that you either make more money than he does or will in the future. Decide who will pay for dinner dates, movie tickets, groceries and vacations. In the beginning, all of this may seem awkward. But, as Dr. Elmore points, out, it just means the relationship is going through the growing pains of adopting an alternative financial script. Remember that though your man is liberated and open to doing things differently, he will still occasionally feel pressure to go back to the old traditional financial script.

- Talk about how each of you will feel if you get a promotion and start earning even more. It's always easier and better to discuss heated topics way before they happen. Alerting your partner to that possibility could diminish future conflicts. Reassure him that money and career status are not the be-all-and-end-all of your relationship.

- Continue to communicate. Relationships work because there is communication and both partners are clear on each other's boundaries. For example, if you begin to employ a power play because you make more, ask your man to call you on it.

- Learn how to talk about money in a gentle, nonthreatening way. When you grill him and demand immediate answers, what he hears you saying between the lines is, "You're incompetent".

- Set limits on disparaging remarks. Women who earn more than their mates may have to nip snide remarks from friends, family or coworkers in the bud. Usually the best way to handle this is to take the gossipers aside and let them know in no uncertain terms that such remarks are off limits.

- Review your expectations. Women who earn more are sometimes concerned when their partner doesn't seem as ambitious as they are. If that's your case, examine what's really going on in your man's life. Is it because he lost his job and can't find another, or is it a natural part of his personality? Not every man is driven to become a millionaire. Don't decide you're going to make him more ambitious. You can't change his basic nature any more than he can change yours.

- Instead, focus on the positive qualities he brings to the relationship. Maybe he is a supportive partner, a great cook, or a wonderful father. The key is to accept him just the way he is. When a person does what he or she does best, they make a much happier partner.

For Men

- Understand that your higher-earning partner is not your enemy. Her goal is not to show you up. It's the exact opposite; to improve the relationship. Asking you to account for the money you two manage jointly doesn't mean she doesn't love and respect you. In fact, she will love you more if you are open and aboveboard with her.

- Renegotiate the domestic workload. Society will continue to hold your partner responsible for the bulk of the household chores no matter how much money she brings home. She, too, may think she's supposed to do all the housework no matter what. You can help her by offering to divide the domestic duties as evenly as possible. After all, chefs are men, vacuum cleaner inventors are men, washing machine repairmen are men, and fathers are men. So sharing the cooking, cleaning, laundry, and child-care burden doesn't detract from your manhood, it adds to it.

Michael's Perspective

Here are some thoughts on how a man can handle the situation when his partner makes more money than he does.

Educate Yourself Financially

A good friend of mine wrote a play about a group of high school buddies who get together for their 20-year reunion. In the play each man talks about his failures and his triumphs and the lessons he has learned. One, a basketball player, ends his story by saying, "Don't let your mouth, your hands, or your feet take you anywhere that your mind can't keep you!" Statistics bear out that a large majority of lottery winners are broke after 5 or 10 years because they're not smart enough to hold on to their loot. Spending money doesn't make money. Investing does. Conflicts that arise when she earns more are definitely influenced by the level of financial education on both sides, because what you don't know or understand, you have a tendency to fear. My advice to men whose mates make more money: Help her learn how to invest it so that both of you benefit in the long run.

Who Has the Power?

Ask any woman who earns more than her significant other if she ever tells herself, "I don't have to take no stuff off of him". If she's honest, she'll say, sure, if worse comes to worse, she could leave because she doesn't need him for his money. I do feel that a woman with a high income feels more "powerful" or "independent" due in large part to the amount of money she earns. But that doesn't mean she doesn't want to have a permanent, loving relationship with a good man within which money is an asset, not a bone of contention.

What Does a Difference in Power Mean?

For some men, a difference in earning means a tilt in the balance of power in a relationship. From childhood, they have been programmed to believe there are certain rights and privileges associated with being the "breadwinner." These men believe that if they aren't the "bread winner" in it's narrowest sense, then they will have to learn how to cook, clean, and manage the house since that's the only other role left. Or that the partner with the most money will have the bigger say in any major relationship or family decisions. These ideas are not necessarily the case in today's changed economic and social landscape. A couple can learn to think differently about the role of money in their relationship.

When Did It Happen?

Issues arising for couples with a big disparity in earnings are also influenced, for sure, on when it happens, or the timing involved. For instance, a married couple starts out with similar earning levels and then the wife gets a promotion or a new job that provides a substantial increase. As a man, I might feel more secure about that than beginning a relationship with a significant difference. The former situation is based on the idea that we're growing together and the event of a new job or earnings increase is a stamp of approval or blessing bestowed upon our union.

How Much More is Too Much More?

In any discussions with men about women earning more, the question, "How much more?" inevitably arises. Most red-blooded guys really don't have issues with women making 10, 20, or $30,000 more than they and shrug off any suggestions to the contrary. However it might be a different story if the woman doubled, tripled, or even made 10 times as much. I think when you get on that order of magnitude, the comfort level starts to waver a bit for men who aren't sure of themselves, of what they want out of life, or of where their power lies. It takes a really secure man to withstand teasing and not allow the financial disparities to result in destructive ego-driven games within the relationship. There are such men who have this type of security and don't have a problem with their mates taking the leading role in money-making. Kurt, Lauren's partner whom we mentioned earlier in this chapter, is one such man. Steadman Graham, Oprah Winfrey's longtime beau, seems to be another. These men bring enough to the relationship to mitigate the money factor. For others, taking second place in the income sweepstakes makes them feel completely powerless. We probably don't hear about the couples that break up under these circumstances. Sad to say, they were unable to make love and money work.

Chapter 13: Making Love and Money Work Action Steps

1. Remember, it's not about the money

2. All that matters is that there is more money in the bank. Get over who makes more.

3. To make love and money work in this situation, you and your partner must change your belief system that says the man must be the major breadwinner.

4. For women, don't use the fact that you make more as a weapon in an argument.

5. Whoever makes the most money **does not** have to have the most power. Adopt an alternative financial script to get rid of that outdated concept. It's what's in the bank that counts, not who put it there.

Notes

Chapter 14

The Singles Money Scene —
How To Play By
The New Rules

"Money Don't Matter Tonight"`—Prince

Cheryl: *Shortly after my separation, I attended a MOBE (Marketing Opportunities In Business and Entertainment) marketing conference in New Orleans. A couple of hours before the evening reception I met Phillip, a marketing entrepreneur, in the lobby of the hotel. After talking for an hour or so with him he invited me to dinner to a popular restaurant in the French Quarter. We were having a great conversation, so I thought this would be an opportunity to continue and see some sights too. We had a nice dinner during which we discussed business, relationships (he was single), and, in particular, what I did for a living. At the conclusion of our meal the waiter placed the bill in the middle of the table. Phillip immediately said, "How do you want to do this?"*

It was the first time in a while I had been on an actual date and I had been under the impression that if the man invites, he pays. Needless to say, I was surprised. But I played it off and said, let's split it. I put half the money on the table and left for the ladies restroom. When I got back from the restroom my money was still on the table and the bill was gone. When I questioned what happened, Phillip said, "That's OK, I invited you to dinner, I'll pay". After returning home from the conference Phillip called a couple of times, but I never returned his phone call.

Michael's Response: *What Phillip might have been thinking or feeling was that he was caught between the old and new rules, and that his situational acuity (in other words, "What am I supposed to do?") wasn't honed enough. What may have happened is that after their dinner conversation Phillip was unsure as to what Cheryl's rules were. These days, a lot of successful women like to exercise their right to contribute to or even pay for the meal. It shows their financial independence. Many women have ridden the wave of backlash regarding dating and paying. Some don't like the idea of a man paying all the time because of what they think the man's expectations will be. Men, therefore, aware of this sentiment may look for signs in a woman that she, in certain circumstances, would like to share equally or even pay for the meal.*

Phillip wasn't sure whether Cheryl wanted to play the power game or not. So when Cheryl got up to go the restroom, he took that as a "cue" that she did not, even though she'd laid some money on the table. By the time she returned he had retraced his steps and offered to pay the entire bill.

Old Money Rule: The Man Pays

Without a doubt men and women are confused on how to handle the bill on a date. The main reason is because we're still operating under the Old Money Rule in a social environment that has drastically changed. As Michael likes to say, old socks, new shoes. So, what is the old money rule? The man pays for the date regardless of who invited whom or how much financial wherewithal the woman has.

Since time immemorial, that's how things worked. Most women lived at home or worked at low paying jobs and waited to be invited out by men who, as primary wage earners, were expected to take the initiative in matters romantic. When they did go  "I can afford her... I can afford her not... I can afford her..." to dinner, the waitperson handed the man a menu with prices and the woman the same menu but without prices. During the meal, the waitperson brought the man a sample of wine to approve. At the end of the meal, the waitperson brought the check to the man. The woman was trained not to ask how much. She was expected to chose that moment to go to the restroom to "freshen up" her makeup.

Money was rarely discussed during courtship. But as time went on, the man assumed that in return for always paying for the date he was eventually entitled to the woman's sexual favors in return. If the woman declined to "put out," as the old saying went, the man felt entitled to drop her. She clearly was not keeping her end of the "bargain", and he was free to look for someone who would.

If a woman did manage to snag a husband whether she followed the old money rule or not, the pattern set by the man continued after marriage. The wife might be given a household allowance and could ask her mate for money to go shopping. But the husband made all the major financial decisions and was considered the head of the household, no questions asked.

How did men acquire that status? Mostly by emulating their fathers. Boys watched Dad pay the dinner bill and were programmed to do the same thing. Girls were taught the same lesson: Father rules the roost. Even now, some women grow up and look for a father figure to continue taking care of them. Have you ever heard of a "sugar daddy"? This is how ingrained the old rule is in our culture.

Times Are Changing

Today, social norms are changing as a result of a number of factors: the mass entry during and after World War II of women into the workplace, the Civil Rights and feminist movements, the softening of the patriarchal bias in this country, and the general benefits of a diversifying economy. Nowadays, a man is no longer expected to be the only partner responsible for "winning the bread." It's not unusual now for a wife to provide as much, if not more, financial support than her husband. Children see this and realize that the days of the father being the sole provider are over. Both boys and girls expect to grow up being self-supporting. Girls know just like boys know that they will have to get a job. When they do, they become able to and entitled to ask a man on a date — and to pay for it.

New Money Rules: The Man and The Woman Pay

If you are a woman, we urge you to considering adopting the following rules. We have a feeling your man already agrees with them:

1) He or she who invites should always be prepared to pay.

2) If there are more dates, you should occasionally offer to pay.

3) Not all invitations are dates.

4) One slipup is no reason to dog your man forever.

New Money Rule 1: He or she who invites should always be prepared to pay

It is perfectly acceptable for you to invite a man on a date – as long as you are prepared to pick up the tab. This is especially true if you make more money than he does. In today's economy both men and women are working hard to earn a decent living, so it's disrespectful to ask him out then expect him to pay.

Men dating women who out-earn them see a major disparity in the Old Money Rule, and are beginning to rebel against it. Many have a difficult time feeling obligated to treat their date to dinner knowing all along that she could probably buy the restaurant. Remember, these are men who were raised believing that the one with the most money pays. So, guess what? If that's you, the rule still applies.

New Money Rule 2: *After the first date, you should occasionally offer to pay*

If he initiates the first date, he will probably insist on paying. But, if there are second, third and fourth get-togethers, you should offer to cover one of those, regardless of whom does the asking. "An offer can go a long way, it's like cash," says relationship expert Dr. Ronn Elmore. "And once you do it you never have to do it again. But if you're late on the offering, it could also mean you end up doing it often. Because when you offer, it shows your heart is in the right place, and it gives him an opportunity instead of an obligation. It's an opportunity to use his power and resources to show you that he is competent. If you don't ask [to pay for the date], it means pressure for him to do something, then it becomes an obligation. When a man begins to sense obligations, his internal get-me-out-of-here alarm goes off. [On the other hand] If there is an opportunity, his senses will tell him to move forward to show how efficient, effective, and accomplished he is."

There are several other ways you, as a woman who makes more than your companion, can participate in financing your dates. One is to split the costs 50-50 after the first couple of dates. Another is to take turns treating each other —he pays for dinner and you pay for the movies or he finances Friday night and you take care of

Saturday night. A third is to go Dutch, each of you responsible for your own expenses.

However, if there is a large discrepancy between incomes, then the higher income earner in all fairness should pick up a greater share of the expenses, whether that is you or your man. Otherwise stick to activities that both of you can afford. While we call this New Money Rule #2, it is not hard and fast. Couples should allow for flexibility and experiment by changing up. Have fun with it. Not only will varying how you pay for dates spice up your relationship, it will also prevent you from getting into a rut, which oftentimes happens after couples get past the first flush of newness.

New Money Rule 3: Not All Invitations Are Dates

Michael and Cheryl:

> *Cheryl's story is a good example of a dinner that may or may not have been a date. She and Phillip had just met and talked for an hour. Their conversation was strictly business. From that perspective, it was not really a date and Phillip was correct in asking Cheryl how she wanted to handle the bill. Cheryl was equally correct in putting money on the table to pay for her half. But when he wasn't sure how to interpret Cheryl's decision to go to the ladies room, Phillip erred on the side of tradition and paid the entire bill.*

> *In this particular case neither party is right or wrong. They handed it in the best way they knew at the time. Which is the primary reason we decided to write this book. We know there are plenty of other single men and women out there who don't have a clue as to what to*

*do and really want to do the right thing without alienating anyone in
the relationship.*

So when is a date a date?

Certainly if there are romantic undertones to an invitation it would be considered
a full-fledged date. Be careful not to mix up romance with business on the same day,
however. It would be better to keep the dinner get-together strictly business, as
Cheryl and Phillip did in New Orleans.

If it's business related or a continuation of an earlier seminar, and if it's a co-
worker or colleague, agree before you enter the restaurant on how you're going to
cover the bill. If it's a client, or a potential client, that's a no-brainer. You pay for the
meal and keep the receipt for a tax-deductible business expense.

If, after the business meal, you're interested in exploring the possibility of getting to know the man better, wait several days to arrange a date when it will be clear
that business is not involved. That's what Helen did with William in Chapter 13.
Keep in mind that it doesn't matter whether he picks you up from your residence,
you pick him up at his abode, or you agree to meet him at a public place, it's still a
date. For security reasons these days, women sometimes prefer not to be called for at
home by a man they've only recently met, or even to transport him to and from a
restaurant where a meal may be accompanied by alcoholic drinks.

Drinks After Work

Speaking of drinks, the New Money Rules for an impromptu get-together are
even less clear than those for a pre-planned date. Our recommendation is that you

each share the cost of a round of drinks or, if one of you has already paid for that round, that the other will cover the next round. This works especially well if it's a first time, get-acquainted date. The one thing you don't want to do is get too caught up in who pays what when you are just beginning to develop your relationship. Thinking about these rules in advance will enable you to be on your toes when these situations arise.

New Money Rule 4: One Slipup is no reason to dog someone.

Michael: *Poor Phillip. He never got farther with Cheryl than that first outing. Cheryl had made up her mind that Phillip flunked the first-date test and should not get another opportunity. As a man, I imagine Phillip sitting by the phone wondering, "Where did I go wrong?" But as we said earlier, neither Cheryl nor Phillip went wrong. Each did what they thought was right at the time. Cheryl shouldn't have dogged him, though. Everyone deserves a second chance and it may be difficult to pick up on an individual's money beliefs in an initial get-together. Phillip may have been uncertain as to whether this was really a "date" or not.*

Communication is the Key

Begin communicating on the subject of money immediately. Get everything out into the open because if you can't talk about it while you are dating, the chances you will not be able to do it while you are in a partnership or married is pretty much guaranteed. It's important to practice financial intimacy as soon as you know things are getting serious.

Here are four ways to bring the subject up:

1. Make talking about money fun. Schedule a special money meeting out in nature-in a beautiful park or on the beach.

2. Ask for financial advice. This works well for women. It's nonthreatening and it will allow you to see what your partner knows about money without embarrassing him. Tell him you need to invest your 401(k) retirement money and need help with selecting the mutual fund options.

3. One partner can volunteer his or her financial information first. If you are a woman with a more solid financial foundation than your partner, be ultra sensitive. Many men feel threatened or inadequate when their partners are more financially successful than they are. Some will say they don't care, but they do. As we said earlier, a man's brain and ego is pre-wired to be competitive, in power and in control of the purse strings-he just can't help himself, it's instinct.

4. Get professional help. We highly recommend premarital financial counseling. You'll have a third party giving financial advice and neither partner has the upper hand or is in more control. It's also less personal, which lessens the possibility of money arguments.

The 17 Dating Commandments

By now we know all of this new information probably has you on systems overload, so we thought we'd end this chapter with 17 commandments we gathered from our single men and women respondents to help guide you through the New Money Rules. Have fun dating!

1. Thou shall not discuss money or income on the first date.

2. Thou shall not pass judgment on a man – or woman! — based on the amount he or she spends on you during a first date.

3. Thou who ask the first date shall pay.

4. Thou shall offer to share the cost after the first few dates.

5. Thou shall not get up and go to the bathroom to avoid paying or participating in the bill – or to give the impression you are avoiding it.

6. Thou shall not order the most expensive item on the menu on the first date.

7. Thou shall not make false assumptions about your date's ability to pay.

8. Thou shall not judge a date by the restaurant you are taken to.

9. Thou shall not fight over the check.

10. Thou shall be prepared to pay if thou are a man, even if thou doesn't have to.

11. Thou shall not suggest a very expensive restaurant unless thou are prepared to pay the entire bill.

12. Thou shall make sure prior to the date that there is enough credit on the credit card to cover dinner.

13. Thou shall not complain about any meal unless the payer also complains.

14. Thou shall not date someone that thou art not interested in just for the "free stuff".

15. Thou shall leave thy bad attitude at home.

16. Thou shall not expect that paying for dinner entitles thou to anything but a "thank you".

17. Thou shall talk about money as soon as the relationship becomes serious.

New Money Rules Will Take Time

Now, that's not to say that we will suddenly cast off old traditions and embrace the New Money Rules. We're definitely in a transitional period as the New Money Rules take shape. At times, men will fall back on what they know and that is: Pay the bill no matter who did the inviting. In addition, many women are still in agreement with the Old Money Rules. In fact, the consensus among the single women we interviewed was still quite traditional. They wanted a man to pick up the bill on the first date even if they'd invited him out. But they did say that on follow-on dates they would share the costs. So, we're glad to note that progress is occurring.

Chapter 15

Money Baggage — We All Carry It!

So you've met someone new, huh? And now you want to move in together…maybe for the rest of your life. Of course, they will bring all their "stuff" with them. And their stuff is now going to be your stuff, including all that mismatched furniture and incompatible artwork. The two of you will probably complete an overall inventory to decide what stays. The excess baggage will just have to go.

But some of the financial "baggage" your new partner brings to the relationship may be just as unpleasant as that chartreuse green couch you said "no way" to. Unlike the couch, the financial baggage won't be obvious at first. True, you know where your partner works, how much he or she makes, where he or she lives, and what kind of car he or she drives. But seeing the full picture of an individual's financial health is a gradual process. Sometimes the signs are easy to read, other times subtle. In addition, because we don't regularly "exercise" our financial antenna, we're not as perceptive at picking up on the vibes as we should be.

So, how to figure out what kind of financial baggage your new love is bringing to this partnership? You could always interrogate them under a bright light, probing their financial background. A bit extreme? Probably. Simple conversations sweetened with genuine concern might be better. Mostly it all boils down to just plain common sense, a little power of observation, and lots of discussion. One thing's for certain: It is just as bad to hide previous financial problems from your new partner as it is to hide previous love affairs.

Nobody's Perfect

Truth be told, it's rare today to find a person with a squeaky clean bill of financial health. Almost everyone has been through a divorce, or a period of unemployment, or some other major change that may have caused financial havoc. Two people bringing significant money baggage into a relationship can find it a difficult hurdle to over-come if it isn't dealt with properly and in advance. This chapter is designed to help you and your partner become more aware of some of the impediments that may crop up and also provide you with common sense solutions to overcome them. Let's start with a list of what they are.

Money Baggage: Seven Common Types

The seven most common kinds of Money Baggage we bring into relationships today are listed below. Which ones do you find yourself carrying around?

1. Surprise! I'm maxed out on my Credit Cards and/or Loans

2. I've earned my degree, Damn it, I just haven't paid for it!

3. My Credit History Is Not So Clean

4. I'm On the Second or Third Go Around – Alimony, Child Support, and Other Family Financial Obligations

5. I'm Between Jobs – Again

6. I Just Can't Say No to My Addictions

7. To Say I Lack Financial Savvy Is an Understatement

Money Baggage 1: Surprise! I'm Maxed Out on My Credit Cards and Loans

If you don't have a solid financial foundation you may fear that your significant other will drop you like a bad habit if the word leaks out. So you don't mention those unmentionables hoping you can solve them "behind the scenes". Actually, poor credit or other past financial missteps in and of themselves are not reason enough for breaking up. It's your lack of disclosure and unwillingness to take steps to correct wayward financial behavior that may result in your partner parting ways with you. The men in our survey said that decisions to discontinue a relationship are not based solely on huge debt or other financial obstacles. But they do want to know how their prospective partners ended up in debt and how they plan to get out of it. We are sure most women feel the same way. Everybody stumbles. The question is whether the stumble is part of an ongoing pattern.

Can you answer the following statements in the affirmative?

- You know your IRS tax agent by name – first name.
- You are a budding entrepreneur – with the loans to prove it.
- You have an address book for your credit card companies alone.
- Your favorite two words are "charge it".

If so, you are lugging around a heavy burden of financial baggage.

Michael – Dot Com and Dot Gone

If credit card debt had a poster boy, it would be me. Like the portraits of presidents on paper money, my mug should be on all credit cards. Of all the stress I've had in my life, nothing has compared to the weight of these cards on my psyche. Now, I could expend lots of words spinning a tale of how I got into this situation, but that could be a book in itself. Suffice it to say, using credit cards to finance a failed business tops the list. Bottom line is, credit cards are like the Alien in that famous movie. They are designed to survive and you cannot kill them very easily once they grow to maturity.

Not only do credit cards survive, they get more expensive. I've noticed that one by one and slowly but surely the issuers are increasing their interest rates from the entry level 9 to 11 percent to the midrange 15 to 17 percent to the penalty-for-late-payment 22 to 27 percent. I asked a major company to lower my interest rate and they flat-out refused. At a later date, I decided to close that account. When I called them to cancel the card, I had to go through the typical "menu" maze until I was finally connected to a "specialist". Would you believe this "specialist" tried to convince me not to close the account because they "might" drop my rate in the future, thereby "saving" me money? I asked when the rate would be lowered but she couldn't give me a definite answer. I said, "No dice." Let me tell you, these cards have been a major factor in how Cheryl and I relate because I worry so much about them.. I've got two bags under my eyes. One is named VISA and the other MasterCard.

I am a recovering Dot-Com entrepreneur. I was seduced by the lure of giga-bucks to be made in the Internet gold-rush that was. As is the case with a lot of entrepreneurial types, initial financing came from a mix of personal savings, loans from family and friends, and credit cards. If you are more skillful than I was, you might have been able to secure a business loan. For sure, there is no pressure like that from a bank or other financial institution that wants its loan money back. Whereas unpaid credit cards can mess up your credit report, unpaid business loans can mess up your house or other assets. Still, whether you are in a relationship or not, maxed out credit cards or business loans are your responsibility, and yours alone, to pay off. None of your partner's money should be used to service such debts.

How to Unpack Your Money Baggage In Full View of Your Partner

- **Start Talking**. If you have maxed out credit cards or loans start talking. Hiding important information such as this is extremely damaging to a relationship if your partner finds out after the fact. Contrary to popular belief, discussing money in your relationship is a wonderful form of intimacy, especially for a man. It's not particularly hard for a woman to talk about money. But a man baring his finances is like, well, it's like a woman baring her body.

- **Complete a Financial Statement**. Along with honest discussion, prospective long-term couples should each do a financial statement (we have attached a sample on the following page). For both of you it's a great way to show you have nothing to hide.

- **Open a Joint Checking Account.** If you're planning on living together prior to the nuptials or if you've set the wedding date for sometime in the future, consider opening a joint checking account now. It will get both of you to the point of knowing how you'll have to work together to handle your finances quicker and better. Practice your joint financial responsibility by contributing an amount to the account based on your respective incomes and paying common expenses out of the account for the next three to six months. Or, if you're not living together before marriage, use the account to achieve common financial goals, such as vacation or wedding expenses. Combining this practice with a commitment to do a monthly budget will put you miles ahead financially by the time the big day rolls around.

Making Love and Money Work Financial Statement

What You OWN		Assets	What You OWE		Debts
Checking			First Mortgage		
Savings/CDs+			Home Equity Loan+		
Money Market Accounts+			**I. Mortgage**	**I. =**	
A. Bank Accounts	**A. =**		VISA		
Mutual Funds			MasterCard+		
Stocks+			Other+		
Bonds+			Other+		
Life Insurance (cash value)+			Other+		
Annuities+			Other+		
Investment Real Estate+			Other+		
B. Investments	**B. =**		**J. Credit Cards**	**J. =**	
Savings - 401(K) & 403(b)			Car #1		
Company Plan+			Car #2+		
IRA+			**K. Car Loans**	**K. =**	
Keogh+			Education		
C. Retirement Plans	**C. =**		Life Insurance+		
D. House (Market Value)	**D. =**		Other+		
Car #1			Other+		
Car #2+			**L. Other Debts**	**L. =**	
E. Cars	**E. =**		**M. What You OWE (I-L)**	**M. =**	
F. Personal Property	**F. =**		**Your Net Worth:**		
Loans Receivable			**H. What You OWN**	**H. =**	
Collectables+			**M. Less: What You OWE**	**M. -**	
Business Interest+			**N. = Your Net Worth**	**N. =**	
Other+					
G. Other Assets	**G. =**				
H. What You OWN (A-G)	**H. =**				

Money Baggage 2: I've Earned My Degree, Damn It, I Just Haven't Paid For It

The cost of higher education has gone through the roof. That sense of urgency on the faces of recent grads is no doubt due to the realization that some amount of indentured servitude will be necessary to completely "own" that degree. Indeed, according to the College Board, 59 percent of the $68 billion in financial aid distributed during the 2000-2001 school year was for loans. And it's never been easier for college students to get credit cards and pile up balances. In 2000, 78 percent of college students had at least one credit card. The average credit card debt per student was $2,748, according to Nellie Mae. It's no wonder students are saying "Hey, I need to earn some money so I can keep these loans at bay".

Unless they were born with a silver spoon in their mouth, anyone who's been out of school from one to five years is looking at a nice sized loan that will be their constant companion for some time. Medical school and law school graduates, add 10 years to that figure. There are ways to get around servicing the loan. You can join the Peace Corps and get some of it forgiven or continue to apply for loan deferments while you take Advanced Basket Weaving at the local junior college. But eventually you have to pay the piper.

Although your school loans can never be considered the responsibility of your partner, the servicing of loans shows up on your credit report. If you are considering achieving financial goals together, both credit reports will be scrutinized and your credit report can be marred if your loan hasn't been paid in a timely fashion.

Money Baggage 3: Not So Clean Credit History

We truly understand how ashamed you can be to reveal to your significant other a poor credit history, but guess what. You have to do it. As we said earlier, you can start by both partners filling out the personal financial statement. The next step is for each of you to obtain your credit history report, because one partner's pre-marriage credit report can definitely hamper your joint financial goals. We know several couples who were unpleasantly surprised when their new home loans were not approved because of one partner's credit report. Once married, both spouses' credit histories will be scrutinized any time a major purchase is made in both names. So any bad debt left over from your fun and irresponsible years will most likely come back to haunt you.

If you live in a community property state (Arizona, California, Idaho, Louisiana, Nevada, New Mexico, Texas, Washington, and Wisconsin), you need to be even more cautious because all debt incurred during a marriage is considered joint debt, even if one partner applies for credit on their own. Therefore, if your spouse defaults on an auto loan that is in his or her name only, you, the other spouse, can be held liable to pay the balance.

Get Your Credit Report Now!

Don't be taken by surprise. Get a copy of your credit report this week. It's easy. There are three main credit-reporting agencies – Equifax, Trans Union, and Experian. Per your request, they will send you a copy of your personal credit report for no more than $8.50 (if you have been denied credit you can receive a copy for free). Here's how to contact the services:

Equifax	**Trans Union Corporation**	**Experian**
P.O. Box 105873	Consumer Disclosure Center	P.O. Box 949
Atlanta, GA 30348	P.O. Box 390	Allen, TX 75013-0949
(800) 685-1111	Springfield, PA 19064-0390	(800) 643-3334
(770) 612-3200	(800) 916-8800	www.experian.com
www.ecoconsumer.equifax.com	(800)682-7654	
	(714) 680-7292	
	www.transunion.com	

If there are any mistakes or inaccuracies in any of your credit reports, get them fixed immediately. The procedure isn't difficult and the individual agencies will tell you exactly what is required. Whenever you tell a credit-reporting agency that your report is inaccurate, the company must check out the claim (usually within 30 days) and present all the facts you state to whatever company is providing the information you are disputing. If this doesn't clear up the dispute, you are allowed to add a brief statement to your credit file, which will be included in all future reports. If any of the negative marks are legitimate (an old forgotten unpaid store charge card, for example), do whatever you can to correct the problem. That means paying it off and not allowing any new bills to go past due.

Be leery of companies that claim to repair your credit report or give you a new and clean one quickly. Unfortunately, there is nothing that will clean up your credit report except time, a history of responsible on-time bill paying, and working with the credit reporting agencies to get your report clean.

There are two reputable nonprofit agencies we do highly recommend: Consumer Credit Counseling Services at (800) 388-2227, and MYVESTA (formerly Debt Counselors of America) at (800) 680-3328 or online at www.myvesta.org. Both agencies can advise you on how to clear up a bad credit report or straighten out an inaccurate one.

Money Baggage 4: Alimony, Child Support, and Family Obligations

First marriages and money aren't easy, so imagine the difficulties of handling money in the second and third marriage, particularly if alimony, child support, or family obligations are part of the picture. They create whole new sets of circumstances. Interestingly enough, when we surveyed people on the kinds of money baggage that affected their relationships, mooching relatives and friends were at the top of several lists, which means this is a major concern that causes a lot of tension in relationships. The way to avoid extreme conflicts over these issues is to follow the same steps we're mentioned throughout the book – lay it all out on the table in the very beginning so there aren't any nasty little surprises.

In most cases, alimony and child support are there to stay for a number of years, so becoming emotionally unglued and resentful does not make for a good relationship. In the case of family obligations, you may have a little more control because in many instances you can simply stop feeling obligated, but that too should be discussed in advance.

Court-ordered alimony and child support payments should simply be looked at as part of the family budget. Factor it in every month just as you would food and water.

Yes, we understand the new partner's income may help make those payments. So what? If they are legally mandated, get over it. Don't fault your new partner for paying them. And as a new partner, as long as you were told in advance there isn't really much you can say because you went in with your eyes wide open. If you were not told in advance, our advice is to sit down and recreate a new budget with the payments. We'll talk more about how to do this in Chapter 17. If need be, get professional financial help. A third party can help you make this a less dicey task.

Money Baggage 5: Ms. Between Jobs and Mr. Unemployed

Nothing describes the concept of limbo quite like the words "between jobs". It's the proverbial halfway house between heaven and hell. In the two-cylinder financial engine that represents a couple, one of the cylinders is not firing properly. And "unemployed" is just a mature form of between jobs. As far as money baggage is concerned these are probably some of the biggest "bags" you can haul. And from a social perspective, they are relatively larger for the man than the woman. But all baggage needs to be claimed. In situations like this, financial matters take center stage. Budgeting, planning, and judicious use of savings are the tools that will help you get through. If you are newly coupled with Ms. Between Jobs or Mr. Unemployed, this is probably not a good time to start living together or commingling funds.

Money Baggage 6: One of You Can't Say No to Addictions

We were hesitant to open this can of worms, but we knew we had to because it appeared heavily on our survey lists. Gambling, weekly lottery tickets, drugs, alcohol, and uncontrolled shopping sprees are all addiction challenges that render it practically impossible to make love and money work.

If you or your partner has an addiction don't lie to yourself, says Dr. Annette Kyle-Vega, an Oakland, California-based psychiatrist who specializes in holistic addiction therapy. Kyle-Vega says that when you get involved with a person who has an addiction you are playing with fire, and there is a great chance you may get burned. "When you are in love with someone with an addiction, you are in love with a triangle—you, your partner and whatever he or she is addicted to. When you love someone with an addiction you are loving someone who will not be able to be completely in the relationship because the regular use of the addictive substance or behavior will rob your partner's ability to feel and be present in the relationship."

Addictive behaviors can be transformed as long as the person is willing to face and heal them. Professional help is generally needed. If you or your partner has an addiction challenge, don't attempt to stop it on your own. Seek professional help right away.

Money Baggage 7: Lacking in Financial Savvy

- No Financial Plan
- Lack of financial discipline – living beyond means

It would be great if everyone who enters into a relationship were already financially savvy, but generally that isn't the case. The majority of people don't have a clue as to what to do with their money. And as we mentioned in Chapter 3, it is a scary subject for many people to tackle. So most enter into a relationship with no financial plan and a general lack of any type of financial discipline, causing them to live paycheck to paycheck and way beyond their means.

Get Smart About Money

Now that you know what the seven Money Baggage mistakes are, making your love and money work means changing those attitudes and getting smart about money. Today, with access to loads of financial information via the Internet, television, radio, and books, it has never been easier. There isn't really a good excuse for not knowing what to do.

In this book we'll briefly cover the financial mechanics – buying stocks and mutual funds and saving for retirement. There are plenty of other excellent books already on the market we suggest you also look at. We've listed a few of them in the Appendix. In Chapter 18, we will show you how to plan a financial life together, which really is the key to financial success in a relationship. Notice that we said together and not separate. It will not work if only one partner in the relationship is gung-ho. It takes two to tango and to make love and money work. You and your partner are a team. Without teamwork, money management becomes a battle of unconnected egos each trying to get their individual needs met. And lack of teamwork works against building family wealth.

When you both enter into the relationship with a clear set of financial goals, you will achieve them twice as fast as doing it alone. A couple with common thoughts on finances has less reason to argue about money. Fewer arguments mean a happier relationship. Read several of the money books we have listed in the Appendix. Surf the web and check out the top money sites (see appendix). Attend financial seminars. Many of the larger full service brokerage firms conduct free sessions for existing and potential clients.

Most of all, take action. Actually do something to make your money better. Invest in a stock or mutual fund. Talk to a professional financial advisor. Create a financial blueprint that you both agree with. Having financial knowledge means absolutely nothing unless you do something with it.

Merging Money

Combining "stuff" may not seem critical to you unless you plan to live together before getting married. If you do plan to cohabit for an extended period of time prior to marriage or simply because you like living together, you should consider dealing with the issue of merged money as soon as possible. The benefit: You will both reveal your individual money styles and can use this positively to see what works best. If at all possible, pursue a common financial goal such as saving for a honeymoon, or vacation, or joint purchase of some sort. Maybe decide that for the next quarter all household expenses will be paid out of the joint account. Scary thought, huh? It needs to be done though, if you're serious. However, we do not recommend joint credit cards at this early stage for any reason. In fact, credit cards are trouble, period.

Most couples combine their money in a joint checking account once they get married. It reinforces a sense of "oneness" and allows them to keep better accounting of the money coming and going. However, one joint account is not always the most logical choice because of the money baggage we've mentioned earlier in this chapter and the money styles discussed earlier in the book. As they say, "you're mileage may vary". We'll go into merging money and joint accounts in chapter 17.

Moving Out

We've talked about money baggage when moving into a new non-married relationship. But financial problems may also crop up when you are moving out of a situation. Moving out can sometimes be as messy as a divorce but without the legal remedies. If you are living together, there are no legal rights for child support or alimony.

Also if you've paid off some debt of a live-in partner and they subsequently disappear, you're out of luck unless you have the repayment agreement in writing. We hate to spoil the romantic fantasy surrounding a new relationship with the black and white details of business transactions, but a repayment agreement in writing offers protection for you and an acid test for your partner. It's always a good idea to have an attorney look at the agreement to give it some stronger legs in court if you unfortunately have to go that route. In Chapter 17 we discuss how to manage money when living together.

Chapter 15: Making Love and Money Work Action Steps

1. Protect yourself and your assets

2. Sit down and discuss your financial goals

3. Share each other's credit reports

4. If things get complicated, seek professional advice

5. Set realizable timetables for clearing up debt

Chapter 16

Getting A Divorce —
It Doesn't Have To Be Nasty

So far, we've talked about how to make love and money work in your relationships, whether you are going together, living together, or married. But we would be less than realistic if we didn't admit that many relationships dissolve and many marriages end. Today, with one million marriages – one out of every two in the United States – breaking up, it seems that divorce has become almost a badge of honor. Many of us are okay with having gone through that particular battlefield. "It's no big deal", and "Everyone is doing it" are some of the comments we hear from our friends and colleagues.

Relationship experts claim the ease of divorce arises with Me-me baby boomers who expect instant gratification. We see something we want, we go for it. If it doesn't work, we throw it away and buy another one. Initially, we didn't agree. But, ironically, as we were writing this chapter our HP 610 Deskjet home office printer broke down. After taking it to the shop we were told it would cost $65 to repair. We said, "thanks but no thanks" and headed straight for CompUSA to buy a new HP 630C Deskjet for $49.99.

We did exactly what the experts said we would do. Are we doing the same thing with our marriages? Tossing them aside the first time they break? Statistics say more marriages tumble over money than for any other reason. So for couples on the verge of breaking up over money, the question becomes whether it absolutely necessary to get a divorce.

While this and the next chapter are on divorce, by no means are we advocates of it. In fact we highly discourage it. Terminating your marriage is far too detrimental in all aspects — emotional, physical, financial, and for your children. No matter how you look at it no one ever wins in a divorce. Yet, despite our thoughts on it, we also realize that divorce has become a staple of American culture. In fact, for some marriages that have gone bad it is the only option. If that is the case for you, we want to alert you in this chapter to some of the financial and emotional realities of divorce. In the next chapter, we outline what you need to know to get a divorce the right way. A way by which no one walks away feeling burned. A way by which the children are not used as weapons to get revenge or more money. A way by which you and your ex-spouse can still be civil toward each other so that your lives are not permanently marred.

Believe it or not, you can do this. But truthfully, if you and your spouse have read this far into the book and you were thinking of splitting up over money, we hope by now we have helped you to reconsider. Money is truly not a reason to end your union. We can both assure you that money issues will not be any easier in the next relationship. If we're too late to dissuade you, however, the least we can do is help make your coming ordeal more bearable.

Cheryl: *While divorce was surely the most horrible time of my life, it was a time of great personal growth. In fact, the divorce was one of the catalysts for this book. Here I was, a well-known financial advisor, advising everyone else on what to do with their money while mine was tied up in divorce court. "If I'm making all these mistakes," I thought, "others probably are too."*

When I went searching for information on how to do it the right way, all I found were books and articles telling me how to hide assets and play other dirty tricks. Where were the books showing me how to work it out honestly? Or to divorce in such a way that everybody was somewhat happy? Finally, I realized that divorce is big business. Think of all the lawyers, judges, and real estate agents who would be out of work. Our loss is their gain. Fewer divorces would mean fewer bucks for them. So, of course they don't want you to know too much about how to work things out financially.

Since the divorce, my ex-spouse and I have moved on with our lives. Our son lives in two homes and is quite happy. He sees it as an adventure. We split all his expenses straight down the middle. If one parent wants to spend more that's up to them. Yes, there were resentments at first but we have since moved past them for the sake of our boy. It was more important to us that we have an emotionally healthy and well-adjusted child than to pay a lawyer five figures to continue to compete in court. Take it from me; divorce isn't fun and it really impacts the children. If you do not have to go there, don't, especially if it is over money. Your relationship and family are more important. And as you will see in the next section, along with the emotional roller coaster there is a major money cost to divorce that will damage you financially for many years to come. It is so damaging that many people never fully recuperate.

---

10 Reasons Why Divorce Isn't The Answer

1. It rarely solves the problem
2. It is a financial disaster
3. It blocks personal growth and maturity
4. It sets you both up to repeat your difficulty with someone else
5. It hardens your heart
6. It weakens your faith
7. It devastes your children
8. It impacts your legacy
9. It increases your loneliness
10. It hurts friends and relatives

Dr. Steve Stephens

The Real Cost of Divorce

The real financial effects of divorce aren't realized until much later. And it isn't just the actual cost of the divorce proceedings (like lawyer fees and court costs) that is expensive. The cost of establishing two households and quickly liquidating jointly held property is great at any financial bracket and has a devastating impact on each former spouse's net worth. Rarely are the incomes and the investments that were divided ever recouped. This is why it is extremely important that couples considering a divorce think long and hard about the financial consequences. We suggest that before you part ways consult a financial advisor who specializes in pre-divorce financial planning before either of you retains an attorney. A financial advisor will present a realistic picture of what you can expect money-wise after a divorce. When you look at the real numbers it may change your desire to split up knowing that you may end up exchanging one set of problems for another.

Women Suffer Most

In most divorces, women are the hardest hit. Typically they earn less money (75 cents on the dollar) yet have full custody of the children. The latest report says the poverty rate for divorced women ages 25 to 34 is nearly 40 percent. For married woman, it's only about eight percent. On the other hand, the standard of living of divorced men is said to increase by 32 percent. Still, men don't come out of divorce unscathed either. Their increased standard of living comes at a price; namely guilt, emotionally unhealthy children, and problems with new relationships. We'll talk more about the emotional aspects of divorce later in the chapter. Right now, let's focus on the actual cost of a breakup.

How Much Will It Cost?

The cost of a divorce depends on five factors:

1. The state where you live.

2. The amount of conflict within the relationship.

3. The method you use.

4. How complicated your household is.

5. And last, but most important, whether or not you stay in control.

Cost Factor 1: The State Where You Live

Divorce costs can vary from state to state and lawyer to lawyer. The amount lawyers charge per hour is typically based on their experience, whether they specialize in matrimonial law, the clients they represent, whether they have their own practice, whether they are a partner in a major law firm, and whether they practice in a rural or a metropolitan area.

Before hiring an attorney we suggest you conduct a survey to determine the going rate in your location for the type of legal representation you feel you need. The following are six questions to ask all lawyers you are considering hiring. The answers will provide you with a general idea of what your divorce will cost.

Cost of Divorce Survey Questions:

1. How much will the divorce cost?

2. For what services will I be charged?
   - Cost of lawyer's time
   - Phone calls to and from the lawyer
   - Phone calls to and from his secretary
   - Cost of duplicating documents

- Court costs
- Research
- Court appearances
- Postage

3. On what basis will I be charged? By the hour, flat fee, or on contingency?

4. Who will pay the lawyer's fees?

5. Will the lawyer accept payments after the divorce is final? Are time payments acceptable?

6. Are the lawyer's fees tax-deductible?

Cost Factor 2: The Amount of Conflict Within The Relationship

The more you and your partner are at each other's throats, the more expensive the divorce. A high level of conflict within the relationship will prevent either of you from trusting each other. Which means you will have trouble negotiating effectively and will be dependent on the judge to resolve everything between you. This will keep the meter running. A high level of conflict also means no one is talking except through the lawyers. Which means you'll talk about your issues at your lawyer's pace, and at your lawyer's hourly rate. The result: Ka-ching! Ka-ching!

Don't Use Scare Tactics

When you are thinking of divorce what you don't want to do is frighten or anger your partner into running to a lawyer and taking the case into conflict. You will both need time to get used to the idea that the divorce is really happening. Don't make any sudden moves without telling him or her about it first. This includes taking items out of the house, withdrawing money, closing accounts, or filing papers. If you are planning to have your lawyer write a letter to your spouse, warn your spouse ahead of time. Receiving an unanticipated letter from a lawyer is shocking, intimidating and can cause the blood to boil.

If divorce papers have been filed, tell your spouse that the papers are on the way. Also let him or her know there is still time to talk before a response is necessary. In addition to talking, put it in writing. Send a letter to your spouse stating you have filed the divorce papers to get the case on record but you have no plans to go further without an agreement from them and a 30 days notice as well. If you already have a lawyer, get your lawyer to send such a letter before the papers are served.

Consider filing the petition so that it requires a marital settlement agreement. State it in a way that you can't go forward without an agreement or an amended petition. These steps let your spouse know that they have time to think things through and talk with you before they must respond. As with every other money issue in this book, communication is the key. And by including your spouse in these preliminary steps along the way, you cut way back on conflict within the relationship. Realize that it is the underhanded stuff that makes divorces so nasty.

Cost Factor 3: The Method You Use

There are basically four ways to get a divorce:

1. Do-it-yourself (least expensive)

2. Uncontested

3. Mediated

4. Adversarial (most expensive)

Do-It-Yourself

Did you know that you don't have to hire a lawyer to get a divorce? If one of your objectives is to save money, you can obtain the necessary forms via software programs or workbooks and do it yourself. Many states today are actually encouraging do-it-yourself dissolutions by lowering the procedural barriers for people who want to file a simple uncontested divorce. The state of Arizona is a prime example. They have set up a divorce self-service center that allows couples to file their own divorces.

But if special handling is needed, such as a division of a large amount of property or concerns regarding custody of the children, the do-it-yourself method isn't the route to take. There may be some important issues that you may overlook, especially with regard to property values and taxes. If your divorce isn't that complicated but will require some legal advice just the same, you can always consult a lawyer on an as-needed basis. That way you will not need to make a large deposit upfront to retain him or her, keeping the cost lower and the control of the proceedings more in your hands.

There is a new concept called **unbundling** available to people who neither want to do their own divorce nor give up complete control to a lawyer. When you use the unbundling method you hire a lawyer for what you need the lawyer to do, an accountant for what you need the accountant to do, and a financial planner for what you need the financial planner to do. The lawyer, accountant and financial planner act more like a group of coaches. If a particular issue comes up in one of those areas you call the accountant or the financial planner directly instead of through the lawyer, the way it is traditionally done. Your coaches do everything that is required, including filing papers and arguing the case in court, if necessary. While you have more control over your divorce this method takes detailed organization on your part. You have to keep track of who is doing what and that it is being done in a timely fashion and at a reasonable cost. Don't use unbundling if there is any friction between you and your soon-to-be-ex-spouse. You'll lose your focus and you won't have enough energy to stay on top of everything. In that case, a lawyer is your best bet.

Uncontested Divorce

By far the uncontested divorce is the simplest, least expensive way to go. It offers you and your partner the chance to end your marriage quietly and with dignity and respect. An uncontested divorce simply means you and your partner are in agreement with the ending of the marriage. Certainly there are still angry and hurtful feelings but you both have agreed to put aside your differences to get through the painful process. The goal isn't about revenge and getting even. It's about separating amicably and then continuing to live your life in the best way possible.

This may sound pollyann-ish to you and you are probably thinking, "There is no way I'll let him or her get off so easy." Let us tell you. Revenge and fighting over money and material stuff isn't worth it. While you may think you are hurting the other person it's you who will be hurt in the long run. It's you who will spend day and night thinking up schemes to get back at your partner for ruining your life. It's you who will waste thousands of dollars on lawyer fees and court costs. All the energy and money you squander would be better spent putting your own life in order. Imagine if you took that same intensity and went back to school to improve your skills, make more money, or start your own business. If you absolutely must get a divorce use the uncontested divorce method if your spouse will agree to it and move on with your life.

The Advantages of the Uncontested Divorce

The most apparent advantage of the uncontested divorce is the cost. With the exception of the do-yourself-divorce, an uncontested divorce that stays uncontested is always the least expensive. We are firm believers in finding the cheapest way to divorce. The less money you spend, the more money you have to live on. The other advantage of an uncontested divorce is that it continues to keep the conflict down in the relationship. It's also more private. All agreements made between you two are filed with the court and made a public record, but the arrangements you make with each other don't have to be. Nor do any of the terms you discuss as you negotiate the agreement that is acceptable for everyone.

The Disadvantage of an Uncontested Divorce

The disadvantage of an uncontested divorce is that one lawyer cannot represent both partners. He or she must represent one and not the other. Which means that one partner will not have a lawyer, creating an unfair advantage for the partner with legal representation. That creates an imbalance of power between the partners.

Here's a way to get around this dilemma if you are considering an uncontested divorce; the partner without representation can hire a lawyer to act as a coach. This lawyer can review the papers, question the client about the facts of the divorce and what they hope to accomplish, and review the options that are available. The partner represented by the lawyer-coach will then have the proper information needed before signing the divorce papers. It's quick and inexpensive and it doesn't create an adversarial battle of the sort that could develop if a lawyer were retained in the traditional manner for the non-represented partner.

Mediated Divorce

A mediated divorce is similar to negotiating a business deal. You and your partner sit down in the same room together with a neutral mediator to work out the terms of your divorce settlement. The mediator does not replace a lawyer and cannot give legal advice. He or she is trained primarily to help you draft your own divorce agreement. Then you each can take the agreement to your individual lawyer to make sure it is reasonable and fair. During the session, the mediator can point out to both partners steps they can take to develop a fair agreement. This open and free exchange of information allows both partners to negotiate with each other in confidence. Since both are working with the same information, it levels the playing field, which shortens the time it takes to negotiate a resolution that is okay with both.

The mediation process is strictly voluntary. There aren't a set number of times you must meet. It will continue as long as all three — you, your spouse, and the mediator—want it to. By the same token, you or your spouse can withdraw at any time. This is one of the main benefits of a mediated divorce. You and your partner are always in control of your own divorce. Because you are both active participants, mediation allows you to get through the divorce with much less conflict than you would experience in an adversarial proceeding. That means less time and less money. It also means you are less likely to go back to court later to fight about something else. Later on in the chapter we'll talk more about the advantages of using a mediator for your divorce.

Adversarial Divorce

Adversarial divorces are expensive, take a long time, and inflict a lot of pain on both spouses. It is the type of divorce we highly recommend you avoid. In an adversarial divorce there are too many lawyers and judges deciding your fate. We understand that in some cases a spouse may need someone to ensure that they receive fair treatment. But in many cases, the adversarial divorce isn't all that it is cracked up to be. Most of the time, neither partner wins.

The Disadvantages of Adversarial Divorces

There is not one positive thing we can say about adversarial divorces, but we have a slew of disadvantages we want you to know about. First and foremost, it costs a lot of money. There are too many people involved and they are all charging by the hour. Every time you meet with your lawyer and your partner meets with their lawyer, and every time the two lawyers meet with each other, and every time the lawyers meets with the judge, and any other time the lawyers spend working or waiting to meet with someone on your case, you and your partner are shelling out big bucks.

When there are so many people involved in your divorce the costs escalate. Plenty of couples have run up bills of $30,000 to $100,000 because they lost control of the process. The average bill falls between $4,000 and $10,000 (still a lot of money) because most couples get tired of fighting, run out of money, or both and end up negotiating a resolution that is dictated by the lawyers.

The second disadvantage is that it takes too much time. With all the parties involved and the conflicts in scheduling meeting times and court appearances, the process gets dragged out for weeks and months. In order for meaningful action to take place in an adversarial divorce all parties need to be present and ready. If one person isn't present and ready, the case gets continued. Which means you'll have to wait several more weeks or months for your next court date. This long stretch with nothing happening except the emptying of your bank account will leave you both feeling frustrated, angry and in limbo. We have heard through the grapevine that these delays are actually a strategy that lawyers use to wear down their clients so they'll finally give in to difficult concessions. Finally, a couple will agree to anything in order to hurry up and get the divorce over with.

As we mentioned earlier, the third disadvantage of an adversarial divorce is that nobody really wins and both partners come out of it feeling burnt. On average, few people are happy with the results of an adversarial divorce and are more likely to return to court to fight over compliance with property settlements, alimony, or child support. With more meetings in lawyers' offices, new petitions, and court hearings, the divorce never comes to a closure.

The fourth and last disadvantage of an adversarial divorce is the horrible affect it will have on your children and other family members. When you have children, you continue to be their parents regardless of the divorce. There will be times when you will need to contact and cooperate with each other, particularly at family social gatherings like birthdays and weddings. With an adversarial divorce, you will both be on edge, ready to attack and seize on anything either of you says for use in litigation. Normal conversations will be next to impossible.

We understand we don't live in Utopia and adversarial divorces may be necessary if your partner is uncooperative and refuses to talk to you away from a lawyer. If that is the case then you really have no choice but to resort to this method. What is key then is to think strategically and always stay in control. Don't allow yourself to get emotionally caught up in the fight.

After a lengthy, down-and-dirty battle, you may secretly be willing to compromise on contentious issues but won't in order to save face. Drop that attitude and make every effort to let your partner know you are always willing to talk. Your children and your health are more important than saving face. You may be really surprised that your spouse wants to do the same thing but just doesn't have the courage. It doesn't matter who takes that first step. What does matter is that the step is taken.

Cost Factor 4: It Depends On How Complicated Things Are

The more complicated the divorce the more specialized help you need so the more expensive the cost. You both will need a lawyer and possibly a CPA (Certified Public Accountant) for each of you. You also may need financial advisors, bankers, insurance brokers, business valuators and a couple of psychologists. While you may need all these people, what will keep the cost down is that you don't lose control over the divorce. Make sure you are both prepared from the very beginning. In the *What's Money To do With It? money journal* we provide you with divorce planning worksheets. The more prepared you are the easier and quicker it will be for the two of you to get down to the issues that really matter.

Cost Factor 5: It Depends On Whether Or Not You Stay In Control

The most effective way to reduce the cost is to maintain open communication between you and your spouse and to stay in control in all aspects of the divorce. Unfortunately, the divorce system is set up to give more power to lawyers and judges. Staying in control is the only way to take back that power. There is no reason for you to be a victim. It's your divorce, therefore you are the one who makes the key decisions, not your lawyer or a judge.

How To Stay In Control

Staying in control isn't as difficult as you think. Here are several things you can do:

1. Reading this chapter is a great start because educating yourself is important. There are several excellent books and web sites that deal strictly with divorce. We have listed a few in the appendix. Talk to family and friends. Just remember every divorce is different so don't compare. But the better your understanding of the process, the more you are in control.

2. If you are planning to use a lawyer make sure you use their time wisely. Don't call them for every little thing. Anytime you consult or ask a lawyer or his assistant to do something for you there is a charge. The average fee for a lawyer's services is $150 to $250 per hour. Telephone conversations are $25 per hour. Court appearances are $175-$300 per hour. And faxes and copies are $1.75 and 30 cents, respectively.

3. Take all legal advice with a grain of salt. Lawyers by nature are adversarial. They're job is to fix what is broken even if it wasn't broken in the very beginning. They'll find a way to break something in order to fix it. Listen to your lawyer's advice, but don't feel obligated to follow it if it isn't the way you want to handle your divorce. The best way to handle it is to consider the other lower-cost, non-confrontational methods of divorce without retaining a lawyer at all. Use a mediator or a lawyer as a coach strictly to look over the settlement papers you and your spouse have already crafted. If later on you find a lawyer is necessary you can retain one at that time.

4. Do your best to put emotions aside and talk. Not talking will only make the divorce process take longer and cost more. It will be more painful in the long run too because things will drag out to the point that you lose total control.

Think before you leap. Before fighting over issues ask yourself the following questions:

- How much is this costing me to fight about it?

- What are the chances I'll win?

- How much is this issue worth in today and future dollars?

You may find that after answering the above questions the issue may not be worth fighting over.

Divorce Money Mistakes

Not only are the potential costs of getting a divorce financially and emotionally debilitating, the financial consequences of divorce are just as devastating. In spite of the scary statistics no one ever expects to get married with divorce in the future. Therefore, dividing assets is the furthest thing from your mind until you are in the throes of the divorce process. And when you're in the throes all rational behavior goes right out the window. This is a time when savvy decisions are pivotal for financial survival, yet your better judgment is clouded, causing you to screw up in any one of several ways.

The Eight Money Mistakes

There are eight common money mistakes we see in divorces today.

Money Mistake 1: Divvying up assets without a thorough inventory assessment. Knowing what you have and how much it is worth are important before you begin splitting up the assets. Make sure to first list all your assets and debts. Or use the divorce planing worksheets in the money journal.

Money Mistake 2: Wasting too much money and time allowing your lawyer to gather your personal information. In the legal world this is called "discovery". During discovery your lawyer searches for financial statements and any information that will help in settling your divorce. The process includes interrogations, requests for production of documents, and requests for admissions and depositions. The cost of all that paperwork can add up quite quickly. In certain circumstances discovery is necessary. If your divorce is one of those, and in order to keep as much control in your hands as possible, inform your lawyer not to send out any interrogatories or requests for documents without letting you look them over first. You may find that the questions and the documents aren't necessary and can be eliminated. The key is to do all the things you can do to save your lawyer time which cuts down on legal costs.

Money Mistake 3: Losing Life Insurance. Maintaining a life insurance policy on the breadwinner is extremely important if young children are involved. While an ex-spouse may be required to have a policy, he or she can allow it to lapse by not paying the premiums. To avoid this from happening and to keep up the coverage, make sure the divorce agreement states that the policy will be transferred to the custodial partner who will then be responsible for making the premium payments.

Money Mistake 4: Both partners sharing a lawyer. A lawyer cannot fairly represent both parties in a divorce. The lawyer will always be biased toward the person who initially hired him or her. Unless you plan to use a mediator or to do the divorce yourself, both partners need their own lawyers to represent them.

Money Mistake 5: One partner not receiving a fair share of the retirement and pension benefits. This money mistake hurts more women than men because men typically make more money and have larger pension benefits and retirement portfolios. According to several divorce lawyers, wives often fail to get the half of their spouse's company pension or other qualified retirement benefits they are entitled to. We'll talk more about dividing the retirement benefits later on in the chapter.

Money Mistake 6: Not sharing college tuition costs. Never assume your ex-partner will pay half of your children's college costs. In many states it isn't required. It's a shame that it isn't. The way to protect your children is to have college tuition costs specifically covered in the marital settlement agreement.

Money Mistake 7: Not dealing with tax consequences. The exchanging of property and other cash assets may have dire financial consequences to spouses undergoing a divorce. Do not sign off on any divorce agreements until you have consulted your financial advisor or accountant to find out the tax impact of the concessions you are making. It's not uncommon for one ex-spouse to get hit with a nasty tax bill they didn't know about several months, or years, after the divorce. Unfortunately, most lawyers and judges don't pay much attention to the tax impact when making their final divorce decisions.

Money Mistake 8: Giving your mate everything they want in hopes they will stay. If there is the slightest inkling that your marriage can be saved, we encourage you to do all you can to keep it together. That's what we are all about —making love and money work. But, if it looks like rekindled love will never happen, wake up and smell the coffee! Don't give your spouse the house, the kids, the retirement accounts and all the cash with hopes that if you are nice he or she will change their mind. By the time you smell the coffee, it's already burnt. Not only have you endured this horrific dissolution you've also been taken advantage of.

Did We Convince You?

Still want to go through with your divorce? In the next chapter, we'll cover in greater detail what you need to know financially to do it right.

Chapter 17

Pre-Divorce Financial Strategies

If you are determined to get a divorce, pre-divorce planning may be the most important financial planning you ever do. It can go a long way towards making the divorce itself run more smoothly as well as provide you with a settlement that's fairer for both of you. Pre-divorce planning will also give you a sense of where things stand before you head into discussion with a lawyer, if you are using one. And it will streamline the settlement process—which definitely cuts down on legal fees. In our *What's Money Got To Do With It?* money journal you will find divorce planning worksheets that will help you organize and analyze your personal and financial information.

Family Dynamics

But before we get into the nuts-and-bolts factors, there are two human aspects of divorce that you need to be aware of.

One is how hard divorce is on children. Most will have to move to a new home, change schools, see less of one parent, lose touch with family and friends, and live on a lot less money. These changes make children feel frightened, sad, and lonely, according to Judith Wallerstein, founder of the Center for the Family in Transition. In her book, "The Unexpected Legacy of Divorce: A 25-Year Landmark Study", Wallerstein concludes that children of divorce are marked for life, with many suffering repeat failure and heartbreak in adult relationships.

So make every effort to put your children's best interests first. One of the best ways to do this is to agree on joint custody. But if joint custody isn't possible, then it's imperative not to use your children as pawns in your fight over sole custody. Never use them to obtain revenge, hurt one another, or demand increased child support payments. We heard from divorce lawyers of spouses who used the other spouse's desire to get sole custody of the children as a bargaining chip to gain an unfair financial settlement. Oftentimes, custody fights are really not about what's best for the kids, but rather about revenge or greed. Don't seek to hurt your ex-spouse by undermining his or her relationship with the children or instigating a custody fight in an attempt to take the children away. You will just end up hurting the kids. Instead, help your children through this difficult time by 1) being attentive to their needs in the midst of your own grief, turmoil and pain, 2) making sure the noncustodial parent maintains a relationship with them, and 3) treating your soon-to-be-ex-spouse with respect.

The other aspect is how hard divorce is on men. Most articles and books on divorce are geared toward helping women get through it intact. Why? Because statistics show that the effects of divorce on men are less severe than on women, due largely to men's greater earning power. While that certainly may be the case, the men we interviewed for this book said it's never easy to deal with a failed marriage. It's a blow to one's ego. It creates a sense of personal failure.

Unfortunately, men sometimes take their anger over the divorce out on their children and ex-spouse. If you're a man, make every effort to prevent your rage from getting in the way of making the right financial choices. For example, vowing you're not going to let your wife get anything doesn't put you in the right frame of mind for negotiating. This kind of mentality prevents any type of equitable settlement. It also sends you and your wife in search of the nastiest divorce lawyers each of you can find. If you don't want your wife's lawyer to "take you to the cleaners" then aim for a fair and equal settlement. Here are three suggestions to help achieve that goal:

- Don't look at divorce as a contest to win or lose. It's really about fairness. And it may not be a 50/50 split, especially when the children are made the priority. If your ex-partner will have full custody of the kids she should rightfully receive some of your money to maintain their welfare. Remember, they're your children, too.

- Share the pension and retirement money. Give it up! Often men don't want to divvy up this asset because they feel they've earned it and should not to have to share it with anyone. That's truly greedy behavior. If your partner was there for you while you struggled to develop your career she is entitled to one-fourth to one-half of your pension depending upon the amount she has saved in her own retirement plan. And if she took time out from her career to raise the children she'll have less in her plan, right? The easiest way to fairly split retirement and pension money is to add it all up and split it down the middle. If one partner does not have a plan, he or she is still entitled to a minimum of one-half of the other's plan.

Preliminary Steps

Now that we've covered those ethical points, here are nine steps we highly recommend you take before you start divorce proceedings:

Step 1: Gather Information

Pre-divorce financial planning begins with knowing what financial assets you have and where you stand financially. So the first step is to get organized. Gather all financial statements and records for joint and separate accounts. Make copies for back up and place them in a safe place. We have prepared a basic divorce financial records checklist (Chart 17-1) that will help guide you in understanding the type of information you will need for any type of legal representation.

Step 2: Secure all liquid investments

Notify the bank to freeze jointly held savings and checking accounts and your home equity line of credit. Do the same with investment accounts, CDs, safe deposit

---

Chart 17-1

Divorce Financial Records Checklist

- Names and social security numbers of you and partner
- Names of employers with addresses, phone numbers, job titles and information regarding salaries, 401(K) and profit-sharing plans, pension plans, SEP-IRA and Keogh plans.
- Bank, savings and investment account statements
- Health insurance papers
- Stocks, bonds and mutual fund statements
- Income tax returns
- Life insurance policies for both of you
- List of separate properties in separate names
- Real Estate held in joint names (home, income property, deeds etc.)
- Real Estate in separate names (business, investment property, income)
- Credit card statements
- Other short and long-term debts, liens and mortgages against assets
- Information on jointly owned family businesses including other owners, financial statements, loan applications, and income tax returns
- Patents, copyrights, royalties
- Vehicle registrations on all cars, boats and other vehicles
- Artworks and antiques
- Trust funds, annuities and inheritances
- Proceeds of legal lawsuits, lottery winnings
- Work assets, including professional licenses or degrees, benefits packages, stock options, deferred compensation, vacation time, sick leave, bonuses, etc.

---

boxes. All new transactions must require both signatures. Each partner should open his or her own checking account for immediate liquid cash to live on.

Step 3: Cancel and cut up all credit cards

Notify the credit card companies in writing that you will no longer be responsible for the charges on any joint credit cards. Pay off all joint debts with joint cash. Split equally any remaining charges.

Step 4: Make a new will and change beneficiaries

After filing for divorce you may not be allowed to change beneficiaries on wills, trusts, life insurance, annuities, CDs, IRAs, 401(k) plans and pensions. Make the new will BEFORE filing for divorce.

Step 5: Signature

Do not sign any financial statements that are blank. Know what you are signing and keep a copy.

Step 6: Taxes owed

Make sure all taxes owed to the IRS, state government or any other taxing agencies are paid to date.

Step 7: Safe Deposit Box

Review all contents in your joint safe deposit box. Make a written list for your records.

Step 8: Employment

Do not quit work. You need to continue to bring in money to maintain your basic living expenses.

Step 9: Family home

Do not move out of the family home without discussing it with a lawyer.

Discovering Hidden Assets

Marital assets that you should be aware of may be hidden for two reasons. Your spouse may be intentionally concealing them in hopes of keeping them after the divorce or they may be overlooked or not considered because you simply don't know such assets can be included in any settlement agreement. The following are common places where marital assets can reside:

- Income, often in the form of cash, that is unreported on tax returns

- Salary paid to a nonexistent employee

- Overpayment of taxes

- Delayed bonuses, stock options or raises

- A custodial account set up in the name of a child using the child's SSN

- Money paid to family or friends for services never rendered

- Loans to family or friends for a phony debt

💰 Delay in signing long-term business contracts until after the divorce is finalized

💰 Expenses paid for girlfriend or boyfriend for gifts, travel, rent, and college tuition

💰 Investments in Tax Free Municipal Bonds or Series EE Savings Bonds

💰 Cash in form of Traveler's checks

💰 Home or office art work or furnishings, antiques, hobby equipment

💰 Cash skimmed from business he or she owns

💰 Tax credits or carryovers

💰 Law firm draw accounts

💰 Foreign asset protection trusts

💰 Patents or trademarks

💰 Unbilled work from a professional practice

If you suspect your ex-spouse-to-be is currently hiding or may hide in the future important settlement assets, experts agree that you should use a little common sense. Start with the obvious areas first. Bank statements, investment broker documentation, loan documents, mortgage statements, tax returns, or even financial records of a business should provide a good start. Tax returns, in particular, provide many areas between the 1040 and Schedules A-E where a whole lot of discovery can be accomplished. Loan applications or personal financial statements, especially with respect to business loans, provide other fertile sources of information. When doesn't a loan applicant put on his or her best "financial face" to obtain a loan? Never.

It's not always easy to flush out hidden assets. If your spouse has a business, take a look at their lifestyle, the types of expenses the business incurs, how money comes in, who receives it, what some of the operating costs of similar businesses are, and how easy it is to skim cash or not report income. We have included a list of sources for more information on this topic in the appendix.

Alimony And Spousal Support

Stephanie and Jordan

Growing up in upstate, New York, Stephanie always knew she would become a surgeon. During the fifth year of her surgical residency she met and married Jordan Trudeau, a junior writer for Time magazine. They were both 26 years old and earning the same amount of money. The last year of Stephanie's residency she was offered a position as the head of surgery at San Francisco General Hospital with a salary five times larger. She and Jordan packed up and headed West. With Stephanie's increase in income, money was no longer an issue so they bought a home and Jordan quit his job with Time in order to write a book.

After two years and no book, Jordan decided to start a local business newspaper. His company lasted 16 years but never made a profit. By this time Stephanie's income was ten times larger than Jordan's. The gap created resentment on both sides and eventually killed the marriage.

When Stephanie and Jordan sat down with their attorneys, Jordan asked for half the proceeds from the sale of the house. When Stephanie didn't agree, Jordan asked not only for half the house, but half of Stephanie's pension and 401(k) plan, as well as spousal support for seven years. After two years of negotiations, Jordan finally got two and one-half years of spousal support and 50 percent of the couple's total assets—a far cry from the original request for half the proceeds from the sale of the house. Stephanie would have been better off accepting his first request and moving on with her life.

Do Your Homework Before You See a Lawyer

Financial support during separation or after divorce comes in many forms. Which one you and your spouse settle on may depend on a number of factors such as the financial status of each of you, the tax implications, your willingness to have an individual "financially" attached to you after divorce, or a spouse's employability.

Unlike Stephanie, you should learn the differences before you file for divorce. Let's take them one by one:

Alimony/Spousal Support/Maintenance – payments made by one spouse to the other during separation or after a divorce. Alimony used to be a one-way street – from the man to the woman. But with changes in divorce laws due in part to the rising income and earning power of women and media coverage of wealthy female celebrities facing the prospect of paying large sums of money in divorce proceedings, courts of law no longer view gender as a consideration. This gender neutrality has changed references to alimony to the more politically correct "spousal support", although the majority of money awards still go from husband to wife. Spousal Support can be temporary or permanent, "rehabilitative" in purpose, or as a reimbursement for putting someone through school. You can also choose to receive alimony/spousal support in a lump sum. Currently, only one of six divorce or separation cases—about 15 percent— involve payments for alimony/spousal support, according to information at www.divorcesupport.com and www.findlaw.com.

Temporary Spousal Support is sometimes used to describe alimony given during the separation period but prior to divorce. Part of its purpose is to maintain a certain previous standard of living for the family although studies show that the overall standard of living decreases when spread over two households instead of one. Permanent Spousal Support is less common than Temporary Spousal Support, but can be awarded depending upon certain factors such as the age of each spouse, length of the marriage, employability or future earnings capabilities of each spouse, tax consequences, or who will have custody of the children. In general, however, any spousal support other than Permanent Alimony/Spousal Support can be assumed to be temporary.

Rehabilitative Support – payment made by one spouse to the other over a specified period of time enabling the supported spouse to become self-sufficient from a career standpoint. Rehabilitative Alimony is sometimes used when a spouse cannot work until a young child is in school full-time or when she or he needs to become "employable". Time is allowed for the spouse to acquire skills, training, or employment in order to become more self-sufficient. The support payments are set for a fixed period of time, through agreement or court award, during which the spouse would presumably get on his or her feet financially.

Lump Sum Alimony – also called alimony in gross, is generally a onetime fixed payment that is an alternative to the periodic payments of other types of spousal support. Lump Sum Alimony is not affected by future events, such as a spouse remarrying, which normally would terminate other types of periodic spousal support payments. Depending on the financial status of the payer, there could be tax advantages to this type of agreement. A lump sum payment would allow the parties to make a "clean break" after divorce and move on with their lives.

Reimbursement Alimony – is designed to reimburse one spouse for expenses incurred while supporting the other spouse. A good example is when a nurse marries and supports a medical student, and any children they may have, only to have her husband leave her for a new "trophy wife" once he completes his training and becomes a full-fledged doctor. The nurse could be entitled to reimbursement alimony for the resources she provided during the medical school years whether she has a current financial need or not. Reimbursement support can be paid over time or in a lump sum.

Insurance and Spousal Support

Life Insurance can be used to guarantee alimony/spousal support payments. An alimony/spousal support payment usually continues until either the payer or recipient dies or the recipient remarries. In order to insure continued support in the event of a payer's death, spousal support recipients may wish to seek an agreement or court order to guarantee support. The usual method is to require the payer to maintain an insurance policy with the recipient as the beneficiary. When Permanent Alimony is involved, the amount of the policy should be high enough to equate to the loss of the future stream of previous payments.

Health Insurance. After a divorce is finalized, a company's health insurance plan will only cover the spouse who had the insurance and any children that were also previously covered. A divorced spouse who wishes can take advantage of a 1980's Federal law requiring most employer-sponsored group health plans to offer divorced spouses of covered workers continued coverage at group rates for up to three years after the divorce. The non-covered spouse has to contact the company within 60 days of the divorce. The covered spouse's employer has to reply within 14 days.

The Tax Ramifications of Spousal Support

Spousal Support is treated as taxable income to the recipient and is a deductible expense for the payer by the IRS. Alimony, which is supposed to be a constant and equal stream of payments, is a deductible expense to the payer and is taxable as income for the recipient. Consequently the IRS doesn't take too kindly to variations in the alimony payment stream while the spouse is legally entitled to alimony. (Of course, we're not talking about termination of alimony due to remarriage or other circumstances.) If the alimony payments you are required to pay decrease or end during the first three calendar years, you may be subject to what the IRS calls the Recapture Rule. The reasons for a reduction or termination of alimony payments requiring a recapture are varied. See your divorce lawyer for help with these complex procedures.

Child Support

How big is Child Support? According to the U.S Office of Child Support Enforcement, child enforcement agencies spent $3.4 billion in 1997 to collect about $13.3 billion in child support payments. In addition to that, there are several million mothers who have not obtained or have not thought to obtain orders for child support. Many of these women had children out of wedlock.

Is Child Support a contentious and divisive issue? You bet it is. We're talking about being financially attached to someone you either despise or are indifferent to for possibly as many years as it takes the children to reach age 18 or more. Can this "connection" be used to continually inflict a little pain and suffering on each ex-spouse as a reminder of how much one thinks of the other? Consider the following facts.

The Census Bureau figures that about half of all parents entitled to receive child support receive the full amount due. Another one-fourth receive only partial payments, and the other one-fourth receive nothing at all. And, although the term "deadbeat dad" has long been a rallying cry among some social commentators, the small percentage of mothers who have to pay child support have a worse payment rate than fathers. Some 57 percent of mothers ordered to pay child support do so, compared to 70 percent of fathers so ordered.

But divorcing couples are not the only ones to blame for divisiveness. Is it not a standard practice for attorney's to warn a sole custody parent to limit contact between the child and the other parent or risk a reduction in a child support award? Do we manipulate kids to manipulate money? Does the system provide an economic incentive for one parent to have sole custody and exclude the other parent from the child's upbringing? We've already discussed in earlier sections and chapters how good people are at hurting each other through money.

Until the passage of federal laws in the 1980, there were no state or national standards on how much child support was fair. The net effect was that child support amounts were generally very low. Now the starting point for determining child support is based on state-by-state guidelines. These guidelines, or more precisely mathematical formulas, consider the income of the parents, number of children, and other factors in calculating an appropriate amount of support. Although in most states the courts do not vary much from established guidelines, some circumstances serve as a basis for increasing or decreasing the amount of child support. To be sure, check with your attorney or mediator, or local child enforcement agency. The main purpose of the state guidelines is to set an appropriate level of support based on the parent's ability to pay. As a result of the federal laws, child support payments increased by about 50 percent. Sometimes the government does do good things.

> *I'm an excellent housekeeper. Every time I get a divorce, I keep the house*
>
> — Zsa Zsa Gabor

Dividing Property, Assets, And Debt

One of the messiest aspects of divorce is the division of marital property and debt. The ideal way to divide the property is best decided upon by the divorcing couple rather than by a judge. But, if a couple cannot agree, they must submit their property dispute to the court, which will follow state law to divide the property. The court will award each partner a percentage of the total value of the property. Each partner is entitled to items the worth of which adds up to his or her percentage.

The court takes one of two approaches toward dividing property: equitable distribution or community property.

- **Equitable Distribution.** This is where a divorcing couple's combined net worth which consist of all assets and earnings accumulated during marriage are split up according to an agreed upon ratio—50/50 to 70/30. The court usually decides that two-thirds of assets goes to the higher income earner and one-third to the other partner. Couples who use this method to divide property must be aware of one problem — taxes. In most divorce cases the agreed upon split is often done without considering tax effects. That can be a costly mistake for one side and a windfall for the other. The reason: Some assets carry a built-in-tax liability while others don't. We'll talk more about taxes in divorce later in the chapter.

- **Community Property.** There are nine community property states: Arizona, California, Idaho, Louisiana, Nevada, New Mexico, Texas, Washington and Wisconsin. In these states all property of a married person is classified as either community property owned equally by both partners or as separate property of one partner or the other. During divorce, all community property is divided equally between the partners, while each keeps his or her separate property.

Okay, So How do You Define Community Property?

Here are the rules the court will use to determine which marital assets are community property and which aren't:

- **Community Property** includes all earnings during the marriage and anything purchased with those earnings, as well as all debts incurred during the marriage.

- **Separate property** are gifts and inheritances given to just one partner, money or stock from a vested pension plan received before marriage, or a personal injury award received by that partner. Property bought with the separate funds of a partner will remain that partner's separate property as well. A business

owned by one partner before the marriage remains his or her separate property during the marriage, but this gets tricky because a portion of the business
may become community property if the business increased in value during
the marriage or both partners worked at the company.

- **Combo property** refers to property purchased with a combination of community and separate funds. It is considered part community and part separate
property as long as a partner is able to show some separate funds were used
in the purchase. Generally, however, separate property mixed together with
community property becomes community property. Case-in-point: You purchased a home when you were single. You marry without a prenuptial agreement and your spouse begins paying one-half of the mortgage. Technically,
the house becomes community property. The way around this dilemma is to
have your new spouse sign a rental agreement. The one-half of the mortgage
he or she pays is now considered rent. You should also create a prenuptial
agreement. (More on this later.)

Dividing the House

Other than determining who gets the children, dividing up the house is by far
the most financially and emotionally difficult decision a divorcing couple will make.
Long ago, if there were children involved, the family home was automatically awarded
to the wife and kids. The theory back then was that it is initially best for the children
to remain in the same familiar place. That was great in theory, but oftentimes expensive for the wife. Here's the problem: In order to keep a home worth $250,000 the
wife has to come up with a way to buy her husband out of his share worth $125,000.
She'll have to bargain away other things to keep the house, only later to discover she

can't afford the mortgage and the upkeep. Remember the story of Jan in Chapter 9, "Searching for a Money Prince Charming"? When her husband, David, walked out on her and stopped paying the mortgage, she lost the house because she couldn't make the payments. Before either spouse decides to keep the house and buy the other out, it is important that they both take into consideration the full cost of the purchase—mortgage, taxes, insurance, landscaping, future selling costs, and other expenses.

Selling the House Before the Divorce

In fact, it may be better to sell the primary family home BEFORE you begin divorce proceedings. If you sell and are still married at the end of the calendar year, you can shelter up to $500,000 of profit from any federal capital gains taxes. There are two ways to qualify for the full $500,000 exclusion. First, by filing a joint return – which means you have to still be married. One or both of you must have owned the home for at least two of the five years preceding the sale. Second, the home must have been used by both of you as your principal residence for at least two out of the five years preceding the sale.

If you're still married and the home is jointly owned or community property, you may also file separate returns and each can exclude up to $250,000 of the share of the gain, provided you both pass the two-out-of-five years ownership and use tests. The best part: This allows you to convert the home equity into tax-free cash and you both can get on with your life. Any gains that exceed the exclusion will be taxed at capital gains rates (20 percent maximum). Another point to remember is that while you may not owe federal taxes on the gain from your home, you still might owe state and local taxes.

Selling the House After The Divorce

If you buy your ex-spouse out, and are newly-divorced at the time of sale, you can still exclude $250,000 of capital gains as long as you meet the two-out-of-five-year residency test. If you remarry and live in the home with a new partner for at least two years before selling, you will still qualify for the $500,000 exclusion by filing a joint return with your new partner.

Keeping the House After the Divorce

If you want to allow your former partner to continue living in the house, you may elect to continue to co-own it after the divorce. But after three years of not living in the home, you, as the nonresident ex-spouse, will no longer qualify for the $250,000 exclusion. That means when the home is finally sold, your share of the proceeds will be fully taxable. The way around this to specify in your divorce papers that as a condition of the divorce, your Ex can continue to live in the house for as long as he or she wants. Or, you can stipulate that the home must be sold or your share bought out after the youngest child reaches age 19. Or whatever is best for you. This agreement means that when the home is finally sold, you can still take advantage of the $250,000 gain exclusion to shelter all or part of your share of the profit.

Keeping Other Real Estate After the Divorce

If you and your divorcing spouse decide to sell your vacation home, rental unit or any other real estate, you will owe capital gains on all profits. But if one of you decides to live in the vacation home or rental unit after the divorce, you can consider it a primary residence. After two years you can then qualify for the $250,000 capital gains exclusion. By the same token, if you remarry and live in the vacation home, rental unit or other unit for two years, you and your new spouse can then sell the place and get the $500,000 exclusion.

Investment Accounts

If you have a large stock and bond portfolio it is imperative you seek advice from an accountant before you and your spouse make a final settlement. The face or market value of the securities may not be the same as the actual property value because of taxes that have to be paid when the securities are sold. That means the 50/50 split sometimes recommended by attorneys is more like 60/40 after taxes are taken into account.

While you are still married you can make tax-free transfers of cash and investment assets held in taxable accounts. Ditto for later transfers as long as they are made per the divorce property settlement. Therefore if the property settlement directs you to give some of your long-held Krispy Kreme shares to your ex-partner there is no immediate tax impact. If the stock was jointly owned or community property, nothing will change tax-wise for the partner after he or she becomes the sole owner of some or all of the shares. If your ex-partner sells, then he or she will owe the federal capital gains tax (probably at 20 percent), plus any state and local taxes.

As you can see, owning appreciated investments comes with a tax liability that many lawyers fail to warn you about. The bigger the gain, the bigger the tax bill. So, from a realistic net-of-tax point of view, appreciated investments are worth less than an equal amount of cash or assets that has not appreciated. To avoid the unequal split use net-of-tax figures to make your property settlement. Your accountant can help you calculate those figures.

Retirement Accounts

Retirement accounts are fast becoming the largest assets for many divorcing couples to split. Both spouses are entitled to a portion of each other's retirement benefits whether they are pension, profit-sharing, 401(k), or stock options. These accounts are generally divided by using a qualified domestic relations order (QDRO), which gives each partner legal rights to receive a designated percentage, usually half, of each other's qualified plan account balance or benefit payments. Any taxes due on the withdrawn money are the responsibility of the receiving spouse, unless it can be rolled over into an IRA rollover.

The QDRO arrangement allows each partner to withdraw his or her share and roll the money over into his or her own IRA. By putting it into an IRA rollover you both are able to be in control of the money and at the same time postpone the taxes until the money is withdrawn.

If you don't use the QDRO arrangement and one partner receives money from the other partner's retirement benefits it will be treated as a taxable distribution to the original owner of the benefits. Which means the original owner could end up owing the IRS money that they are giving away. Sound confusing? Here's an example. Let's say you have $100,000 in your qualified retirement account. Your ex-partner will receive $50,000 of it. If you do not have the QDRO arrangement, the $50,000 will be treated as a taxable distribution to you. Of course, your ex-partner will love you because he or she gets a tax-free sum of money at your expense.

Here's the scary part. Not only will you be responsible for paying the income taxes on the money your ex-spouse gets, but you may also get hit with the 10 percent early withdrawal penalty if you are under the age of 59 ½. Now you see why you need a QDRO. Make sure it is so stated in your divorce papers. We suggest all couples play it safe and consult an accountant with divorce experience to make sure the required lingo is included. Don't automatically assume your divorce lawyer knows how to handle the QDRO arrangements. Many don't.

IRAs and SEPs

A QDRO arrangement isn't needed to split up your IRA accounts, but there are rules you must follow to avoid any tax problems. You can roll over money tax-free from your IRA to an IRA set up for your ex-partner as long as the transfer is authorized by the divorce property settlement. The ex-partner can now manage his or her own money and defer the income taxes until the money is actually withdrawn. When it is withdrawn he or she will be responsible for paying the income taxes— not you. The same rules apply for the SEPs (simplified employee pension) accounts because they are treated as an IRA.

Stock Options

Not so long ago, when stocks were at their high and stock options were really worth some money – at least on paper — they were the trophies of many a divorce negotiation. During that time, greed really reared its ugly head. Talk about some nasty fights. There were cases when a divorce settlement was reopened because one partner decided to go after options that he or she was not awarded in the original property settlement.

Nowadays, there is still some emphasize on stock options but less than before. The difficulty remains in deciding how to divide them up, especially since it's hard to determine their exact value. The additional challenge is how the IRS calculates the taxes on employer-granted stock options. According to the IRS, there is no tax problem if option stocks are given to an ex-partner after the divorce under the terms of the divorce settlement. The ex-partner will owe the taxes if the stock is later sold for a profit.

The challenge is the options themselves. The IRS states that the option holder will be taxed on the equity in an employer stock option transfer to the ex-partner. Even worse, the tax is at the regular tax rate (up to 39 percent), because it is considered income instead of capital gains.

Avoiding the Stock Option Tax Bite

There are three ways you may be able to avoid the stock option tax bill. First, find a way *not* to transfer any employer stock options to your ex-partner. Instead, agree to give him or her cash or some other type of assets tax-free. Second, if possible, exercise the options right away with little or no tax liability (depends on the type of option and the current market value of the stock). Then you can give your ex-partner the actual shares instead of the options. This will not cause a tax-problem. Third, if you live in one of the nine community property states you can claim that your ex-partner owned one-half of your options from the day you received them. That way, transferring 50 percent to him or her should not trigger negative tax consequences. Ideally, this should be done while you are still married. It's better to do it during a year when you are filing a joint tax return.

Credit Cards and Other Debts

With 6.6 trillion dollars in consumer debt outstanding in this country, many divorcing couples have as much debt as they have property. Getting free in divorce is as much about assigning responsibility for debt payment as it is dividing up the property. There are several ways to deal with debt payment in a divorce. We have listed them in order of preference:

- Agree to pay off all joint debts before the divorce. If there is available cash, or property that can be sold for cash, paying off the debt now is simpler — and safer — for both of you. It's also a clean break for both of you. You can start your new financial lives without the threat of debt hanging over your heads.

- One partner agrees to be responsible for the debt the two of you shared and in return gets compensated with other assets. It is then up to the partner that takes on the debt to decide what property to liquidate and when to pay off the debt. Be careful with this method. Whichever spouse agrees to pay off the debt should hold the other spouse harmless. The only caveat is that the indemnity is only binding on you two, not on third parties. If the debt doesn't get paid, the credit card people will still come after either or both of you.

- Both partners agree to share equal responsibility for payment of the debt. This is the worst choice. The relationship remains entangled and therefore vulnerable to conflict. You have to talk to your ex-partner about money every month at a time when you are trying to build a new life. It's better to divvy up the debts in some roughly equal fashion so each of you knows which bills you are responsible for paying off.

Business Ownership

Dividing a business between a divorcing couple is an entire book in itself. We are not lawyers so we don't want to approach this subject lightly. If you and your partner own a business we highly recommend you engage the services of a matrimonial lawyer and a CPA with experience in dealing with the division of a business in divorce. We do know that if the business isn't properly divided both parties can suffer dire tax and financial consequences.

Taxes

Earlier we touched on the tax implications when property and assets are divided. Let's briefly reiterate. Generally, splitting up ownership of your assets has no immediate federal tax consequences. You can make tax-free transfers of houses, cars, other real and personal property, investments held in taxable investment accounts, and business ownership interests while still married or as part of the divorce settlement agreement.

But divorce has serious tax implications and pitfalls galore for unsuspecting couples. Most divorce lawyers aren't schooled in taxes, so don't expect much help from them. It's pretty much up to each partner to educate himself or herself on the subject before a final divorce agreement is reached, because once the papers are signed, it may be difficult to make corrections. We suggest you get help from an experienced CPA on this issue.

What's Timing Got To Do With It?

Everything! The marital status of parting couples for purposes of their tax return is set as of the last day of the calender year. So, if you are contemplating a divorce, consider whether you would be better off making your divorce effective before the end of the year which would allow you to file as single taxpayers next April. Or, it might be better to make the divorce effective the following year, which will allow you to still file a joint return April of the following year.

Our recommendation is that despite the tax advantages of filing jointly you should file separately. Why? If you are not financially savvy, you risk being held liable if there are errors on the joint return. However, if you and your spouse do decide to file a joint return before the divorce is final, it's important that you have your accountant review the return before you sign it.

Divorcing The Right Way

If we seem biased in this section, you are right. This book is about making love and money work so we recommend the method that allows you to come out of a divorce as financially whole as possible. Two lawyers fighting an adversarial divorce in court will not only leave you and your ex-partner financially broken but spiritually and mentally scarred as well. The lawyers are really the only winners in this type of divorce. So what is your alternative? Divorce through mediation.

What Is Mediation?

Divorce through meditation is a procedure that a couple agrees to take part in with the help of a trained mediator for the purpose of reaching a divorce settlement on their own. Mediators don't replace lawyers; they will neither make your decisions nor give you legal advice. They are trained simply to help you draft your own divorce agreement. Then you each take the agreement to your individual lawyer who will review it and make sure it is fair and reasonable. You are both still using a lawyer but there isn't a need to retain one at great expense. In this instance, your lawyer is more like a legal coach.

Does My Case Qualify for Divorce by Mediation?

We understand that if your divorce is not pretty cut and dried, a mediator may not work. Here a few guidelines upon which you can decide to use a mediator:

- You both have agreed to the divorce.

- You both want to arrive at a fair and reasonable settlement without using the court system or the divorce settlement to "get even" or punish each other.

- You both feel somewhat equal in power financially and don't feel you need to have a legal battle.

- Your property, money, and child custody issues are straightforward and do not require all-inclusive advice from tax attorneys, and accountants.

- There isn't any major infighting in the relationship. You both need to be mentally clear to agree to the terms of the divorce with a mediator.

- The mediator is fully aware of the balance of power in your relationship and supports and protects you both when needed.

- The mediator has been recommended from someone you trust and you both feel comfortable and safe with him or her.

- The mediator stays abreast of the negotiating meetings with accurate records of what is or isn't agreed upon from week to week. There is no need to waste time and money going over the same issues each time.

Be aware that divorce mediation will not work when there is an overwhelming imbalance of power within the relationship. If one partner has been controlling and intimidating during the marriage, he or she will be the same way during mediation. In that situation, it's better to engage a lawyer.

Areas to Settle in Mediation

When you are going through a divorce there are many areas to be discussed and decisions to be made. It is the responsibility of your mediator or your lawyer-coach to alert you to those important areas. Many of them we have already discussed. Here are additional points to consider as you go through your negotiating sessions. Variations in state laws may affect whether some of these items apply to you:.

- Alimony/spousal support

- Child support

- Custodial arrangements for children

- Visitation rights/parenting time

- Division of family home

- Division of other real estate or real property

- Medical, dental, hospital expenses for the children

- Medical insurance or COBRA for a former partner for up to three years after the divorce judgment

- Pensions, 401(k) accounts, IRA and SEP accounts, Qualified Domestic Relations Order

- Cars, boats and other motor vehicles

- Furniture, art, and other valuables

- Income taxes-joint filings and liabilities for payment of taxes

- The discovery of hidden assets

- College education expenses for children or ex-spouse

- Life insurance for protection of child support payments, alimony/spousal support, and property payments in the event of a death

- Hold-harmless clause in case one partner does not live up to financial obligations

- Fees for mediator, lawyer, accountant and any other needed experts

- Bankruptcy protection in case one partner decides to file BK

- Payments for summer camps or other special needs involving children

- Provisions to review in certain situations with regard to child support and/ or spousal support.

Mediation Can Be Good For Everybody

In spite of what you hear in the media it isn't necessary for divorce to be nasty. That's a choice you and your soon-to-be ex- partner make. We've covered a lot of material in this chapter and by no means is it everything you need to know about ending your marriage. We wanted to give you the basics and show you ways where you both can financially win in a divorce. No, it isn't easy and it's hurtful no matter how you do it. Using a mediator is the best way to lessen the pain.

Divorce mediation style allows you both to control the terms of your divorce. It stresses a win/win rather than a win/lose approach. You are able to invest energy in arriving at fair terms rather than fighting each other. Divorce settlements through mediation also tend to require less time and expense. And since both partners are a part of the negotiating process there are fewer feelings of victimization once an agreement is reached. Instead there is openness and cooperation. Overall it can be less stressful, and more financially and psychologically healing, which helps both partners exit gracefully and move on in life.

Healing Yourself After A Divorce

Divorce is financially difficult for both men and women. Going from a two- income household to a one-income household isn't easy, especially in states where the cost of living is inordinately high. It's been said that after a divorce you either grow and evolve or simply give up. Why not look at your divorce as a new beginning? It could be the perfect time to start your own business or develop a new career. It's also an excellent time to start fresh with new financial goals. Here are seven steps to help get you back on your financial feet while the healing process goes forward:

- Complete a new personal balance sheet (Financial statement, see chart 15-1) listing all your assets and liabilities. If your liabilities exceed your assets, work to decrease your debts and increase your assets. The balance sheet will also let you know the amount of money you have available for retirement. This is particularly important for divorced non-working women who usually have absolutely nothing saved up and are dependent on obtaining part of their husband's retirement benefits from the divorce.

- Draw up a new will, especially if you have children. The easiest way to do this is to consult a lawyer. If your estate is large, chose a specialist in estate planning.

- Establish a new monthly spending plan. Now that your income is cut in half you need to know the exact inflow and outflow of your money. You may find that you have more going out than coming in. Meaning, you may need to cut back on some of the activities you were doing while married and/or find a higher paying job. A financial mistake many divorcees' make is trying to maintain the same lifestyle they had before. This effort is as much emotional as financial. By keeping things the same the divorce doesn't seem as painful. Unfortunately, this is the quickest way to the poor house. We know of several divorced women who received lump sums of cash as part of their settlements as opposed to monthly checks. Guess what? They went through the entire amounts within the first two years. Better to scale down and put more into your savings and retirement plans until you are fully back on your feet. It usually takes about a year to financially recover from a divorce.

- Eliminate and stay out of debt. More than likely you and your ex-partner divvied up your marital debt. So your new goal will be to get rid of your share and to discontinue using all credit cards except for emergencies. Several excellent books are available to help you manage your credit and get out of debt. We have listed some of our favorites in the appendix.

- Determine your new insurance needs. Make sure you are protected by automobile insurance, homeowner's/ rental insurance, health insurance, life insurance, and disability insurance.

- Set new financial goals. Ones that really matter to you. Are there any goals you wanted to achieve but sacrificed while you were married? A dear friend of ours always wanted to start his own nightclub but just couldn't do it when he was married. Today he is divorced and following his dream. Every Friday he rents out a local nightclub and draws anywhere from 200 to 300 people.

- Start building or add more to your savings, investment and retirement plans. Now that you are on your own you want your money to grow the best way possible. Put the maximum amount into your employer 401(k) plan, invest every month into a mutual fund to build your investment portfolio, and add $20 to $100 every month to your emergency cash fund. If investing your money is new to you learn all you can by taking an investment class, attending seminars and logging onto the Internet. It's full of great money and investment advice. Learning about money has never been easier. We list the top money websites in the appendix.

Time to Move On

Even though your marriage has dissolved, do your best to maintain goodwill toward your former spouse. Even if you feel sad and angry that your deep trust was broken, don't act on or seek out revenge. Don't point fingers or assign blame. No matter how heartbroken you may be, try to realize that healing your hurt, not hurting your partner, is what will bring you peace and help you move on.

Retaliation during or after a divorce is an irrational impulse; it's a knee-jerk reaction of a scared and confused mind. Don't waste time by becoming embroiled in legal power plays to destroy each other. If children are involved make every effort to maintain a respectful relationship. If children aren't involved take time off from each other — at least a year, if possible. With time, the scars will fade. As philosopher Sam Keen says so succinctly: "Even soul mates may come to a fork in the road where their paths diverge, and they must grant each the hardest gift of fidelity—a loving divorce."

Chapter 17: Making Love and Money Work Action Steps

1. Remember, there is no need for divorce to be financially nasty.

2. If after reading this book you find you still must get a divorce—let it be uncontested. It's the least expensive and emotionally damaging.

3. Don't use money or children as a weapon in a divorce; it's destructive for everyone involved.

4. Use a divorce mediator if at all possible.

5. Be fair when dividing property.

6. After the divorce, complete a new personal balance sheet, draw up a will and establish a new monthly spending plan.

7. Eliminate and stay out of all short-term debt.

8. Protect your family and assets by obtaining new life, automobile, home/rental, disability and health insurance.

9. Set new financial goals and persevere until you meet them.

10. Begin your new future by starting investment and savings accounts. Also, put the maximum contribution possible into your employer sponsored retirement plan.

11. Don't waste time retaliating against your partner. Concentrate on healing emotionally, spiritually and financially. It's time to get on with your life!

Chapter 18

Making Love And Money Work 101

> *Love is when you give 60% and take 40%.*
>
> —— Unknown

We are at the end of *What's Money Got To Do With It*, but by no means is it the end for you. It's actually the beginning of how you and your partner will make your money work in your relationship. Up until this point we have made you aware of several financial issues that will, or probably already have, come up in your relationship. We've offered techniques for dealing with these issues. In this chapter we want to sum it all up and show you the correct way to make love and money work.

We'll begin by discussing how to manage money when you are living together. We have found that many living-together couples rarely if ever bring up the subject of money in their relationship. Could this possibly be the reason why 50 percent of living-together couples break up? It may not be the only reason but it is definitely a contributing factor. We'll show you how to develop a financial plan and a live-in budget.

Next, we'll show you how to design your financial life together. Is it my money, your money or our money? Should you have separate or joint accounts or both? What about starting a business together? And don't forget how important it is to set financial goals that make love and money work without debt. All of this and more will be covered in this section.

And last, we'll talk about the art of making love and money work in your relationship. We'll show you how to build financial security while maintaining a healthy love affair. Romance and finance can work with the right recipe and the freshest ingredients. Our list of the 25 keys to making love and money work are those ingredients. It's up to you and your partner to follow the recipe and mix the ingredients properly to have a wonderful and satisfying financial partnership. The secret is that you both must take charge of your money together. By following the steps in this chapter you will be an unstoppable couple on your road to wealth.

Living Together: Look Before You Leap

Making love and money work in a marriage is tricky. But living together and managing the money is even trickier. It takes a lot of finesse from both partners to make it happen. Money trips up many live-in couples because the guidelines aren't as clear as in a marriage. Married couples pay the bills from a joint bank account, stash money away together for retirement, and buy things together that belong to both.

When you live together, money confusion crops up because now you're managing finances the way two non-romantic roommates would, but you're not non-romantic—you're in love. So who will pay for the glamorous stuff like dinners and movies out? Who will pay for the dull stuff like plumbing repairs? How will living expenses such as rent or mortgage, water, gas, garbage, and electricity be covered? These are the types of money issues that need to be addressed way before the move-in date.

Living together is an increasingly popular lifestyle choice. The number of unmarried couples who live together skyrocketed from 439,000 in 1960 to a staggering 4.2 million in 1998, according to the Marital Status Living Arrangements report of the U.S. Census Bureau. The 2000 Census did not ask about living arrangements, but based on past data predicted the number of couples living together has increased to at least 5 million.

The Financial Drawbacks Of Living Together

It's been said that living together is a dress rehearsal for marriage. That's true as long as you enter into the arrangement with your financial eyes wide open. Living together does offer some positive financial perks. The two major benefits are 1) sharing the cost of household expenses and 2) avoiding responsibility for each other's debts. But those same benefits also contribute to the financial drawbacks of living together. The one that fouls up most couples is a lack of financial cohesiveness. Which means you and your partner don't really create a secure financial foundation together. You don't sit down and share financial goals or write up a financial plan that will serve as a blueprint to help you manage your money and build wealth. Instead you each do your own financial thing. Here's what happened to Anita and George. They have since learned the lesson and now sit down together and write out their financial goals.

Anita

We experienced this very thing in our own relationship when George did not consult with me before investing $1,000 on a hot tip stock recommended by an associate. When we finally did discuss the investment, it was after the fact – and after he lost the $1,000. If we had been married he probably would have sat down with me before buying the stock. But since it was "his" money, not "our" money he saw no reason to include me in on the decision-making.

George

I've now learned that a financial plan will serve as the glue that keeps you both tuned into each other. Without one, it will be much easier to give up on the relationship when the financial going gets rough. That may be okay when marriage is not in the cards. But if marriage is a possibility in your future, the money decisions you make as a live-in couple are a huge indication of your commitment —or lack of it— and set an important precedent should you ever decide to marry.

Legal Protections When You Live Together

Don't think for a minute that by living together you will avoid the legal issues entailed in marriage. In many respects living together can actually be more complicated due to the inconsistency of laws regulating live-in couples. As of yet, the laws aren't well defined. That's why couples thinking about moving in together may want to protect themselves financially with a cohabitation agreement.

What Is A Cohabitation Agreement?

A cohabitation agreement is similar to a prenuptial agreement except it is for non-married couples. It is a friendly, mutually agreeable but formal contract between two parties who are not covered by marital laws. It is a written document that spells out the terms governing the relationship including what happens if it dissolves.

This living together agreement is a relatively new legal instrument. Before 1970 it didn't even exist in the United States. In fact, before 1970, living together was illegal in all states. Even today, there are still a few states where the law remains on the books although is not enforced.

What A Cohabitation Agreement Does

The cohabitation agreement is the only legal document that will protect the finances of couples living together. Couples without one are taking a big risk since live-in partners have no legal basis for compensation unless a cohabitation agreement is in place. In other words, you can live together for years and not have a legal claim to your partner's assets upon the breakup of the relationship or death. Here's what a cohabitation agreement can do for your living-together relationship:

- Establish a legal relationship while living together

- Protect personal assets

- Protect assets you want to pass down to children from a previous relationship

- Clearly state how joint property is to be divided

- Prevent expensive legal challenges in the future

- Spell out the couple's financial arrangement

- Discuss the details of jointly assumed loans

- Determine whose name(s) will be listed on any rental leases or agreements

- Establish the financial arrangements for children of the relationship

- Discuss how legal fees incurred during a breakup will be paid

- Decide who will get the pet(s) and seasons tickets

As you can see, living together isn't really easier than marriage. You aren't free from all legal ties. And if you move in without a well-thought out financial and legal plan, you may find yourself in court to protect assets that are similar to those of a married couple. The best thing to do is to set up protections before you take the leap. You will not only prevent catastrophic financial consequences but you will make ending the relationship much easier to handle.

Drawing Up Your Financial Blueprint Together

Hopefully, we haven't scared you away from moving in with your soul mate. Surely that was not our intention. We simply want to give you a heads-up to make living together fun and enjoyable and not stressed out over money. If this is the direction in which you want to take your relationship, then the next step is to draw up your financial blueprint together. We suggest you do it before you move in or immediately thereafter. Don't wait!

Stage One: Decide Where To Live: His Place, Her Place, Or Our Place

The first stage of creating your financial blueprint begins with determining where you will live: His place, her place or our place? Where you live can have a major impact on your relationship. Here are our four recommendations:

- **Recommendation 1:** A neutral place, one that isn't, or hasn't been, either partner's. You should both pick it out. This will allow you each to feel equal in the relationship. One partner moving into the other's place can work, however, as long as the new partner isn't made to feel like an outsider. That is why it's important to follow recommendation 2.

- **Recommendation 2:** Make the place comfortable and homey for both of you, especially if one partner is just moving in. Change the furniture around, buy some new accessories, and make space for some of the new partner's things. Living in a place where a previous lover or spouse lived may feel awkward to the new partner. Get rid of anything that might remind him or her of past relationships.

- **Recommendation 3**: Make the place "our" place. Spend time together getting your home in shape. It needs to be a joint effort. Not only is that way more fun, but also good practice for working as a team.

- **Recommendation 4:** If renting or leasing, put both names on the agreement. It's important that you both have joint responsibility for your home. State in your cohabitation agreement what you will do with the home if the relationship ends. Without that clause neither partner can rightfully ask the other to leave.

Should We Buy A Home Together?

Buying a home together when your marital status is still legally "single" can be as complicated, expensive, and life altering as buying a home together when you're married. Yes, we know you've decided to live together rather than get married because "We don't need a piece of paper to prove our love." That's all well and good. But when buying a home together, you really do want a piece of paper to protect your combined interests. As a live-in couple, you don't have the same options that a married couple has. Therefore all legal matters must be airtight before you and your loved one take out a mortgage.

Get Everything In Writing

A cohabitation agreement is an absolute must if you are thinking of buying a home together. Particularly if either of you has been married before or brought substantial assets or debts into your current relationship. Here are a few things to consider when writing up a contract to buy a home together:

Take 'Stock' in Your House: If you have widely different incomes and assets you may want to buy the house differently than through the traditional 50/50 split. Think of the purchase price of the house as equal to 100 shares of stock. If one partner is paying the bulk of the down payment she or he should "own" a larger portion of shares in the house, say 70 percent. The portion of the down payment contributed by the other partner then equals 30 percent. If the "junior" partner later contributes to the increase in the value of the property by making more house payments or paying for remodels or upgrades, he or she is allowed to purchase some of the down-payer's share of stock. This arrangement is spelled out in the legally binding cohabitation agreement. Same goes for selling the house. Whatever percentage of "stock" each partner "owns" in the house at that time is the percentage of the proceeds they should receive from the sale.

Parting Company: Breaking up is hard to do, and doubly harder when there is a house to divide. You know how smart companies always have a clause in their business plan to cover a decision to dissolve the company? They know it is easier to arrange in the beginning when everyone is still getting along. You and your mate need to think of your arrangement as being similar to the company's deal. Make sure when you buy a house that you agree on how to split it up if you later part ways. We know of one case where one of the partners bought the other's share of the house and remained in the home. Since both partners had equally contributed to the down payment the partner who stayed in the house paid the other 50 percent of what the house was worth. In another case, the couple split the equity in half minus the state fees and Realtors' commissions that would have been paid had the house been sold.

Advance planning and writing it down are the only ways to avoid a "war of the roses" battle over who keeps the home in the event things don't work out.

The Process Of Buying A Home

The decision to buy a home together is the easy part. The challenges are finding a home you both like and then actually qualifying and making the purchase. The really sticky area is the financing of the home. Unfortunately, there are no laws that prevent a lender from discriminating against a non-married couple so you may encounter problems when applying for a home mortgage.

Lenders require non-married couples to apply as separate applicants. If there are problems with one partner's application you may not get approval for a mortgage loan. Most lenders require both partners to qualify. That becomes easier if you are married. Banks and lenders consider married couples as one unit, which allows one person's qualification to allow the couple to buy. The real issue here, it seems, is that banks and lenders haven't developed a system to process an unmarried couple's application. We predict this will change as more couples take up housekeeping together. Until then, you'll have to abide by their outdated process.

Setting Up The Title Of The Property

Normally, when a married couple buys property, the title of the property is placed in both names as joint owners with rights of survivorship. Unmarried couples may want to set it up differently. Here are the two options that are available:

Option 1: Joint Tenancy with Right of Survivorship (joint ownership). As mentioned previously, this is the title that married couples often select when buying a home or other property. Joint ownership allows an easy transfer of the property to the surviving partner or spouse in the event of death. The property automatically transfers to the surviving partner or spouse and inheritance tax is avoided because the property doesn't go through the estate. However, if the property is titled this way one partner cannot sell his or her share or choose to leave his or her share of the house to anyone other than the other owner.

Option 2: Tenants In Common. This option gives you more flexibility, by making it possible to have multiple owners with unequal shares. Also, each owner can leave his or her share of the property to whomever he or she chooses. Therefore, it is critical for each partner to have a will. Tenants in common with no rights of survivorship is an excellent choice for partners who want to leave their share of the property to their children from a previous relationship. The drawback with this title is the inheritance taxes, because the portion of the house that belonged to the deceased partner must go through his or her estate. So, things could get a little hairy.

If You Decide To Marry And Then Buy a House — A Prenuptial Agreement

If after living together for a while you decide to marry, you can choose to keep your cohabitation agreement and house title as before. However, marital attorneys recommend you obtain a prenuptial agreement and retitle the property as husband and wife. In case there is a judgment against one partner it will not affect the house. That isn't the case if you are unmarried. Either you or your partner's creditors can attach a judgment to that percentage of the house each of you owns.

In the preceding paragraph, we mentioned "prenuptial agreement." Before we go any further, let's pause here to explain that term. Let's start with Marcia Lopez's story.

Marcia Learns the Hard Way

After three unsuccessful marriages Marcia, a sales manager for an insurance company, realized that making more money than her partners has been an issue in her relationships. When she met husband No. 3 she had been working for 10 years, owned two houses, was putting money into her 401(k) plan and was building a pension. On the other hand, her new hubby was a widower with no career, no money, no investments, an 11-year-old Volkswagen, some clothes and a large jazz collection. So how come after 12 years of marriage he walked away with one of the houses, half of her 401(k) retirement fund, and one-fourth of her pension?

Marcia admits she was love-struck and really wanted this relationship to work so she didn't ask the widower to sign a prenuptial agreement before they jumped the broom. "This relationship was supposed to work, so I thought, why not show good faith?" she said later. "Never mind that he doesn't make as much money as me. I went into thinking, I don't care, I'm going to help him."

This sentiment sounds great but seldom works out and usually backfires. Which is exactly what happened to Marcia. When she initiated divorce proceedings, her husband took her to the cleaners. And under the laws of her state, there was not a thing she could do about it.

Today, Marcia has bounced back financially. After that disastrous experience she decided to focus her energies on rebuilding her assets. Now she owns two homes again and has over $500,000 in her company 401(k) plan. Her advice: "You can love somebody whether they have money or not, but don't let that cause you to make foolish decisions. [If you bring substantial assets into a second or third marriage] keep romance and finance separate. Don't mix sex with money." And, we might add, be sure you and your lover-boy or girl signs a prenup!

Why a Prenuptial Agreement?

Prenuptial agreements get a lot of bad press. When we hear about one, it's usually about a rich business tycoon, celebrity or athlete in the middle of a nasty divorce whose prenup is being challenged.

Remember when San Francisco Giants baseball star Barry Bonds' first wife, Sun, (Yes, that is her name) took him to court after their divorce? Sun said Barry took advantage of her when they first married by having her sign a prenuptial agreement she didn't understand. The judge eventually ruled in Bonds' favor, but you can bet that before his second marriage he made sure his new wife understood the terms of any prenup she was asked to sign.

Then there's Michael Douglas, the aging movie star, who married Catherine Zeta-Jones, a much younger actress. According to the celebrity magazines, their prenup specifies that Zeta-Jones will receive a large sum of money for every year she remains married to Douglas. If true, that payoff seems kind of creepy to us, but we guess it's just like any other business arrangement. If she does divorce him some day, she'll know up-front what she'll lose, money-wise.

We want to put a more positive spin on prenuptial agreements. Such a document can play a very positive role in making love and money work in your relationship. How? By laying everything financially on the table well before the wedding day. (Not, as we have heard, on the day before or the day of the wedding. We are going to safely assume that the people who are that underhanded aren't reading this book.) And by serving as a financial blueprint for couples just starting out or going into their second or third marriage.

What Is a Prenuptial Agreement, Anyway?

A prenuptial agreement, also known as a premarital agreement or an "antenuptial" agreement ("ante" as in before something happens, not "anti" as in against something) is a legal contract signed by the two partners before the marriage. It is designed to establish a couple's marital property rights and financial responsibilities before they marry and should they subsequently divorce. It also determines the rights of the surviving partner upon the death of the first partner. Particularly in second or third marriages where there are children from prior unions, a prenuptial agreement assures that assets brought into the relationship will remain with each partner or passed down to heirs from the previous unions in the event of divorce or death.

The Benefits of a Prenuptial Agreement

In order for a prenuptial agreement to be valid both spouses must fully disclose all financial information before the marriage. Doing this is a great benefit for any couple wanting to start their financial life off the right way by entering into the marriage fully aware of where they each stand financially. As we mentioned earlier in the book, a relationship where both partners are on the same financial page makes a world of difference. Sure, you'll still have your disagreements, but money fights will not play a central part in the marriage. Instead, you'll be able to sit down every month and discuss your financial goals, pay your bills on time, and invest and grow your money the right way.

The prenuptial agreement will also show each spouse's shaky financial areas. Sometimes we don't want our future partners to know we have too much credit card debt or no savings account. Well, you know what? You got to get over keeping financial secrets. They are murder on a relationship and certainly do not make love and money work. You both need to see each other's financial weaknesses and strengths. That's what a relationship is — a coming together to support each other financially, emotionally and spiritually. If your partner is good at managing credit, then he or she needs to be responsible for that area. If you are good in the investment arena, then you should handle most of those decisions. The key is, of course, that you both discuss those decisions and are in agreement with handling your finances in that manner.

What Do I Have to Do to Obtain a Valid Prenuptial Agreement?

First, you must draft an agreement together. It must be a full disclosure of each other's assets and liabilities, written well in advance of the wedding. Both partners must have ample time to read over everything before signing. Each must enter into the agreement freely and voluntarily. If there is even the slightest hint of duress to sign or fraud, the prenuptial agreement is subject to being thrown out.

Second, the prenup should cover the following:

- Prior marital history and family background

- Property each partner is bringing into the marriage and who will own the investment income from that property.

- How the income from each partner will be handled

- What happens in the event of death of one partner

- What happens with property that one partner inherits

- How you will file tax returns — jointly or separately

- Where you will live

- If there is a divorce what type of support is expected

- Who will pay for the debt brought in before and after the marriage

- If this is a second or third marriage, what assets will go to children from a previous marriage(s) and what will go to the new partner.

If you live in a community property state and you don't want the assets to be evenly divided, use a prenuptial agreement to alter the division of marital property. It is legally okay as long as the agreement meets state law. The state will allow a properly made, full disclosure prenuptial agreement to alter the typical rules for the division of marital property upon divorce or death. In the prenuptial agreement both partners must agree upon the rights each will have to the property they bring into the marriage and/or acquire during the marriage.

Third, each of you should have your own lawyer look over the draft and make any needed corrections. In some states, a prenup may be considered invalid if either partner claims he or she did not have their own lawyer approve it.

Buying a House, Married or Not

Bottom line: Whether you are married with a prenuptial agreement or just living together right now, buying a house is serious business. Make sure you both research and talk to realtors and banker/lenders about the process. We've heard plenty of stories of couples whose relationship disintegrated while buying a house because of the stress of the innumerable details. The key is that you both agree to what you are doing and are willing to talk your way through the process. Happy house hunting!

Stage Two: Create A Joint Financial Plan

The second stage of the financial blueprint for living-together couples is to create a joint financial plan. This written plan will detail the financial arrangement you have decided on. There are several ways to handle your household money. They include:

- One partner pays for everything.

- Divide all living costs down the middle.

- Split expenses based on the percentage of each partner's income in relation to the total household income.

- A mixture of the three or a method you both decide upon that suits your needs.

The best way to avoid resentment and to make sure one partner is not being taken advantage of is to share equally down the middle. However, if one partner is substantially out-earning the other, a fair way to work as a real partnership is to contribute according to your earning power.

Stage Three: Develop a Living Together Spending Plan

The third phase of the financial blueprint is to create a workable spending plan. We have included worksheets (Chart 18-1) to help get you started. Ideally, you can use one of the popular money software programs. If you don't have access to a computer we suggest you use the money journal or notebook to keep track of the inflow and outflow of money. In fact, any and all information regarding money—goals, spending plan, information on savings and investment accounts—should be kept in this money journal.

Living Together Spending Plan Worksheets

When creating the spending plan, make sure you both are in agreement with it. If it isn't doable for one of you it could start money conflicts. If it isn't, go back and make adjustments.

Joint or Separate Accounts When Living Together

The biggest money question you may have when living together is whether or not to open a joint checking or savings account. We recommend you keep separate accounts until you are officially married. There is no commingling of money and each person is responsible for paying his or her share of the expenses from their own checking account.

We also recommend you keep separate credit cards. And don't put joint purchases on each other's cards unless you have an agreement in writing from the other partner that he or she will pay their share of the bill by a mutually agreed upon date. To avoid this messy type of managing the money, we suggest you pay cash for all joint expenses. No credit cards! It keeps you both out of debt and it's a clean and easy way to manage the money.

Loaning Money To Each Other

Remember we said earlier that you should treat your living together arrangement like a business partnership. This means when either of you borrows money from the other; you draw up a document with repayment terms outlined. This is the proof you will need in court if you break up before the loan is repaid and you need to pursue payment.

Chart 18-1: Spending Plan Worksheets			
Item	**Current Amount**	**Target Amount**	**Difference**
1. Housing			
Mortgage or rent	$	$	$
Property taxes	$	$	$
Insurance	$	$	$
Utilities	$	$	$
Yard maintenance	$	$	$
Phone	$	$	$
Household purchases and supplies	$	$	$
House cleaning and household help	$	$	$
Home improvements	$	$	$
Other housing costs	$	$	$
Subtotal, housing	*$*	*$*	*$*
2. Food			
Home	$	$	$
Restaurant	$	$	$
Children's lunches	$	$	$
Work lunches	$	$	$
Warehouse club or food co-op membership	$	$	$
Other	$	$	$
Subtotal, food	*$*	*$*	*$*
3. Clothing			
You	$	$	$
Children	$	$	$
Subtotal, clothing	$	$	$
4. Transportation			
Lease or car note payments	$	$	$
Insurance	$	$	$
Fuel	$	$	$
Maintenance	$	$	$
Other transportation	$	$	$
Subtotal, transportation	*$*	*$*	*$*

Chart 18-1: Spending Plan Worksheets (cont.)			
Item	**Current Amount**	**Target Amount**	**Difference**
5. Dependent Care			
Daycare	$	$	$
Baby-sitter	$	$	$
Summer programs	$	$	$
Support of relatives/others	$	$	$
Other	$	$	$
Subtotal, dependent care	*$*	*$*	*$*
6. Education/school tuition and fees			
You	$	$	$
Children	$	$	$
College savings	$	$	$
Subtotal, school	*$*	*$*	*$*
7. Healthcare			
Well childcare, immunizations	$	$	$
Health insurance premiums	$	$	$
Medicines	$	$	$
Dental care	$	$	$
Eye care	$	$	$
Subtotal, healthcare	*$*	*$*	*$*
8 Insurance not listed above			
Disability	$	$	$
Life	$	$	$
Other	$	$	$
Subtotal, insurance	*$*	*$*	*$*
9. Recreation/entertainment			
Your club memberships	$	$	$
Children's club memberships	$	$	$
Zoo/museum/park memberships	$	$	$
Personal care and improvements	$	$	$
Vacations/travel	$	$	$
Hobbies	$	$	$
Movies and video rentals	$	$	$
Other	$	$	$
Subtotal, recreation	*$*	*$*	*$*

Chart 18-1: Spending Plan Worksheets (cont.)

Item	Current Amount	Target Amount	Difference
10. Goodwill			
Gifts, children	$	$	$
Gifts, others	$	$	$
Charitable contributions	$	$	$
Children's allowances	$	$	$
Subtotal, goodwill	*$*	*$*	*$*
11. Consumer credit debt reduction			
Mastercard	$	$	$
Visa	$	$	$
American Express	$	$	$
Discover	$	$	$
Gas cards	$	$	$
Department store	$	$	$
Other	$	$	$
Subtotal, debt reduction	*$*	*$*	*$*
12. Retirement plans (other than those automatically deducted from your salary)			
IRA	$	$	$
Other	$	$	$
Subtotal, retirement plans	*$*	*$*	*$*
13. Taxes			
Federal income tax	$	$	$
State income tax	$	$	$
Social security/FICA	$	$	$
State disability/ unemployment	$	$	$
Subtotal, taxes	*$*	*$*	*$*
14. Other expenses not listed above			
Investment (payments to savings, etc.)	$	$	$
Miscellaneous	$	$	$
Subtotal, other expenses	*$*	*$*	*$*
TOTAL EXPENDITURES (ADD SUBTOTALS)	*$*	*$*	*$*

Part II

Designing Your Financial Life Together

> *We have two choices: we can make a living or we can design a life.*
>
> — Jim Rohn, Author

In previous chapters we dealt with several of the emotional and psychological issues of money. Now it is time to get down and dirty with making love and money work in your relationship. Our goal is to provide you with concrete financial steps to assist you and your partner with growing money and building wealth. We want you both to be on the same path and heading in the same direction.

We have broken Designing Your Financial Life Together into six steps that will serve as your road map to keep you on track. They aren't at all difficult to follow, in fact they are simple and easy to implement. Patience, discipline and an ironclad commitment are what the two of you must bring to the table.

The Six Steps To Designing Your Financial Life Together

1. Setting financial goals together

2. My money, your money, our money: Creating a money management system

3. A spending plan that works

4. Making love and money work without debt

5. Building assets and wealth the fun and easy way

6. Insurance-It does your money good

Step 1: Setting Financial Goals Together

Ever heard that old saying, "If You Don't Know Where You Are Going, You'll Probably End Up Somewhere Else"? That's very true when you don't set financial goals. Now is the time to pull out your money journal. You and your partner are going to embark on an exciting adventure of setting your financial goals together.

This is the time you both can let your imagination run wild. This is the fun part of Making Love and Money Work. Couples who have fun with their money have a much higher chance of staying happy while becoming wealthy together because setting and writing down financial goals really works. Don't believe us? Well, numerous studies have proven the value of setting goals.

In a Harvard University Business School Study on goal setting and planning, each student in a graduating class was asked whether they had a clear, specific set of goals written down with a plan for achieving them. Only three percent had written goals and plans outlining exactly what they wanted for their future. After 20 years the researchers went back and interviewed all the graduates. They discovered that the three percent with written goals were worth more, in financial terms, then

> *If you go to work on your goals, your goals will go to work on you. If you go to work on your plan, your plan will go to work on you. Whatever good things we build end up building us.*
>
> — Jim Rohn

the other 97 percent combined. They were happier, healthier and more successful than the graduates with no written goals. As you can see goal setting is extremely powerful.

So let's get started by writing down in your money journal the financial goals that are most important to you. We encourage each partner to have both individual and joint financial goals. Here are seven tips to keep in mind as you develop your goals, followed by a worksheet that will help you create your Designing Your Financial Life Plan.

Tip 1: Make sure the goal is something you both truly want

That's because achieving it will require a great deal of time and effort. You both must want it so badly that failure is not an option. Remember how we talked about money values in Chapter 4? Look at yours again and base your goals on the values that you listed. The closer your goals are to your values, the more likely you will achieve them. Wouldn't it make sense to plan your spending and investing around the things that really matter and that will help you and your partner grow and live prosperously?

Tip 2: Make your goals and plans specific, detailed and with a timetable

Saying, "We want to be wealthy" isn't enough. The word wealthy is too vague. There isn't enough information to help you and your partner focus on what you need to do to actually become wealthy. By what year do you want to be wealthy? How much is enough to be wealthy? $100,000? One Million? 10 Million? What are you going to do to get wealthy? Why do you want to be wealthy? What will you do with your money once you are wealthy? The goals need to be clear and precise. Look what happens when we describe the goal in this manner: "Within the next five years, we will create an investment portfolio worth over $100,000 by investing $1,500 into a stock mutual fund that has had an average return of 12 percent over the past three years." This goal is specific, measurable and with a timeline. You can both see the goal. When you can see it, it's easier to design a plan to make it happen. And because it is measurable, you can track the progress you are making toward its achievement.

Tip 3: Put your financial goals in writing

Based on the Harvard Study we shared with you earlier you can see why writing your goals down is important. Goals in your mind are merely pipe dreams. Written goals, on the other hand, take the wishing out of a dream and make it concrete. Now the dream is in black and white and you both have basically signed a contract that says you are committed to turning your dreams into reality. You need to know in advance how much money the goal is going to cost you. So ask yourself, what is this goal going to cost? How much should we save every month, quarter or year? Once you have a figure you can set up a systematic saving and investment plan to accumulate the money you will need to reach that goal. Chart 18-2 will help with getting your goals down on paper.

Tip 4: Work on just a few goals at a time

Setting too many goals at one time can become overwhelming and cause you to lose your focus. Don't set simultaneous goals such as retire early, buy a vacation home and pay for your children's college education. Instead, aim for five goals over a period of five to ten years. That's a more practical timetable.

Tip 5: Break your goals down into baby steps

Don't look at each goal in its entirety, it may seem too overpowering. Instead, break it down into sub-goals that are much more quickly attainable. For example, if you want to save $500,000 by the age of 65, you may want to break that goal into a series of smaller conquests—$150,000 by age 45, $350,000 by age 60 and so on. Impatience and goal achievement don't mix. Couples who are successful at reaching their goals don't go for the get-rich-quick programs. They reach their goals by patiently and consistently working toward them

Tip 6: Start taking action toward your goals within 24-48 hours

You've heard it a thousand times but it's worth repeating here. With apologies to the Duke, goal setting don't mean a thing if you ain't got that (follow-through) swing. So along with breaking it down into sub-goals, take initial action on it within the next 24 to 48 hours. Do one thing to get you moving in the right direction. Take the previous example of saving $500,000 by age 65. Once you have set that goal you can start the process immediately by going on the Internet to find information on investing. Or you can call and make an appointment with a financial adviser to map out a plan. By taking this specific action immediately your goal becomes more plausible. You can actually see it. This excitement creates energy, which keeps you both pushing toward making your goals a reality.

Tip 7: Don't try to reach your goals alone

Most couples today are so busy trying to balance work, family and relationships that they really don't have enough time to devote to their financial well-being. Face it; it's too difficult to do alone. So don't even try. There are financial advisors, bankers, lawyers, insurance agents and accountants that can assist you on your path to reaching your goals and making love and money work. Use them. Sure, the Internet is full of great information but the challenge is knowing where to find the valid information and what do you do with it. Study on your own and become more knowledgeable about the ins and outs of finance, but also seek out financial professionals.

Chart 18-2: Designing Your Financial Life Plan				
Short Term Goals	**Costs**	**Desired Date**	**Total Money Needed**	**Monthly Savings Required**
1.	$	$	$	$
2.				
3.				
4.				
5.				
6.				
7.				
8.				
9.				
10.				
Intermediate Term Goals	**Costs**	**Desired Date**	**Total Money Needed**	**Monthly Savings Required**
1.	$	$	$	$
2.				
3.				
4.				
5.				
6.				
7.				
8.				
9.				
10.				
Long Term Goals	**Costs**	**Desired Date**	**Total Money Needed**	**Monthly Savings Required**
1.	$	$	$	$
2.				
3.				
4.				
5.				
6.				
7.				
8.				
9.				
10.				

They may assist you in reaching your financial goals quicker than you can do it on your own.

Step 2: My Money, Your Money, Our Money; Creating A Money Management System

In the majority of marriages, money is shared. Most couples have joint checking, savings and investment accounts. As for credit cards, each partner usually wants their own. And today's independent wife wants her own checking account as well. Most wives feel they lose control and power when they have all their money tied up in joint accounts. Having a separate account allows them to feel more secure in case the relationship doesn't work out.

On the other hand, psychologists claim that when men want to merge money it is their way of letting their woman know they want more intimacy and togetherness. *In the case of Renee and Paul, a couple we know, it was actually a marriage proposal. They had been together for five years when Paul suggested they open a joint savings with the money he received from the sale of his home after his divorce from his first wife. "It was $25,000 and I couldn't believe he wanted to put my name on the account" said Renee. "This was the first sign that Paul was really serious about our relationship."*

Joint Accounts Are About Trust

Commingling money in a relationship makes a statement about trust and commitment. When an account is held in both names, either partner is able to withdraw funds from the account at any time. The key with joint accounts is that both partners know what's going on with the money. Partnerships without trust regarding money are doomed before they ever begin. There is no way the union can sustain itself in times of financial challenges.

Love Won't Balance The Checkbook

Once you've made the decision to have a joint account the next area to decide on is who's going to pay the bills and balance the checkbook? And who's going to make the investment decisions and decide on a spending plan? Ideally both partners should be equally involved in all financial decisions. In most relationships that generally isn't the case. Since opposites do attract, one partner is likely to be more involved than the other. They may enjoy paying the bills and following the stock market every day. If this is how it is in your household, that's fine. Who pays the bills and balances the checkbook isn't what is really important. What matters is that everyone knows what is going on and one partner doesn't feel he or she has all the financial responsibilities.

What works for most couples is to divvy up the financial workload. Maybe you both can sit down every month and pay bills or one does it online and shares a report with the other. Again, experiment with different money management systems and stick to the one that works best for the both of you.

A Money Management System That Works!

After surveying several couples, we concluded that the money management system that seems to work best comprises separate checking and savings accounts for both partners and one joint account. Each partner deposits a set amount each month into the joint account to pay for household expenses like rent, utilities, groceries, health and dental care, insurance, savings, and retirement planning. The amount you each contribute to the joint account should be proportionate to your income levels. If a joint expense pops up that's out of the ordinary and more than your joint account allows for that month – a major house repair, new tires for the car — treat it separately by writing checks to cover it from your personal accounts to the joint account. Most likely you'll use your separate accounts for discretionary items such as clothes, gas and oil, and personal upkeep like haircuts and manicures.

Step 3: A Spending Plan That Works

Here's a variation on the saying about getting where you want to go that we mentioned in Step 1. This one says**, "If You and Your Partner Don't Plan Where You Are Going You'll Get There."** In other words, if you don't plan on going anywhere, you'll get nowhere. It is important to plan how to spend your money in a way that makes you both happy. Otherwise, you'll spend a lot of money in search of happiness and fulfillment without finding it. No matter how much money you and your partner make, it will never be enough if it is spent on poor choices. And poor choices *will* be made if there isn't a plan in place to make better choices.

In the vast majority of money management books, such a plan is called a "budget". Based on past experiences with clients, we think calling the plan a budget is too restrictive and sounds like punishment. Most

> *Relationship isn't a competition. If your partner wins, you win. If your partner loses, you both lose.*
>
> — Martha Bolton

people treat budgets like a diet. They start off with good intentions, but don't follow through because budgets focus on what we can't do rather than what we can do. Diets say, "don't eat". Budgets say, "don't spend". It's gotten to the point today that when a financial advisor recommends a client create a budget they don't even try. And those who do eventually give up. Which is why we prefer to recommend a "spending plan."

The purpose behind the spending plan is that within the limits of your available money you spend it freely on the things that have the most meaning for you and your partner. Your spending plan is designed to be proactive not reactive. It is positive ("yes, do spend") rather than negative ("no, don't spend"). The spending plan doesn't need to be complicated. It's simply a tool that provides your relationship with financial direction. It assists you and your partner in making good spending choices way ahead of time. The way to handle a financial emergency is to have a plan in place to take care of it. Your spending plan pays off in successful and meaningful money management.

A top-notch spending plan will have three basic parts: 1) Developing a Making Love and Money Work mission statement that explains why you and your partner spend money. 2) Determining priorities and understanding when to say yes or no, and 3) having a way to track where you are financially, based on your spending.

Making Love and Money Work Mission Statement

As soon as you enter into a permanent relationship, pull out your money journal. Write a mission statement on how your spending will express who you are and what things you want to accomplish financially. The statement reflects the money values that are important to you, your partner and your family. If nothing is important to you, then having all the material possessions in the world will not be meaningful. Creating your mission statement helps orient your life around the fulfillment of the things that matter the most. It puts you in charge. Money becomes only a tool, a means to achieving the goals and dreams we talked about earlier in the chapter.

In writing out this mission statement refer back to your goals list. Become extremely clear and specific by asking yourself the following questions; What do we

want our money to do for us? What material possessions give us the most fulfillment? Remember to focus on your passions and not money just for money's sake.
Recall the biblical saying, "What good will it be for a man if he gains the whole
world, yet forfeits his soul?" (Matthew 16:26). Believe it or not there are many
unhappy millionaires out there. They have the swank mansions, fancy cars, unlimited
vacations and all the companionship money can buy. Yet many have lost their mission
and purpose in life.

Cheryl: *At one point I forgot my mission and purpose. When I initially
wrote and self-published my first book, I did it not for the money but
to share my knowledge of money with women to empower them to
become financially savvy. Once I turned over the rights to a major
publisher, suddenly the money became more important than the mission. The focus was on how many books I sold this month as opposed
to how many women I financially empowered. While I made a lot of
money, I actually grew unhappy. I developed writer's block and to
top it off my marriage fell apart. I began to question whether I had
sold my soul to the devil. I prayed and meditated on it for over a year
until I finally came to the conclusion that I must get back to my
original mission. Once I did that my writer's block disappeared and
money became secondary not primary.*

Determining Priorities

Successful money management choices require setting priorities. Many of
your priorities will be determined by your Making Love and Money Work mission
statement. Some priorities will be set based on your current money circumstances

which are based on your past choices. If you and your partner are in serious debt, it is because of the buying choices you made in the past. Have you heard the saying, "You are in life exactly where you want to be"? I'm sure you're thinking, "No way! Why would I want to be in so much debt, living paycheck to paycheck"?

You are there because of your past choices and now you have new choices. You *can* get out of debt and you *can* stop living paycheck to paycheck. You can either get a new job making more money or you can stop overspending. The choice is yours. So understanding what your money has done for you, or to you, in the past will help you and your partner make wise trade-offs today.

Check Out Your Spending

After you are your partner have determined your priorities the next step is to prepare a spending plan. This is done by creating a spending plan chart for each of you and also for joint spending decisions. Use the spending plan chart 18-1 we provided earlier in the chapter. Or you can simply use your money journal. Go through your checkbooks for the last six months and using the categories below, place the amount of the check into its appropriate category. Make sure you keep a receipt for purchases made with cash or credit cards and itemize them for six months, also. The categories are as follows:

- Automobile, gas, insurance, and annual registration

- Charitable giving

- Clothing

- Credit card/loan repayment

- Entertainment and recreation

- Food/groceries

- Hair care and/or personal trainer

- Housing/ rent cost—include taxes, interest, principal, homeowner's insurance, renter's insurance

- Life Insurance

- Savings

- Retirement Accounts

- Medical / dental insurance

- Phone

- Investments

- Utilities

Instead of a miscellaneous column break down all other recurring expenses. Example, childcare, exercise club, etc. This exercise will show you how you've been using money. Pay attention to categories where there is overspending. Does the overspending in this area contribute to the Making Love and Money Mission Statement you both agreed on? If not, you know that someone, maybe even both of you, have been saying yes to the wrong things. Now that your priorities have changed, the way you spend money will change as well.

Stop The Leaks

Here are some of the common spending plan busters that affect relationships:

- Sneaky little expenses. That daily latte and banana nut muffin from the trendy coffee bar cost $4.00 a day. Keeping the video rentals an extra night runs about $3.00. These expenses are minimal, but together and over time, they really add up—to the tune of $1,140 a year for the latte and muffin and $394 for the video, if you rent one per week and incur a late fee. This adds up to a total of $1,534 per year. If you were to invest that money in a mutual fund earning an average 10 percent a year, you'd have $3,980 in 10 years. Instead of going to the coffee bar daily go once a week. And make sure you return your video(s) on time. Take the money you are saving and invest it into a mutual fund (more on mutual funds later in the chapter).

- Periodic, recurring expenses. Monitoring the monthly bills is pretty straightforward. But we often forget to set money aside for semiannual or annual bills like household insurance and car registration, or irregular expenses like home repairs. Unless you have a money cushion to draw on, you may be forced to put these bills on your credit card.

- Gifts. Holidays aren't the only time that wreaks havoc on your spending plan. Birthdays, anniversaries, graduations and christenings also require gifts. And because most of us are too busy to shop for sales, we pay top dollar for presents. When creating your spending plan, plug this major leak by compiling a list of people or events you will need to buy gifts for and guesstimating the amount you will spend. Carry the list with you just in case you run into a sale. You may be able to purchase great gifts at great savings.

- Vacations. People today are so happy to get away from work that they go crazy spending all kinds of money while on vacation. It's not the trip itself that is the problem; most people are good at planning those expenses. It's the incidentals that pile up. Souvenirs, T-shirts, admission fees to museums and amusement parks, the constant flow of ice cream cones, soft drinks, and other snacks. These items add hundreds of extra dollars to your vacation bill and need to be worked into the vacation-spending plan in advance.

I Can See Clearly Now

You now have the makings of a true spending plan. You and your partner know where you are financially and how you got there. You can clearly see the choices that have led you both to this financial position. Now that you both understand why it is important to set spending priorities and why you must have a Making Love and Money Work mission statement, the next step is to practice following the plan you establish by:

1. Paying your bills and financial obligations
2. Getting rid of your debt
3. Saving money to buy a home or start a business
4. Spending only on things that really matter
5. Tracking the inflow and outflow of money

Spending Money Wisely

Many couples today are trapped in the "too much month at the end of the money" syndrome, brought on by the high-end lifestyle created during the expansive "dot.com" economy. But as we all know, economies fluctuate from year to year and there is no guarantee that what's up today will be up tomorrow. Which is why it is important that you and your loved one spend your money wisely.

The most painless way to get out of the "too much month at the end of the money" syndrome is to focus on simplifying your lifestyle to reduce costs. All the showy "stuff" **you,** think you have to have — name-brand clothing, electronic "toys" —isn't really necessary if you have to buy it on credit. We aren't saying you shouldn't have it, only that you not go into debt to get it. Spending your money wisely means prioritizing what matters most in your relationship. Regardless of how much income you make, you'll find that when you do that, your true needs can be met.

Follow The Millionaires

> *If you want to be a millionaire you have to think like one.*
>
> — Dr. Johnnie Coleman

Even though we mentioned earlier how some millionaires lose their mission and purpose in life, it is useful to look at how millionaires in general manage money very, very well. Often we think of the very rich as people who inherit wealth or obtain it by sheer luck. But based on a study by Thomas J.Stanley, Ph.D. and William D. Danko, Ph.D., authors of the best selling book, "The Millionaire Next Door," that's often far from the truth. The 20-year study of millionaires found that they have two things in common; frugality and smart spending habits. Millionaires know how to spend their money wisely. See how close you and your partner's spending habits are to those of millionaires. Take the following Millionaire Spending Habits Quiz.

Millionaire Spending Habits Quiz

1. How many credit cards do you and your partner have?

    a.   Two or Less

    b.   Three to six

    c.   More than six

2. How much time do you spend each week tracking your investment portfolio and personal finances?

    a.   None

    b.   One to three hours per week

    c.   More than three hours per week

3. How much of your total net worth is invested in stocks, mutual funds or real estate?

    a.   None

    b.   1- 10%

    c.   10 - 20%

    d.   More than 20%

4. How much do you save each month as a percentage of your income?

    a.   1-5%

    b.   5-15%

    c.   More than 15%

5. Do you spend more than:

    a. $400 for a suit or dress

    b. $150 for a pair of shoes

    c. $250 for a watch

    d.   None of the above

6. Does your household have a monthly spending plan?

7. Do you track the money spent on food, clothing, and housing every month?

8. What's the age of your latest car?

    a.   1 year or less

  b. 1- 3 years

  c. Older than 3 years

9. How much did you pay for your latest car?

  a. $15,000 or less

  b. Between $15,000 and $25,000

  c. More than $25,000

10. Divide your mortgage balance by your pre-tax household income. (For example, $300,000 / $60,000=5) or

10a.Divide your monthly after-tax income by your monthly rent.

Do you and your partner have millionaire-spending habits? Total up your score.

Scoring

1. 2 points for a, 0 for b and c

2. 2 points for c, 0 for a and b

3. 2 points for d, 1 point for c, 0 for a

4. 2 points for c, 1 point for b, 0 for a

5. 2 points for d, 1 point for selecting a, b or c, and 0 if you select 2 or more

6. 2 points for yes, 0 for no

7. 2 points for yes to all three, 1 point for two of three

8. 2 points for c, 0 for a and b

9. 2 points for a or b, 0 for c

10. 2 points if your answer is 2.5 or less

10a. 2 points if answer is 4 or more

Total points

20 points: Excellent! You have millionaire- spending habits. Even if you don't have or aren't worth a million dollars yet, with your good habits you soon will be.

15-19 points: You're close! There are a few money habits and financial lifestyle changes you need to make.

> *Never spend your money before you have it.*
> ——Thomas Jefferson

0-15 points: Watch out! If your score is low, you are really heading in the wrong financial direction. Start today to rethink your priorities and make developing millionaire spending habits a <u>must.</u>

Step 4: Making Love and Money Work Without Debt

Our consumer-based economy and its partner, the advertising media, have taught us we can have everything we want right now whether we can afford it or not. We have more shopping centers than high schools and over 11,000 magazines urging us to buy! buy! buy! And buy is exactly what we do. But if we don't have a spending plan, we can easily fall into one of three debt traps – or all three: The "I don't want to wait!" trap; the "Keep up with the Jones's" trap; and the "I deserve it!" trap. Which one have you been following?

The "I Don't Want To Wait!" Trap

Patience, once considered a virtue, is now a vice. The "I don't want to wait" trap snaps shut when we acquire something without the cash to buy it outright. So before you and your partner go into debt, don't ask, "do we want this today?" Ask, "Will this be worth paying double for tomorrow?"

A great antidote to the "I don't want to wait!" trap is the "frozen asset" technique used by several couples we know. You place your credit card(s) in a container of water and put it in the freezer. When you get the urge to use a card it's so inconvenient to thaw it out that you'll probably decide to use cash or forget the purchase entirely. That's good because studies show that people who pay cash spend about 30 percent less than people who use credit cards. Another way to escape the "I don't want to wait!" trap is to ask the store to put the desired purchase on hold for a day. This will give you time to consider if you really "need" it or just "want" it. When we do this, we either forget about it or don't feel like going back to the store the next day to buy it. This method helps us eliminate impulse shopping.

The "Keep Up With The Jones's" Trap

Men and women are equally notorious for falling into the "Keep up with the Jones's" trap. You will know you have fallen into this trap when you hear yourself whining, "But everybody else has one." The majority of people buy things because other people already have them. If our friends, coworkers, neighbors, or relatives have it, we want it too – by hook or crook.

Again, our consumer-dependent economy sets the "Keeping up with the Jones's " trap. About 70 percent of the nation's gross national product is based on the manufacture and sale of consumer goods. When we stop buying, the economy slides into a recession. So, the media bombard us with celebrity life-styles of affluence and fashion. We see athletes and movie stars wearing designer clothes, driving fast foreign cars and living in large, expensively decorated homes. But because these lifestyles are far beyond what most people can afford, we use our high-interest credit cards to keep up. We think we can have the same lifestyle as whomever we compare ourselves to – until, that is, we max out.

The "I Deserve It!" Trap

When the economy was robust a few years back, it led to a "Life is Good" philosophy and created an attitude of "I deserve it!", particularly among the Baby Boomers and Generation X'ers who had made fast money in the dot.com industry. "I want it" and "I gotta have it now" were words that were recited when they shopped online or at one of the many outlet malls. Although things have changed recently with the high-tech meltdown, old habits die hard.

We are just never satisfied with what we already have, so we feel compelled to buy more. The only way out of this trap is to become more patient, responsible and to develop wealth-building self-discipline.

Let's begin with the cold, hard facts about getting out of money troubles and debt:

1. Believe it or not more money is never a solution to financial challenges. When it's difficult to handle what you already have, it will be even more difficult to handle more. And don't think having a big line of credit is financial freedom. It's not. It's really more like dragging around a ball and chain.

2. To escape and really take charge of your debt you must first admit and acknowledge to yourself that because of your poor control of your money, you have fallen into debt entrapment. Feeling ashamed and sorry for yourself is

> *Do less acquiring and pay attention to what you already have.*
>
> — Lee L. Jampolsky

not going to help you. But developing a get-out-of-debt plan and following through on it will. Right now you and your partner must make a firm decision and commitment to get out of debt and to take the necessary action steps to do it.

Here is a **9 Step Reduction Plan** to help you get out of debt and on the road to financial freedom:

Step 1. Determine why you fell into debt entrapment in the first place. Did you or your partner fall into the "I Don't Want To Wait!", "Let's Keep Up With The Joneses" or "I Deserve It Trap!"? Knowing how and why you got into so much debt will help you and your partner not repeat the same mistake once you get out of it. This is the time you want to hold each other accountable for your desire to change the thing that contributed to your debt entrapment.

Step 2. Be a cheering section and support for each other. Sabotaging each other's efforts to change the way you handle money is a definite walk down the divorce aisle. If there is ever a time when a couple must stick together, it is during money challenges. A clear head on the part of both partners is needed to get over any financial trouble. Take the time to sit down and have a heart to heart family discussion on the sacrifices that must be made and the reasons for those sacrifices. You want to create a spirit of teamwork so that your family can support and encourage each other. Next, you want to have a family agreement to stop using credit cards unless it's for an emergency and you have no other way to pay for it.

Step 3. Develop a spending plan to monitor and keep track of where your money is going. (Use the spending chart 18-1)

Step 4. Make a list of all your debts. The key to getting out of debt is knowing exactly how much debt you have. List each of your loans, how much you owe, the minimum monthly payment, and the interest rate on each loan. If you haven't both passed out yet, move on to the next step.

Step 5. Get ready to make major lifestyle changes. It will take more money to get out of debt than it did to get in, so plan on living off 70% of your take-home pay so that the remaining 30% will go to debt reduction, savings and investments, and giving. Living on 70% of your take-home pay is probably a huge reduction for many of you and will entail a major lifestyle change since the majority of us are already living on 110% of our income – the reason we got into debt entrapment in the first place. But it is absolutely necessary in the beginning to put a dent in the debt.

If living off 70% right now is a stretch, that's okay. Just start with what you can. A small amount can make a big difference. By paying an extra $25 a month on a $5,000 credit card balance at 21%, you will pay the loan off in less than 9 years instead of 25, and with the decrease in time, it will lower your cost from $8,000 to $13,000. If your income isn't enough to develop a workable get-out-of-debt plan, you have two options: 1) increasing your income and 2) spending less money. Increasing your income, possibly through a second job, may seem like the quickest solution but there are other factors you need to consider. Sometimes a second job can actually add additional stress and expense, especially if the job will take you away from your family, or if there will be additional costs such as child care, clothing, or transportation that will eat away at the extra income.

The truly best option is to reduce your current living expenses. You and your partner must brainstorm and come up with ways to cut expenses without a major lifestyle overhaul. And both of you must be willing to make necessary sacrifices so that each is responsible in getting out of debt. Maybe it is to cut out a big vacation for the next couple of years. Or maybe you won't buy a new car every two years. It is these types of expenses that continually keep you in debt. Unless you absolutely need to buy something new, don't! Focus all your effort on paying off your debt and building wealth.

Step 6. Find extra income by any legal means necessary. Our homes and garages are full of "stuff" we can sell to raise cash to make an extra payment on a credit card. Work overtime or if you're self-employed, sell more of your products or services. Whenever my (Cheryl) hairstylist, Denise Brown of Ringlets Salon in Oakland, needs extra money to pay her property tax bill, she'll work on a few of her off days to bring in more cash. Get creative and focus on money solutions instead of worrying about the problems. When you stop worrying and allow your thoughts to come through, you'll think of plenty of ways to make money to pay off your debts. A book we highly recommend on the subject is *Grow Rich While You Sleep* by Ben Sweetland (Wilshire Book Co.)

Step 7. Make laddered credit card and debt payments. This is the best and consistent way to reduce debts. Begin by making the minimum monthly payment on each bill. Make sure you have reserved extra cash in your spending plan to apply toward paying off debt. Add the extra cash to the minimum payment of your smallest loan. Continue to do this every month. This method will accelerate the reduction of that debt. Once it is paid off, apply the extra money to the next smallest debt's monthly payment. Continue this process until all your debts area paid off. And remember, in order for this to really work you must discontinue the use of the cards.

Step 8. Seek debt counseling. If you and your partner are feeling overwhelmed by debt, getting outside help may be necessary to relieve the stress. There are two services you should check out. The first is Debt Counselors of America (1-800-680-3328 or on the internet at www.dca.org). It offers affordable resources to help with debt. The second is Consumer Credit Counseling Services at 800-388-2227 or on the web at www.nfec.org. This is a nonprofit agency with counselors to assist in creating a debt reduction plan. They will also work with your creditors to renegotiate better repayment plans. The cost is affordable and they have offices nationwide.

Step 9. Don't wait another day to get out of debt. Get started immediately! Relationships and too much debt are like oil and water, they don't mix. Too much debt causes far too many money arguments, sleepless nights, and appearances in divorce court. This is the reason why it is extremely important that you and your partner discuss credit cards and debt in the very beginning of the relationship. Relationships are tough already. You certainly don't want to add anything that will make it more difficult.

Step 5: Building Assets and Wealth The Fun and Easy Way

> The philosophy of the rich versus the poor is this: the rich invest their money and spend what is left; the poor spend their money and invest what is left.
>
> — J. Paul Getty

Hopefully by now you can see a light at the end of the money tunnel. You have set goals for exactly what you want, created a spending plan, know where every penny is going, and on your way out of debt. Now it's time to put your money to work. Building wealth and accumulating assets is the next step in designing your financial life together. Not only that, its fun and exciting.

The key to building wealth in your relationship is to develop an automatic investment plan devoted solely to funding your goals and priorities. With an automatic investment plan you and your partner commit to putting in a specific dollar amount into a selected investment on a weekly, monthly or quarterly basis. Thanks to technology, particularly the Internet, it's never been easier to research different investment options and set up your own automatic investment plan. Today, you can buy stocks and mutual funds using an automatic investment plan with as little as $50 a month. In the following pages we'll discuss the two wealth building investment options we recommend- mutual funds and stocks. We will also provide you with a selected list of mutual funds companies we recommend you add to your wealth-building portfolio. Many of them will allow you to start your investment with $50 to $100 as long as you enroll in their automatic investment plan.

It really doesn't take much money to build wealth but it does take discipline and consistency. The automatic investment plan will help you in that regard. Once you've set it up, the mutual fund or financial firm will automatically deduct the money from your checking or savings account on a predetermined date. It's the automatic aspect that makes this work. Most people just aren't disciplined enough to manually write and mail a check every month to their investment accounts. Don't fool yourself thinking you'll do it. Even the most sophisticated investors admit they probably wouldn't "get around" to it.

How Much Money Will It Take?

The amount of money you contribute to your building wealth accounts is totally up to you. The faster you want to get the ball rolling the more you should put in. Ten to fifteen percent of your take home pay would really help to build a generous nest egg. But you don't have to start that high. We suggest you start with five percent of your after-tax income. So before you pay your bills, have five percent of your take home pay automatically placed in your building wealth accounts. If five percent seems too much to begin with that's fine. Start with two to three percent or whatever is most comfortable for you. What's important is that you start the process. We know from experience that if you think building wealth is hard and requires a lot of sacrificing, chances are you probably won't stick with it. So in the beginning, make it easy for yourself.

Once you have the money automatically taken out before you pay your bills you will be amazed at how quickly it adds up. And once you've become comfortable with the amount being taken out we suggest you increase it. There are a couple of ways you can do that. The first way is to go for the gusto and increase it a full five percent in six months and then another five percent the following six months. The second way is to do it gradually by increasing it one to two percent every six months until you reach 10 to 15 percent of your take home pay.

Where Should We Put The Money?

Deciding where to put the money is the fun and exciting part of building wealth. There are literally thousands of ways to invest. And because there are so many choices the majority of people become confused and overwhelmed and end up doing absolutely nothing. We want to make building wealth easy for you, so in this section we will only focus on stock mutual funds and common stocks. They aren't complicated and over the long term have outperformed most of the others. If you want to know about the other investment choices, we've listed several books and Internet sites in the appendix that we recommend for more information.

> *The safest way to double your money is to fold it over and put it in your pocket.*
>
> — Kim Hubbard

Why Stock Mutual Funds?

The most difficult decision to make when buying stock is – surprise! — what stock to buy. Between the New York Stock Exchange, NASDAQ and smaller exchanges around the world there are thousands of stocks to choose from. Even with the Internet it is time consuming to research and select your own portfolio. Stock mutual funds are a good choice for people who aren't interested in doing their own research.

Chart 18-3: Look What Saving a Little in Mutual Fund Will Get You!

End of Year	$10 Monthly Deposit At End of Year To	Annual 8% Earnings (Combined Div. & Appreciation Will Amt. To)	Total Accumulated Earnings	Combined Accumulated Deposits & Earnings
1	$ 120	$ 5.14	$ 5.14	$ 125.14
2	240	15.15	20.29	260.29
3	360	25.96	46.25	406.25
4	480	37.74	83.99	563.99
5	600	50.15	134.14	734.14
6	720	63.87	198.01	918.01
7	840	78.58	276.59	1,116.59
8	960	94.47	371.06	1,331.06
9	1,080	111.62	482.68	1,562.68
10	1,200	130.15	612.83	1,812.83
11	1,320	150.17	763.00	2,083.00
12	1,440	171.78	934.78	2,374.78
13	1,560	195.12	1,129.90	2,689.90
14	1,680	220.33	1,350.23	3,030.23
15	1,800	247.56	1,597.79	3,397.79
16	1,920	276.96	1,874.75	3,794.75
17	2,040	308.72	2,183.47	4,223.47
18	2,160	343.02	2,526.49	4,686.49
19	2,280	380.05	2,906.54	5,186.54
20	2,400	420.07	3,326.61	5,726.61
21	2,520	463.26	3,789.87	6,309.87
22	2,640	509.93	4,299.80	6,939.80
23	2,760	560.33	4,860.13	7,620.13
24	2,880	614.75	5,474.88	8,354.88
25	3,000	673.53	6,148.41	9,148.41
26	3,120	737.01	6,885.42	10,005.42
27	3,240	805.57	7,690.99	10,930.99
28	3,360	879.62	8,570.61	11,930.61
29	3,480	959.59	9,530.20	13,010.20
30	3,600	1,044.96	10,575.16	14,175.16

Table 1 – Appreciation of a $10 monthly investment over time at 8% compounded annually

End of Year	$20 Monthly Deposit At End of Year To	Annual 15% Earnings (Combined Div. & Appreciation Will Amt. To)	Total Accumulated Earnings	Combined Accumulated Deposits & Earnings
1	$ 240	$ 19.08	$ 19.08	$ 259.08
2	480	57.95	77.03	557.03
3	720	102.64	179.67	899.67
4	960	154.03	333.70	1,293.70
5	1,200	213.14	546.84	1,746.84
6	1,440	251.11	797.95	2,237.95
7	1,680	389.77	1,187.72	2,867.72
8	1,920	448.68	1,636.40	3,556.40
9	2,160	552.54	2,188.94	4,348.94
10	2,400	671.42	2,860.36	5,260.36
11	2,640	808.14	3,668.50	6,308.50
12	2,880	865.36	4,533.86	7,413.86
13	3,120	1,146.16	5,680.02	8,800.02
14	3,360	1,354.09	7,034.11	10,394.11
15	3,600	1,593.20	8,627.31	12,227.31
16	3,840	1,868.18	10,495.49	14,335.49
17	4,080	2,184.40	12,679.89	16,759.89
18	4,320	2,548.07	15,227.96	19,547.96
19	4,560	2,966.27	18,194.23	22,754.23
20	4,800	3,447.22	21,641.45	26,441.45
21	5,040	4,000.30	25,641.75	30,681.75
22	5,280	4,636.34	30,278.09	35,558.09
23	5,520	5,367.79	35,645.88	41,165.88
24	5,760	6,208.97	41,854.85	47,614.85
25	6,000	7,176.30	49,031.15	55,031.15
26	6,240	8,288.75	57,319.90	63,559.90
27	6,480	9,568.07	66,887.97	73,367.97
28	6,720	11,039.27	77,927.24	84,647.24
29	6,960	12,731.17	90,658.41	97,618.41
30	7,200	14,676.85	105,335.26	112,535.26

Table 2 – Appreciation of a $20 monthy investment over time at 15% compounded annually

A stock mutual fund is a diversified collection of stock that is professionally managed. If you join a stock mutual fund you don't decide what stocks to buy or sell. A portfolio manager does that for you. The portfolio manager will take the money you deposit into the fund and manage it according to the fund's style (we'll talk about fund styles later on). In return, you pay a small management fee for the professional advice and trading.

Investing in stock mutual funds is an excellent choice for partners, married or living together, who want to build substantial wealth over the life of their relationship. (Check out chart 18-3, Look what saving a little in mutual funds will get you!) Stock mutual funds are convenient and relatively risk free. By participating in stock mutual funds you can diversify your money among many different stocks without the time and expense of buying a few shares of many different companies. And more important, diversification is the best way to reduce risk.

In our opinion, there are five key reasons why you want to build wealth using stock mutual funds:

1. **Simple to invest in.** As we mentioned earlier, many mutual funds will allow you to open an account with $50 as long as you sign up with the automatic monthly investment program. Generally there isn't a cost when you set up the program directly with the mutual fund company, a discount brokerage firm or other financial/insurance institution.

2. **Immediate diversification.** Because a stock mutual fund makes many investments, rather than a few, you get the advantage of diversification. Which means that even if some of the investments are not performing as well, others may be doing better. For example, a typical stock mutual fund may own shares in more than 100 companies.

3. **Professional money management expertise.** Professional money managers direct the funds, continually buying and selling. They do the research and attend the company shareholder's meetings to stay abreast of what is going on with the company. As an investor, you will receive profits and losses in proportion to the number of shares you own. You either get your profits as a distribution – a check to you — or you can tell the mutual fund to plow your profits back into more shares.

4. **Low fees.** There are basically two types of mutual funds, no-load and load. No-load funds are purchased directly from the mutual fund company, and through discount and online discount brokerage firms who don't charge a commission. Load funds are purchased through a full-service financial or brokerage firm that charges you a commission ranging from two to nearly nine percent. Both no-load and load funds also charge a management fee of one to two percent of the assets managed.

5. **Easy to liquidate and keep track of.** Mutual stock funds are priced daily and posted in the newspaper. So you're able to follow your fund everyday if you want to. Selling the fund is easy as well. You usually get your money within two to five days after you sell your funds.

Stock Mutual Fund Styles

There are six stock mutual fund styles we believe you should consider when building a mutual fund portfolio. We have listed them in the order from most conservative to most risky.

- **Index Funds.** These are great for both first-time and experienced investors. Index funds are stock mutual funds that mirror specific indexes like the most commonly quoted Standard & Poor 500 (S& P 500) or Wilshire 5000-stock average of large companies. This type of fund makes an excellent investment because it is simple, inexpensive and easy to set up. With minimal hands-on management, the fees of the index funds tend to be low and the performance matches the performance of the market as a whole. In the appendix, we have provided a list of some popular index funds. Before you invest any money make sure you read the prospectus. These funds work so well we recommend you put 50 to 100 percent of the money you want to invest in them.

- **Large Capitalization Value Funds.** These types of funds invest in companies whose outstanding stock has a total value of $5 billion per company or more. These companies tend to be more established and secure. Many pay their shareholders dividends every quarter. This type of stock mutual fund looks for large undervalued stocks that are selling at bargain prices. The objective is to invest when the stock is down and hold on until it returns to its full value. By investing in this type of fund, you get a consistent return, a possible dividend and low volatility. T. Rowe Price Value fund (www.troweprice.com) and Dreyfus Premier Core Value A (www.dreyfus.com) are two such funds.

- **Large Capitalization Growth funds.** These types of funds invest in companies whose outstanding stock value is also $5 billion or more per company, but the difference is that these stocks are growth oriented and not undervalued. These stocks rarely pay you a dividend. All the company profits are reinvested back in the company to use for research and new product development to expand the company further. Some examples of large-cap growth stock companies are Microsoft, Walt Disney, AOL-Time Warner, and Home Depot. Over the last few years these types of stocks have outperformed the other mutual fund styles.

- **Medium Capitalization Funds.** These funds invest in companies with an outstanding stock value of $1 billion to $7 billion per company. The risk of investing in these companies is a little higher but so is the potential for a higher return. The companies are usually newer and therefore tend to be more volatile. But don't let that scare you. We highly recommend that everyone's portfolio contain mid-cap stock funds. One to consider Vanguard Capital Opportunity fund (www.vanguard.com)

- **Small Capitalization Funds.** Small capitalization funds invest in companies whose outstanding stock values range from $250 million to $3 billion per company. The stocks of these companies are more risky which means a higher return for the investor. Small cap-stock funds are ideal for the young investor with time on his or her side. If there is a downturn in the market they have the time to sit it out. If you aren't a young investor you can invest in this fund as well. We suggest you invest no more than 25 to 35 percent of your assets in a small capitalization fund.

- **Global and/ or International Funds.** These funds invest in stocks in the overseas market. Global stock funds have approximately 60 percent of their assets invested abroad; the other 40 percent is invested in the United States. The International stock funds invest strictly in foreign stocks. We recommend at least 10 to 15 percent of your portfolio be invested in a global or international fund.

- **Sector Funds.** These funds invest in stocks in one particular industry like technology, health care, electronics, or biomedical. Because these stocks are all within the same industry, the risk-level is greater but so is the potential for reward. The stocks within the same industry tend to follow the pack. If one stock is down the others tend to go down as well. Of course on the flip side, if one stock within the industry has outstanding earnings and goes up the rest tend to follow as well. We recommend no more than 25 percent of your money be invested in sector funds.

Building Wealth By Investing In Common Stocks

Now that we've covered mutual stock funds, let's turn to individual stocks. There is now a great way to buy individual stocks using an automatic investment plan. The plan is called the Dividend Reinvestment Program (or DRIP). The plan allows investors to buy quality stock in easily affordable amounts directly from the company without a broker. Approximately 1,100 publicly traded companies offer the plan.

When you set up a DRIP account you are able to continue to buy more stock automatically and have any stock dividends reinvested automatically, generally with no commission. The additional purchases may be as little as $10 or $50. Some DRIPs permit investments of up to $100,000 per year. DRIP programs are excellent for building wealth because you can start buying blue chip stocks like Coca-Cola with an investment as little as $10 a month. The majority of DRIP programs have minimums of less than $100 per investment.

Setting Up A DRIP Program

It's very easy to set up a DRIP program. You first need to become a shareholder. You do that by buying at least one share of stock. We suggest you buy through a discount brokerage firm or an online brokerage firm. Some of the DRIPS today will allow you to purchase the first share directly through the company. This is called a direct purchase program. For more information on DRIPS, we recommend you go to www.dripinvestor.com or www.moneypaper.com. These sites list all the companies that offer DRIP programs.

Building Wealth With Your Own Business

Maybe all this talk of investing in mutual funds or individual stocks is interesting to you. But maybe your real dream is to start and own your own business. What better than to have a partner who understands your dreams and goals, and shares a passion for that life and work? It takes a lot of courage for a couple to start a business together. The challenges you face can bring out a person's worst traits. All of a sudden you become more aware of each other's idiosyncrasies, many of which you will not like. You begin to see the real person. It is at this time that you will need to accept each other for who you are. To make the relationship and business work, both of you will need to get past your fears and take off the mask of vulnerability. Just remember you're in this together.

Couples in business are becoming a growing demographic according to Aziela Jaffe, author of *Honey, I Want to Start My Own Business: A Planning Guide For Couples* (HarperBusiness). She bases that belief on the surge of entrepreneurial spirit and the emergence of women as equal business partners.

Cheryl and Michael:

We aren't going to lie, starting a business together has been a rough ride. The biggest issue is our different working styles. Cheryl is impatient and wants things to happen immediately. Michael, being the numbers and computer wiz, is more methodical. So needless to say, we clashed. It was necessary to become acclimated to each other's working style. When money was tight and the pressure was tough, we both thought of throwing in the towel. But we didn't. We found the courage to stay instead of run. We both knew going in that it wasn't going to be easy. Starting a business with or without a partner rarely is. Yet somehow when you're in the throes of it you forget all the work that is necessary to make it a success. Now that we have completed the book and gotten through the financial crunch, we both have an attitude of "Well, if we could get through this, we can get through anything!" So not only has it strengthened our business but our relationship as well. And that is the biggest advantage when a couple decides to start a business together to build wealth. You both will grow by leaps and bounds even if you don't plan to. And when you both learn to communicate with and understand each other and to accept your strengths and weaknesses, a lasting bond will form.

What We Are Learning

If starting a business together to build wealth is high on your list here are a few lessons we learned. We suggest you follow them to make your relationship and the business a success:

- Always remember your relationship comes first, before any business or project.

- Carve out quality time for the relationship as well as for the family. This will help you to maintain balance.

- Expect the unexpected. Be able to adapt to change as it enters your life. Stay flexible and go with the flow. Working as a team will make the task seem less like work.

- When working on a project together, combine your strengths to make it successful. Also clarify your roles. Each partner must know what aspect of the business he or she is responsible for.

- Support each other in everything that you do. Especially when there are money challenges. Don't throw up your hands. It's usually when things are at their roughest point that a turnaround is just around the corner. Stay with it.

- Make sure you share a passion and vision for the company. If it's one-sided the business may never get off the ground. You have to share a common goal.

- Don't take everything too seriously. Laugh at your mistakes. When the business becomes challenging, humor is a great healer.

- Take vacations. Lots of them. Don't allow the business to consume you; it will create major relationship challenges.

- Take breaks from each other. Working together 24/7 can get old real quick. Everyone needs his or her own space at times.

- Butting heads is normal. Remember you are two different people, bringing two different perspectives to the relationship and the business. You both must learn to back down and compromise.

- Leave work at the office. Set up rules or guidelines governing when to talk about work during dinner or on the weekends. It's important to separate your personal life from your business life. You need time to focus on your relationship and your family.

Toni and Bill

Toni credits her mother for her bodacious entrepreneurial spirit. Her mother, from the Philippines, had only been in the United States for seven years when her husband passed away. A thick accent and limited skills became a barrier to finding gainful employment for the single mom of two daughters. To make ends meet she sold everything from fish to wigs to other Filipino families until settling on real estate several years later.

Today, Toni is following in her mother's footsteps. She and her husband, Bill, are partners in a seven-year-old health and wellness network marketing business based in Northern California. The business is thriving.

Toni and Bill actually had no intentions of building a successful business together. It was Toni's business in the beginning. It took Bill, a high-powered Chicago attorney, more time to be a believer and jump on board. Six months to be exact. It only took six months for Toni's income to surpass the monthly paycheck Bill brought in from his 70-hour work weeks. " I was burned out and didn't like my job," Bill recalls. "It seemed that no matter what I did it wasn't helping people. I saw Toni changing people's lives and making more money than me." Toni suggested Bill stop what he was doing and work with her.

And is he ever glad he did. Their business has over 6,000 customers and distributors and provides them with a substantial five-figure monthly income. Having traveled around the world their new goals are to build a financial empire and to send their two children to a college of their choice, loan-free.

Managing The Money

Money has never been an issue of contention in their marriage. They have always had joint accounts, neither will make a big ticket purchase without the other, and when they do spend money it's on things they both like to do. The only problem is that they had never used a spending plan until recently, when they decided to get serious and take charge of their money. "We know in the beginning of our business we spent foolishly," Toni says. "It was nothing for us to spend $2,000 on ski equipment or to just blow $1,000. We found the more the money came in, the quicker it went out."

Toni and Bill both admit their personal money histories influenced their earlier behavior. Toni's father, a lavish spender, bought mink coats and designer clothes and toys for the family. They were the best dressed in the neighborhood, yet when he died he left no life insurance or retirement fund. In the meantime, her devoutly Catholic mother told Toni and her siblings that they couldn't afford anything, didn't deserve anything, and that money was the root of all evil. Throughout her childhood Toni's father's free-spending ways contradicted what her mother was saying. "This has caused me to have a confused state of mind about money," Toni says. "I always wanted to make money but would sabotage myself because I didn't believe I deserved nice things."

Bill, on the other hand, learned about money from his wealthy grandparents on his mother's side. Growing up in New York, Bill's grandmother took him and his two brothers to the toy store every Saturday where they were allowed to buy whatever toys they wanted. "She showed her love and affection by giving us gifts and money,"

Bill says. "It was great back then, but now I see how it has made me terribly con-fused about money."

Now that Toni and Bill understand how there past money history is impacting their present money history, they've conquered half the problem. They are taking the necessary steps to manage their money better as well as to become financially educated. Their priority right now is to build enough wealth to afford their family a stress-free lifestyle and to be able to pass their assets on to their children.

Toni and Bill's Advice To Make Love and Money Work In Business

- Feed off each other's strengths. Initially, Bill was strong in taking care of the financial end of the business. Toni was the marketer. It was easier for Toni to get out and talk to people to build up clientele. Now both are active in handling the money.

- Don't sink a ton of money into the business in the beginning. Work at it and reinvest the earnings to build it up slowly.

- Maintain separate business and personal accounts. Don't commingle money.

- Stay organized. Keep your office and files in order. Make sure the office accommodates both partners' organizational style.

- Hire your children. Pay your children or other youngsters to stuff envelopes and do odds and ends. You're teaching your children to become entrepreneurs and it's a great tax benefit for your business.

- Set clear business and personal goals. When the money is coming in it's easy to get off track. Make building wealth and taking care of your family a priority.

- Take one-fourth of the business income and invest in mutual funds and real estate. You need a security fund for emergencies and slow months.

- Pay cash. Don't assume future income will pay off charge cards.

- Guard against the business consuming your life. Don't talk about business at dinner or when you go to bed.

- Be flexible. Sometimes you'll need to switch off roles. If Toni is on the phone in the evening talking to a customer, Bill will put the children to bed.

- If you work from home, treat the business like a business and not a hobby. A hobby business generates a hobby income.

- Create and stick to a spending plan for the business and your personal money. When the money is rolling in fast, you're more likely to blow it. Question every dollar you spend. For example, should you spend $25,000 on a new automobile or put it in a college fund.

Making love and money work in your own business is definitely possible. Toni and Bill are in love, having fun and making money!

Step 6: Insurance-It Does Your Money Good

We are well aware that insurance is a topic that people would rather put on the back burner, please don't. Insurance protection is extremely important to have as you and your partner are accumulating assets and building wealth because one catastrophic event can easily wipe out your entire savings and investment accounts. The potential for financial and emotional devastation from not having the proper protection is far too great to ignore.

In this section, we'll briefly discuss the six major types of insurance that you will need for the protection of your life and assets. Our chief goal is to make you more aware of the key issues about insurance so that when you talk to an insurance agent or financial advisor you will make the best possible decisions. The information we are providing isn't all-inclusive, so we recommend you seek professional advice regarding all of your insurance needs.

The Benefits of An Insurance Specialist

Buying insurance on the Internet is easy today, but we suggest you use extreme caution. With so many new insurance products on the market, it can be confusing and you may end up purchasing the wrong type of policy. That's why having an insurance specialist on your team of financial advisors can be invaluable when you're making decisions on such complex insurance products such as disability, and long-term care. These both are the fastest-growing and most complex areas of insurance you could imagine. More than likely, you couldn't make a well-reasoned decision about these types of insurance without a specialist who has special expertise.

This isn't to say that you shouldn't do your own homework. You need to learn at least the basic issues about the different types of insurance so that when you meet with a specialist you'll have a better understanding of their recommendations. Make sure to ask a lot of questions. In this section, we'll put some of the key issues on the table for you, but don't stop here. In fact, this is where the Internet could be of great benefit. Check out the insurance websites we've listed in the resource section before you meet with an insurance specialist.

The Major Six Kinds of Insurance

The six types of insurance you want to include in your financial portfolio are as follow:

1. Automobile insurance
2. Homeowner/rental insurance
3. Health care insurance
4. Life insurance
5. Long-term care insurance
6. Long-term disability insurance

Automobile Insurance

Many states now require that you carry a minimum amount of liability coverage, and if you still have an outstanding loan on the car, the lender will require full coverage to protect their investment.

Automobile insurance is very similar to homeowner's insurance in that it covers your property (the car), medical payments and liability for bodily injury or damage to another person's property.

If and when you have an accident and you're at fault your insurance plan will cover the damage. The insurance will also cover events such as theft and vandalism. You will either be paid the cost of the repairs or the actual cash value, whichever is less. The actual cash value is the depreciated value of the auto before the damage, not the replacement value. In many cases the actual cash value is a far cry from the replacement value. If you have an older car check with your agent regarding the collision and comprehensive coverage. Collision covers damage to your car caused by a collision with another auto or object. And it doesn't matter whether the object is moving or not. For this coverage there is a deductible, which is the amount you must pay before the insurance company kicks in its share. The higher the deductible, the lower your premium. The normal deductible ranges from $100 to $500. Comprehensive covers damages made by entities other than automobiles such as fire and theft.

Your liability coverage is the most important. It covers bodily injury, death to others, property damage, medical payments and uninsured or under insured motorist. Since this coverage protect you for medical injuries and loss of income make sure to choose the highest amount possible. For example, liability coverage is typically stated as "100/400/100." The 100 refers to a $100,000 per-person injury limit that is paid for losses from an accident. The 400 refers to a maximum payment of $400,000 for bodily injury per accident. And the 100 refers to the maximum amount of $100,000 per accident paid for property damage.

The cost of auto insurance varies. Essentially, it depends on age, gender, driving record of driver, the type of car, and the area where the car is insured. We suggest you shop around and compare rates. If you live in a large city, expect your rates to be 2-4 times higher than in a small city with less traffic. Research has also shown the cost of automobile insurance for the same car and driver can vary over 300 percent in the same city or region of the country.

Homeowner's/ Rental Insurance

The normal homeowner's insurance offers two types of protection: The first type covers losses of your home and personal property, and what it costs you to live while your home is being repaired or replaced. The second type covers your liability for injury to others. This will cover you if you are sued for damages that occur when an individual is on your property.

What's really important about homeowner's insurance is that you want to be sure you have adequate coverage to replace your home and the contents in the event of complete loss due to perils such as fires, vandalism, or other damaging events. Don't make the mistake that many do and only get the lender's minimum required insurance coverage. It will only be enough to pay off the mortgage and not protect any of your belongings let alone build you another house. Insure for 100 percent of the expected reconstruction cost, minus the costs of the foundation and underground pipes. Don't go by market value, which includes the land as well as the house. You want to use the cost to rebuild from the foundation up.

The best policy is a "Guaranteed replacement-coverage" not a "cash value" policy. This coverage keeps you fully insured for the right amount. The "cash value" policy means you will get up to the current market value of the house, which probably may be a lot less than what it would cost to rebuild your home.

Also include in your policy an automatic inflation protection. It cost extra, but it keeps your coverage up-to-date and not far behind the actual cost to rebuild your home. Every year the replacement value of your home will automatically rise to account for inflation.

Flood And Earthquake Insurance

We also suggest you consider two disasters not automatically covered: flood and earthquake, if you live in an area where these are common. Most insurance companies offer earthquake coverage. Coverage for flood is offered through a federal government program. Contact your insurer for additional information.

Keep Records of Inventory and Don't Undervalue

Other things you don't want to do are to undervalue your personal belongings and not keep an inventory of what is inside your home in a fireproof location. Otherwise you are leaving yourself open to major financial disaster. We recommend you take a video camera and video every room in the house pointing out different items and saying what they are and how much they cost, then put the videotape in your safety deposit box at your bank. Yet, more important, make sure your policy states it will replace your personal belongings at the current cost, not the depreciated value (flea market prices).

Liability Insurance

As we mentioned earlier, the liability coverage will cover you for damages if someone or something is injured on your property sues you. The basic policy probably includes $100,000 of liability coverage. This isn't much, especially if you own a swimming pool. It's wise to get additional coverage. With a small additional fee, you can have from $300,000 to $1,000,000 of additional coverage.

If this isn't enough protection, you can purchase "umbrella insurance", which covers losses in excess of the limits on both your homeowner's and auto policies. The ceiling can be $5 million or more. This extra coverage is good for high-net worth couples or individuals in high profile careers.

Renter's Insurance

If you are renting an apartment or condominium you definitely need insurance coverage. Don't skip on this, the cost is typically minimal and it's well worth it for peace of mind. You should have a plan that covers your personal property as well as liability for injury to others. If someone is injured in your apartment they can sue you as well as the landlord. Just recently one of my client's (Cheryl) experienced the effect of not having renters insurance. She and her two sons were renting a town house when her oldest son accidentally hit and set off one of the fire sprinklers with a basketball in his bedroom. Firefighters came but were unable to turn off the water for close to 30 minutes. It led to over $4,000 in water damage to the town house. Unfortunately, the damage was not covered by the homeowner's policy because the renter created it. My client had to personally shell out the money to pay for the damages. If she had renter's insurance it would have been covered.

Health Care Insurance

With today's astronomical health care cost no one can afford to be without health care protection. But what's sad is that many people are without health insurance due to unemployment, only part-time work and the prohibitive cost. If you are working full-time consider yourself fortunate, because your employer covers the bulk of your health insurance costs. But this may not always be the case. With the aging of the 76 million baby boomers today, employers are really beginning to feel the pinch of medical costs and may require the employees to foot more of the bill in the near future. So it's a good idea for you to stay on top of the changes in health insurance. Keep abreast of the changes in your policy, the cost of the premiums, deductibles and co-payments. Usually every year your company will allow you to evaluate and update your coverage. The options are usually between an HMO, a PPO and traditional medical insurance. How do you choose which is the best for you? We suggest you talk to your insurance specialist for guidance. If this isn't possible, start by comparing the costs and the coverage of the various options. Make sure you read the fine print. Decide whether or not you want the ability to select your own doctor or can the plan just assign one to you. Stay away from health care policies that only cover specific diseases. You also don't want a hospitalization policy that pays directly to you on a daily basis.

Talk to a professional. An insurance specialist can really assist in choosing the right type of health coverage. An injury or sickness and the wrong type of medical coverage can run up your medical bill into millions of dollars and put your financial well-being immediately in the poor house. Check out these resources for additional information.

Health Insurance Association of America, (202) 824-1500

The National Health Council, (202) 785-3910

Health Care Financing Administration, (800) 638-6833

The National Committee for Quality Assurance, (800) 839-6487

Life Insurance

Life insurance, guess what? It isn't for you! It's for the financial needs of the loved ones' that you leave behind. We know it's difficult to talk about death and life insurance but you really need to get over it. There have been far too many horror stories of families not having adequate insurance protection and truly paying the price for it with a drastic reduction of their lifestyle; children not being able to attend college, the family home having to be sold, and the list goes on and on. This is easily avoidable with the proper amount of life insurance coverage in place.

Insurance Terms to Know

To better understand life insurance, here are a few terms you should know before talking to an insurance specialist:

- **Death Benefit** (face value)—the amount of money that is paid to the beneficiary if the insured person dies.

- **Premium**—the amount you pay to the insurance company for coverage. It can be paid monthly, quarterly, or annually.

- **Policy Term**—the period of time you are covered by life insurance. It can range from one year to your lifetime.

- **Surrender Charge**—a fee charged by the insurance company if the policy is cancelled. Be sure to ask your insurance specialist whether or not your policy has a surrender charge.

Term Life Insurance Versus Whole-Life Insurance

Life insurance comes in many shapes and sizes. The two primary types are term (temporary) and permanent. The former provides a death benefit only; the latter, a death benefit plus a savings component.

Term Insurance

Term insurance is good for only a specific period of time with no frills or a savings plan. The coverage provides protection only, and pays when the insured person dies. The terms can vary from one to twenty years. As far as cost, it is the most cost effective life insurance that you can buy and the least expensive. The annual premium is based on the length the term, and your current age and health when you apply for the insurance. For example, if you are a healthy forty-six year old woman who doesn't smoke, a twenty-year term life policy with a $500,000 death benefit would cost about $80 a month.

The drawback with term insurance; it has no cash value if you decide to cancel your policy. When the policy runs out it can be renewed but the cost will be based according to your new age, health and the length of the term. The higher your age, the higher the premium because you are now closer to your probable age of death. If you were to renew the above-mentioned policy at the age of 70, the annual premium would run $12, 684, $1, 057 a month. As you can see the cost would be prohibitive.

There are three types of term insurance.

Annual Renewable Term

This is insurance with a term of one year renewable yearly. The premium begins at a low rate, and increases each year, the younger you are the lower the beginning rates. This is the least expensive of the three types of term insurance and the one we recommend. It is annually guaranteed renewable as long as you continue to pay the premium.

Decreasing Term

Decreasing term is used as insurance to pay off your mortgage in the event of the breadwinner's death. The annual premium stays the same, yet the amount of the insurance declines over time. This insurance is expensive for the amount of protection you receive.

Level Term

With level term insurance you prepay the premiums for the beginning years. The premium and the protection stays the same throughout the term of the policy. If you cancel the policy you lose the upfront premium payments. With the availability of so many other life insurance policies with better protection, we don't recommend level term.

Permanent Insurance (cash value)

Permanent insurance provides a death benefit plus an investment option. There are three types of permanent insurance: whole life, universal life and variable life. The initial premium on a cash value policy are higher but don't increase as long as the policy continues. Unlike term insurance part of the premium is invested to obtain a higher savings return. All cash value that accumulates can be borrowed from the policy or used to pay the premiums or increase the death benefit. If you cancel the policy, this savings accumulation remains yours. If you borrow against it you pay an interest rate stated in the contract. To keep the policy in force, continue to pay the premiums. When there is a death, the insurance company will deduct the amount of the loan from the amount it pays the beneficiary.

Whole-Life Insurance

Whole-life insurance has been around the longest and is the most conservative. It is will remain in force regardless of how long you live. The insurance company will invest your premiums, but you have no control over how and where the money is invested.

Universal Life

Universal life insurance is similar to whole-life in that a portion of the premium pays for insurance while the other portion goes into a savings fund. It differs in offering more flexibility than whole-life, since interest earned on the savings plan can be either at a fixed rate or placed into mutual funds. The more money the investment plans make, the more you can borrow and the quicker your death benefit grows. If you have the money for the initial premium and want a conservative investment opportunity, look into universal life.

Variable Life

With a variable life policy, a portion of the premium is invested in mutual funds and other managed accounts. The higher the investment grows, the higher the death benefit. This policy also carries a minimum death benefit in case the investment portfolio doesn't do well. If you don't mind the ups and downs and want higher returns for your insurance premium, you should consider variable life. While it's great to be able to invest part of your premiums it can also be confusing. Talk to your insurance agent and read the prospectus before you invest.

How Much Life Insurance Do We Need?

There are several formulas to calculate your death benefit needs, ranging from simple to complicated. The simple formula is to purchase six to eight times your annual salary. If you don't make a lot of money this figure may be too low. We recommend the amount to be enough for your family to maintain their lifestyle by living on the interest and dividends that comes from investing the principal.

Insurance Formula

The formula we suggest is to obtain $100,000 in insurance for every $500 of monthly income required, including income taxes. (Although a death benefit payment from the insurance company will not be taxed, but the income you make from investing the money will be taxed). Here's an example; you need $5,000 a month to cover all expenses and income taxes. Your heirs will need the entire $5,000 to live on as well. You take the $5,000 and divide by $500 and get 10, so your insurance policy should be 10 times $100,000, or $1,000,000 worth of insurance coverage.

Get More Information

There are good sites on the Internet to get quotes and to figure out how much insurance you need. We have listed them in the appendix. The best thing to do is to talk and develop a relationship with an insurance specialist; they will help you weigh out the pros and cons of the different options for your family. Take the time to research and study the different options so that you are able to ask the right questions. And review all your insurance needs annually.

Long-Term Care Insurance

Long-term care (LTC) insurance is fairly new yet becoming increasingly popular. Thanks again to the baby boomers. But it is still the one insurance people seem most resistant to purchasing. Yet, it is the one that you and your partner most will probably need because, chances are one of you may need to spend time in a nursing home after the age of sixty-five.

Long-term care is designed to pay for care for senior adults in a nursing home or in their own home. We have found that if there is a long-term health problem, most people prefer the long-term care in their home.

Long-term care policies are somewhat complicated and expensive. Nevertheless, you really need it, since your health insurance will not pay for long-term care. It's rare if Medicare covers it, and if it does, it will only pay the full cost of a nursing home stay for only twenty days and partially pay the cost for another eighty days, after that you are on your own. You may qualify for Medicaid to pay it but it comes with a price, you have to be financially destitute.

Who Should Buy Long-Term Care and When?

Unless you've got plenty of money and have a high six-figure retirement portfolio you need a long-term care policy to shelter the assets that you do accumulate from depletion. With the high cost of a private nursing home stay (in some areas the costs is about $4,500 per month. The more upscale nursing homes run around $9,000 a month) it isn't uncommon that the health problems of one partner wipes out the couples life savings. So if you want to be certain that a debilitating illness or illness doesn't destroy your partner's financially, or if you want some of your assets to go to your heirs, consider long-term care insurance coverage.

The time we recommend you buy a long-term care policy is when you are still young, around fifty-nine. Even forty isn't too young, because the insurance premiums are based on how old you are when you purchase the policy and the projection of how well you will stay for the lifetime of the policy. Once the policy is put into force, the premium payments stop and the cost of the insurance is free the entire time the benefits are being used. This is the one insurance you don't want to put off because the longer you wait, the more it will cost. In the appendix we have included a few of the top insurance companies that provide Long-term care insurance.

Long-Term Disability Insurance

One of the most valuable assets you and your partner have is your ability to work and earn an income. The chance of one of you becoming disabled by an accident far outweighs death. With a decrease in income for a long time or even permanently and most likely an increase in medical bills, poor financial preparedness definitely could create chaos in your life. To avoid such a disaster, disability insurance is available to take care of your income if you aren't able to work. The insurance will usually pay 60 to 70 percent of your current salary.

Don't depend solely on workers' compensation to take care of your financial needs if you become disabled. It only covers you if you are injured on your job. The long-term disability policy will pay whether you hurt yourself on the job, on vacation or at home.

Social Security offers limited disability coverage with a restrictive definition of disability; in that your case might not meet their guidelines to make you eligible. If you are eligible, you must wait six months before you receive the money.

Long-term disability insurance is similar to long-term care insurance in that it is complicated and expensive. Many employers and trade associations offer long-term disability insurance for their employees as part of a benefit package. Most of these companies offer one of two disability plans. The first pays benefits for a short period usually up to one year. The second is the long-term plan intended for more serious disabilities. The latter generally provides a certain percentage of your earnings, and payments can last five to ten years or until you reach the age of sixty-five. Similar to Social Security there is a waiting period before the money kicks in. Typically three to six months after you become disabled. Check with your benefits department to see which plan you are covered by. If neither you nor your partner is covered we suggest you obtain an individual policy. The cost is based on your age, health and income. Research various insurance companies and compare coverage's and annual premiums. Start with the companies we suggested for your long-term care insurance.

Part III

A
New
Beginning

Now It's Your Turn!

We've covered a lot in this section. Designing your financial life in your relationship is extremely important today. And it isn't as complicated as you think. It's simply having a plan and following it. We've given you the tools now it is up to you to take them and use them to make love and money work in your relationship. Be consistent yet flexible. Building wealth takes patience. It will not happen overnight. But it will happen when the two of you come together and decide you aren't going to live in financial deprivation any longer. And remember; no one will ever care more about your money than you so never depend on anyone to take charge or control of your money.

"United We Stand, Alone We Go Broke"

The quote above sums it all up. Teamwork is the name of the game to make love and money work. Your relationship is successful when both of you handle the "dirty" work; paying the bills, doing the banking, selecting insurance plans, and managing the investment portfolio. When both of you are financially self-reliant you will bring confidence, knowledge and a sense of equality and financial well being to the relationship, while at the same time maintaining your sense of self while enjoying the benefits of togetherness.

Both win when the male partner of a working -woman does an equal amount of housework and childcare. When the woman gives solid support to her partner and makes sacrifices along the way as he strives to build a new business or start a new career. To achieve that kind of parity, you must both open your minds and hearts to accepting and embracing your differences. Money in our relationships must follow a different path from that of previous generations. One partner can no longer be overly dependent on the other financially or emotionally. Don't expect perfection from your mate because when you don't get it you feel hurt and you're ready to quit. You were looking for your partner to give you what you couldn't give yourself.

When love and money is working you and your partner experience deeper intimacy, greater satisfaction and longer happiness in the relationship. Why? Because by accepting, respecting, and supporting each other, you can discuss differences, share dreams, and value your individual personalities. Instead of pointing out the faults and quirks of your significant other, spend time working on your own character flaws. By doing this you are making your relationship a safe place for growth and change. You send a message that you're willing to cooperate in order to make money and love work better.

While choosing a partner based at least partially on financial compatibility may seem unromantic, it is smart. Relationships are like business alliances; there must be economic benefits for both. What are those benefits? Everything we talked about in the previous section; creating and building wealth, starting a business, getting rid of all financial debt, developing a six figure investment portfolio, and saving for your children's college education.

One thing we have learned from experience is that you can't change a person no matter how much you love them. If you find you and your partner aren't moving forward financially or simply can't see eye to eye on how to make your money work the bold thing to do is to develop your own wealth -building plan. Get out there and pursue your own dreams of financial independence. If you don't take control of your own financial future, you may end up in the poor house.

The ideal making love and money work relationship is a lot like sex: if you want it to be good, you have to talk about it. Earlier, we mentioned how talking about money is still taboo, yet sex isn't. Look at the extremely popular HBO drama, "Sex and The City." When was the last time you saw a television show that dramatized making money work in relationships? You haven't and probably won't.

If you want to make love and money work in your relationship, you must first begin with a meeting of the minds. You both must clearly recognize and scrutinize all the issues you'll need to clear up to build a solid foundation of wealth together. And this financial foundation begins with a solid commitment that both of you will be upfront and truthful about money matters. Secrets no longer allowed.

Knowing about each other's finances requires full disclosure on both sides. That means cleaning up any unfinished business from the past. Are there any legal, financial, relationship or career messes that you haven't dealt with? You can't afford to let these linger. This unfinished business is the baggage we talked about in chapter 15. Like dead weight around your neck, it will drag you and your new relationship down.

Assets that are created within the relationship should be held in both names. You both must also agree on the relationship's investment philosophy. If an investment is being considered and one partner feels it's too risky, he or she should speak up! Don't go along with it just to keep the peace. This is how resentment builds in the relationship. If need be, go to a financial coach or planner. A third party will help neutralize any tension that may arise and keep the discussion focused, productive and non-judgmental.

Schedule A Money Talk

Now that we've reviewed some of the main ingredients for Making Love and Money Work, it's now time to make good on the "money talk" we mentioned earlier. The money talk offers an opportunity for you and your partner to give each other honest feedback on your money issues. Because the first money talk will lay the groundwork for your investment relationship, you need to go in with a written agenda, just as you would with any other business relationship. The agenda will keep you both focused and prevent you from feeling overwhelmed. Here are some issues and topics you will want to discuss:

- Each partner's money skills. If one is weak in a certain area decide on a way to help her or him become more knowledgeable.

- Your financial future. What does it look like? How much money are you planning to grow together? How many credit cards will you have? When are you planning to stop working or a make a major career in your career? What type of lifestyle do you envision for the two of you?

- Debt. Are you living in credit card hell and paying high interest charges? If yes, what steps are you taking to get out of debt?

- Assets you both have now in your wealth-building plan. Will your future income allow you both to live out your wildest dreams?

> Making Love and Money Work
> - Make a commitment to stay together and be faithful
> - Pray and worship
> - Communicate, even when you don't feel like it—especially when you don't feel like it.
> - Practice forgiveness
> - Help one another, and bear each other's burdens
> - Take time away
> - Fight the tendency to drift apart
>
> Gary C. Collins

- Major future financial expenses; college for children, retirement, taking care of elderly parents.

- How you will select investments. Will you have an individual as well as joint investment portfolio?

- What name(s) the investment assets will be held in.

- The goal of the investment portfolio. How much money do you both want to accumulate for the future and why? Retirement; start a business; buy a house; other.

- Who will be in charge of monitoring the investment portfolio? And how—computer, discount or full service brokerage firm?

- Whether the returns from the investments will be reinvested in other investments or used for some other purpose.

- Whether or not you will use a financial coach. If so, will each partner meet with the coach on an individual basis as well as together?

> *Remember, it takes two to get an argument going. Invariably, the one who is wrong is the one who will be doing most of the talking.*
>
> — Ann Landers

- Wills and estate planning.

These topics will get the money conversation rolling. As you both get all your money concerns on the table, no matter how difficult it is, it will take your relationship to a new and higher level. It's not like sex, where there's lots of fantasy. Instead, it's romantic because making love and money work in your relationship leads to real intimacy. As you and your partner formulate, implement, and track your plans together, you'll have the time of your life while developing a deeply spiritual and long-lasting relationship. Consider the experience of Oliver and Antoinette

Oliver and Antoinette

Oliver and Antoinette are making love and money work in their relationship. Married six years, both were previously married to financially irresponsible partners. This time, they are determined to get it right.

When the bank Antoinette worked for merged with another bank, she decided to take the buy- out package, start a consulting business and help Oliver with his dental practice. She was well positioned financially thanks to the savvy money management habits she learned from her father. "He taught me to save most of my annual raises, buy a $50 Savings Bonds each month, and take advantage of 401(k) programs and company matching savings or stock purchase programs," she says. "I did all of them. In addition, I had stock options which all came due when the merger took place. Those that I could have exercised, I never touched. Instead, I invested all but a small percent."

Oliver thanks the U.S. Navy for helping him learn to manage his money while building a dental practice that serves well-known sport figures and entertainers. Oliver says he wouldn't trade his time in the military for anything in the world. "Working on an aircraft carrier with 5,000 crew members provided a great training ground for dentistry, good benefits, and a chance to save money," he says. As soon as he was discharged, getting out of debt was his priority. He paid off his student loans early, and used cash instead of credit cards.

Today Oliver and Antoinette's smart money management style is paying off quite handsomely. They own a beautiful 4,000-square-foot home with swimming pool and Jacuzzi in Tampa, Florida, run a financially thriving dental practice, have a high six- figure investment portfolio, and take several vacations a year. When we interviewed them, they had just returned from a 12-day Mediterranean cruise to Greece and Italy. "We are financially where we are today because we took time in the beginning to create a financial plan," Oliver says. "We both always worked hard and did extra work in the early years to make extra money. Also, we don't depend on just one source of income. And by serving on corporate and nonprofit boards, we enjoy other benefits such as travel at little or no cost." Antoinette even makes a little extra money as a part-time radio announcer. For four hours every Sunday, she hosts a jazz brunch segment on the local jazz station in Tampa.

Oliver and Antoinette each have their own checking account. However the accounts include both their names so either can access them in case of an emergency. They also have a joint account for household expenses. They each have credit cards, but rarely use them and when they do, pay them off within 30 days. The investment accounts are set up in joint names except for one that is in Antoinette's name only. Her accountant and attorney recommended she have that one for tax and estate purposes. Both spouses know that each has a separate account, but neither knows how much the other has in that account. "It's not being sneaky or secretive, however, you just never know," says Antoinette. "But deep down we really consider ourselves to be financial soul mates."

Oliver and Antoinette make every dollar count and follow specific steps to stay financially in check. They use coupons, pay cash and get a copy of their credit bureau report annually. They also research before they buy any big-ticket items. "We usually find the best product at the right price and try to find ways to cut the 'middle' man out," they say. "This saves lots of money!" They recommend couples know when to buy the cheapest and when to buy something that may be a little more expensive but last longer.

When they make travel reservations they book in advance and ask for discounts. For hotels they call the 1-800 number or sometimes the hotel direct. "Oftentimes one offers specials that the other doesn't!" When shopping at their favorite stores, they get to know the managers who can authorize deals that sales clerks can't.

Even though they are financially comfortable, Oliver and Antoinette find ways to curtail spending. They have stopped buying more "stuff" and instead make do with what they already have. " I guess in our 'old age' you start to look around and see how much you've wasted money on things you no longer use," Antoinette says. She recommends couples clean out their closets and garages and take the good items to a consignment shop or nonprofit homeless shelter.

Oliver and Antoinette are extremely grateful for their financial accomplishments and show their gratitude by giving time and money to the community. Antoinette also inherited the $2.00 bill habit from her father. She always carries a crisp $2 bill in her wallet and puts one in every gift and birthday card she gives to friends and relatives. She says it's a sign of prosperity and good luck.

Oliver and Antoinette's advice on making love and money work

- Faithfully follow your spending plan.

- Know that it can take 35 years to pay off a $5,000 credit card debt when you make only the minimum monthly payments. "You'll be old and gray by the time it's paid off and the item will be long outdated."

- Make every dollar count. Pay cash whenever possible.

- Have a goal for monthly savings. Get excited about reaching it.

- Pay for things with paper money and put the change in a jar. "You'd be surprised how much money you accumulate in one month. Put the jar money in savings."

- Be careful of "get rich quick" investment schemes. "There are more and more folks out there trying to rip you off."

- Stay away from finance companies.

- Learn to be happy with yourself—money does not buy happiness.

"I guess we're fortunate to have one another," Oliver says. "We both think the same when it comes to saving money. As my mother always said, "Romance without finance is a nui-sance."

Wow! Isn't Oliver and Antoinette's story great? That's why we made it the last story in the book. They represent the epitome of making love and money work. If you follow their advice along with the principles outlined in this book, you too can make love and money work in your relationship.

25 Action Steps To Making Love and Money Work

Now we really are at the end of the book. And it's now time for you to put everything you have learned into practice. It's time for you to make love and money work in your relationship and take it to the next level. This book is your blueprint to take control, create a solid financial foundation, and build true wealth with your partner. If you aren't in a relationship today, that's even better, because when you do find that special person, your eyes will be financially wide open. Be sure to share this guide with you new partner so that you both enter into the relationship ready to work as a team to financially improve your life.

The Ultimate List

At the end of each chapter we gave you action steps to take as you traveled along your financial journey. We believe it is a good idea to restate some of the steps and give you additional ones as well. So we conclude Chapter 18 with the 25 most important action steps to Making Love and Money Work in your relationship. Until we meet again…God bless and may you and your partner have a wonderful, fulfilling and prosperous life.

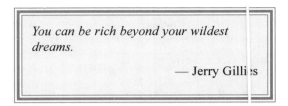

> *You can be rich beyond your wildest dreams.*
>
> — Jerry Gillies

The Steps:

1. **Take care of business.** Each partner in the relationship needs to have defining financial roles they are accountable for. Decide who will pay the bills and who will oversee the investment portfolio and savings accounts.

2. **Schedule monthly money talks.** Discuss your financial vision of the future and set financial goals. Partners that dream together, stay together.

3. **Get organized together.** Develop a financial filing system to store your canceled checks, deposit slips, and important documents and receipts needed for filing your income taxes. Having both partners develop the system will eliminate many future arguments.

4. **Take stock.** Make an inventory of all the personal belongings you each bring to the relationship as well as the assets accumulated in the relationship. By having this information you'll have a better idea of how much property insurance you should purchase and with this information it will be easier to file a claim if anything is lost, stolen, or damaged.

5. **Keep track of your spending with a spending plan.** Your spending plan will allow you to take control of your money. Remember, it's not the amount of money you earn that matters; it's how you manage what you have. Live within your means.

6. **Build a money cushion.** All relationships need a financial cushion in a money market or bank account. These funds will come in handy if you lose your job or suffer other unexpected emergencies.

7. **Get rid of credit card and short-term debt.** Total up the amount owed on each card and determine what action steps you must take to pay off the balances.

8. **Maintain your own credit cards.** To maintain a credit rating in your own name, each partner should keep one or two separate and active credit cards.

9. **Pay yourself first.** Put your building wealth program on automatic pilot by signing up with your bank or employer to have money automatically deducted from your paycheck and transferred into your account. It's the painless way to save money without having to physically write a check and mail it in.

10. **Build wealth together.** Building a long-term investment portfolio must be a priority for a making love and money work. Start the portfolio by having money deducted electronically from your paycheck or checking account and put into a mutual fund, DRIPS account or online brokerage account.

11. **Plan you estate.** Each partner should update and review wills and trusts documents. Meet with your attorney at least once a year to insure that your estate is in order in case of a death.

12. **Get financial help.** Becoming financially free isn't always easy on your own. At one point you will need the help of a professional team–an accountant or bookkeeper, financial advisor, banker, attorney, and insurance agent. Look for a professional with at least 10 years of experience who comes highly recommended from friends, relatives or members of your financial team

13. **Be supportive of each other during money challenges.** Avoid name-calling and blame games during financial crises. It's a time when both partners are vulnerable. Saying or doing something hurtful may cause irreparable damage to the relationship.

14. **Money isn't everything.** Often in our quest to amass more money we forget what is really important and our relationships and health suffer. Put your relationship, family and health first. When you do the right thing the money will come.

15. **Take care of unfinished financial business.** Unfinished financial baggage can weigh heavily on a relationship causing stress and arguments. If there is unfinished business in the relationship clean it up as quickly as possible.

16. **Develop an <u>Our</u> money philosophy.** Each partner must take his and her ego out of the relationship. Get over who makes more money. What matters is that you are a team building financial wealth together.

17. **Share the expenses.** If both partners are working, the expenses should be shared. If one partner makes less, set up a balanced sharing arrangement equivalent to each partner's income.

18. **If considering a divorce, ask yourself is it really the only option?** Talk to an experienced matrimonial lawyer, financial advisor and marriage counselor before throwing in the towel. You may be financially glad you did.

19. **During a divorce don't use children or money as a weapon.** It's damaging to everyone.

20. **Assess your money personality, as well as that of your current or future partner.** While opposite money personalities attract, it's just more difficult. Ideally, you want a partner with similar life and financial aspirations.

21. **Each partner must get clear on his or her values, beliefs, life-styles, needs and goals.** Discuss these before and during the live-in relationship or marriage. Both partners need to be on a similar page to make love and money work.

22. **Get rid of destructive personal feeling and fears about money.** Money wounds aren't permanent and they will hinder you in reaching your financial goals. Try to heal them.

23. **Plan quarterly and annual making money and love work retreats.** Get out of town to a quiet spot — a resort or bed and breakfast inn — to discuss the changes you want to happen in your life and with your money. This helps to create a common vision for the relationship.

24. **Don't bet on a Money Prince or Princess Charming to sweep in and financially rescue you.** That's pure fantasy. Take the time to get your own financial act together before and while you are in a relationship.

25. **Follow the Making Love and Money Work money formula.** Divide 10 percent of your income between your religious affiliation and other charitable organizations; put 20 to 25 percent in short and long-term savings and devote the other 65 to 70 percent to living expenses, including taxes. If you spend less than you make you will always have money to build a solid financial foundation.

The Making Love and Money Work Commitment

If you are serious about getting your financial house in order, you and your partner should fill in and sign the Making Love and Money Work commitment form below. Make two copies. Keep one in a prominent place in your home and send one to Romance and Finance Counseling Group (the address may be found on page 393.)

To get our financial house in order, we realize we must do our part in building our wealth. We hereby make the following commitments:

1) We commit to changing the attitude and lifestyle that keeps us in financial bondage, and we dedicate ourselves to managing our money to build wealth.

2) We commit to getting out of debt and to stop overspending on credit.

3) We commit to establishing a surplus account by spending less than we earn and setting aside up to one-fourth from each paycheck.

4) We commit to reaching our financial goals and dreams.

5) We commit to following the 25 steps to Making Love and Money Work

6) We commit to following our monthly spending plan.

7) We commit to building wealth through savings and investments

8) We commit to staying focused.

Signature: _____ Date: _____

Signature: _____ Date: _____

Please print:

Name: _____

Address: _____

The End

Appendix

RELATIONSHIP RESOURCES

American Association for Marriage and Family Therapy
202-452-0109
www.aamft.org

Prevention and Relationship Enhancement Program (PREP)
800-366-0166
www.prepinc.com

National Institute for Relationship Enhancement
800-432-6454
www.nire.org

The Institute for Equality in Marriage
www.Equalityinmarriage.org

The Stepfamily Association of America
www.Saafamilies.org

The Gottman Institute—Couples' Retreat and Products
206-523-9042
www.gottman.com

Coalition For Marriage, Family and Couples Education, LLC
202-362-3332
www.smartmarriage.com

Passionate Journey- Couples' Retreats
408-847-0406
www.mountmadonna.org

ORGANIZATIONS

Coalition of Black Investors
P.O. Box 30553
Winston-Salem, NC 27130-0553
888-411-2624
www.cobinvest.com

National Center for Women and Retirement Research
P.O. Box 393
Sag Harbor, NY 11963
631-725-3583
www.agingfocus.com

National Urban League/ ICI Education
Foundation Partnership
(Investing for Success Program)
1401 H Street, NW Suite 1200
Washington, DC 20005
202-326-5800
www.ici.org/investing_for_success/index.html

American Association of Retired Persons
601 E Street, NW
Washington, DC 20049
800-424-3410
www.aarp.org

INVESTMENT CLUBS

National Association of Investors Corporation
711 West Thirteen Mile Road
Madison Heights, MI 48071
877-275-6242
www.better-investing.org

FINANCIAL EDUCATION

Association for Financial Counseling and Planning Education
614-485-9650
www.financialcounseling.net

Alliance for Investor Education
www.investoreducation.org/

American Association of Individual Investors
625 N. Michigan Avenue, Suite 1900
Chicago, IL 60611
800-428-2244
www.aaii.com

Forum for Investor Advice
7200 Wisconsin Avenue, Suite 709
Bethesda, MD 20814
301-656-7998
www.investoradvice.org

Investor Protection Trust
1901 North Fort Myer Drive, Suite 1012-1014
Arlington, VA 22209
703-276-1116
www.investorprotection.org

National Endowment for Financial Education
5299 DTC Boulevard, Suite 1300
Englewood, CO 80111
301-589-5600
www.nefe.org

National Foundation for Consumer Credit
8611 Second Avenue, Suite 100
Silver Spring, MD 20910
301-589-5600
www.nfcc.org

National Institute For Consumer Education
559 Gary M. Owen Building
300 W. Michigan Avenue
Ypsilanti, MI 48197
734-487-2292
www.nice.emich.edu

Securities and Exchange Commission
Office of Investor Education and Assistance
800-SEC-0330
www.sec.gov/oiea1.htm

CREDIT-REPORTING COMPANIES

Equifax
P.O. Box 105873
Atlanta, GA 30348
800-685-1111, 770-612-3200
www.ecoconsumer.equifax.com

Experian
P.O. Box 949
Allen, TX 75013-0949
800-643-3334
www.experian.com

Trans Union Corporation
Consumer Disclosure Center
P.O. Box 390
Springfield, PA 19064-0390
800-916-8800, 714-680-7292
www.transunion.com

DRIPS (DIVIDEND REINVESTMENT PROGRAM)
www.dripinvestor.com
www.moneypaper.com

MUTUAL FUNDS

Mutual Fund Education Alliance
100 NW Englewood Road, Suite 130
Kansas City, MO 64118
816-454-9422
www.mfea.com
Morningstar
Ranks Mutual Funds
www.morningstar.com

www.mutuals.com

Investment Company Institute
1401 H Street, NW, Suite 1200
Washington, DC 20005-2148
202-326-5800
www.ici.org

ON THE WEB

www.personalfund.com
www.smartmoney.com
www.fundmaster.com
www.indexfundsonline.com
www.fundalarm.com
www.vanguard.com

MUTUAL FUND COMPANIES

Ariel	800-292-7435	www.arielmutualfunds.com
Aim	800-959-4246	www.aim.com
American Century	800-345-2021	www.americancentury.com
Dreyfus	800-373-9387	www.dreyfus.com
Fidelity	800-343-3548	www.fidelity.com
Franklin Templeton	800-342-5236	www.franklintempleton.com
Janus	800-525-8983	www.janus.com
Invesco	800-525-8085	www.invesco.com
T.Rowe Price	800-638-5660	www.troweprice.com
Strong Funds	800-368-1030	www.strongfunds.com
Vanguard	800-851-4999	www.vanguard.com

FINANCIAL/ MONEY WEBSITE

www.nasdaq.com
www.edgaronline.com
www.marketguide.com
www.morningstar.com
www.quote.com
www.stockselector.com

www.valueline.com
www.valuestocks.net
www.ragingbull.com
www.quicken.com
www.theonlineinvestor.com
www.thestreet.com
www.fool.com
www.finance.yahoo.com
www.financecenter.com
www.quicken.com
www.gomez.com

ONLINE/DISCOUNT BROKERAGE FIRMS

Ameritrade	866-857-6048	www.ameritrade.com
E-Trade Financial	800-ETRADE1	www.etrade.com
Charles Schwab	866-339-0399	www.schwab.com
T.D. Waterhouse	800-tdwaterhouse	www.tdwaterhouse.com

LEGAL EDUCATION

Academy of Family Mediators
4 Militia Drive
Lexington, MA 02173
617-674-2663

Nolo Press
www.nolo.com

www.findlaw.com

INSURANCE RESOURCES

National Association of Insurance Commissioners
120 Twelfth Street, Suite 1100
Kansas City, MO 64105
816-842-3600
www.naic.org

Financial Strength of Insurance Companies

A.M. Best
800-424-2378
www.ambest.com/

Standard & Poors
212-208-1527
www.insure.com/ratings/tabframe.html

Moody's Invesor's Services
212-553-0377
www.moodys.com/economic/ecoindex.htm

Duff & Phelps
312-263-2610

Life Insurance on Internet

Ameritas
800-552-3553
www.ameritas.com

E-Insure Services, Inc.
312-663-9663
www.einsurance.com

Insweb Corp.
650-298-9100
www.insweb.com

MasterQuote of America Inc.
800-337-5433
www.masterquote.com

Quotesmith.com, Inc.
800-556-9393
www.quotesmith.com

TermQuote
800-444-8376
www.termquote.com

Select Quote
800-343-1985
www.selectquote.com

Insurance Quote Services
800-972-1104
www.iquote.com

Life and Disability Insurance

Aetna U.S. Healthcare
800-636-2386
www.aetna.com

Mutual of Omaha Insurance Company
402-397-3200
www.mutualofomaha.com

Northwestern Mutual Life Insurance Company
414-271-1444
www.northwesternmutual.com

State Farm Mutual Automobile Insurance Company
309-766-2311
www.statefarm.com

Long-Term Care Insurance

General Electric Capital Assurance Company
800-844-6543
www.gefn.com

CAN (Continental Casualty)
800-775-1541
www.can.com

John Hancock
800-732-5543
www.jhancock.com

UNUM Provident
800-227-8138
www.unumprovident.com

FINANCIAL ADVISORS/PLANNERS

Romance & Finance Couple's Money Counseling
4110 Redwood Road, Suite 103
510-482-5129
www.romanceandfinance.com

The Financial Planning Association
800-322-4237
www.fpanet.org

National Association of Personal Financial Advisors
800-366-2732
www.napfa.org

Financial Planning Association
3801 E. Florida Avenue, Suite 708
Denver, CO 80210
800-322-4237
www.fpanet.org

FINANCIAL REGULATORY AGENCIES

Securities Industry Association
212-608-1500
www.sia.com

Securities Investor Protection Corporation
202-371-8300
www.sipc.org

NASD Regulation, Inc.
202-728-8958
www.nasdr.com

RECOMMENDED READING

Girl Get Your Money Straight; A Sister's Guide To Healing our *Bank Account and Funding our Dreams In 7 Simple Steps*, Glinda Bridgforth (Broadway Books, 2000)

The Black Woman's Guide To Financial Independence; Smart Ways To Take Charge of Your Money, Build Wealth, and Achieve Financial Security, Cheryl D. Broussard (Penguin Books, 1996)

The 6 Secrets of a Lasting Relationship; How to Fall in Love Again——and Stay There, Mark Goulston, M.D., with Philip Goldberg (A Perigee Book, 2001)

Women, Men & Money: The Four Keys for Using Money to Nourish Your Relationship, Bankbook, and Soul, William Francis Devine, Jr. (Harmony Books, 1998)

Creating A Spiritual Relationship, Paul Ferrini, (Heartways Press)

Fall In Love Stay In Love, Willard F. Harley, Jr. (Fleming H. Revell, 2001)

Love Busters; Overcoming Habits that Destroy Romantic Love, Willard F. Harley, Jr. (Fleming H. Revell, 2002)

His Needs Her Needs; Building an Affair-Proof Marriage, Willard f. Harley, Jr. (Fleming H. Revell, 2001)

Rich Dad Poor Dad, Robert T. Kiyosaki with Sharon L. Lechter C.P.A., (TechPress, Inc. 1998)

Rich Dad's Guide To Investing; What The Rich Invest In, That the Poor and Middle Class Do Not!, Robert t. Kiyosaki with Sharon Lechter, C.P.A., (Warner Books, 2000)

The CashFlow Quadrant; Rich Dad's Guide To Financial Freedom, Robert T. Kiyosaki with Sharon L. Lechter, C.P.A., (TechPress, Inc., 1999)

Retire Young Retire Rich; How To Get Rich Quickly and Stay Rich Forever!, Robert T. Kiyosaki with Sharon L. Lechter, C.P.A., (Warner Books, 2002)

Loopholes of the Rich, Diane Kennedy, C.P.A., (Warner Books, 2001)

Creating Money; Keys To Abundance, Sanaya Roman & Duane Packer, (HJ Kramer, Inc., 1988)

The Complete Idiot's Guide To Living Together, Rosanne Rosen, (Alpha Books, 2000)

The Mastery of Love; A Practical Guide to the Art of Relationship, Don Miguel Ruiz, M.D., (Amber-Allen Publishing, Inc., 1999)

The Millionaire Next Door, Thomas J. Stanley, Ph..D., (Longstreet Press, Inc., 1996)

The Millionaire Mind, Thomas J. Stanley, Ph.D., (Andrews McMeel Publishing, 2000)

How to Love a Black Man, Dr. Ronn Elmore (Warner Books, 1996)

You Paid How Much For That?!; How to Win at Money Without Losing at Loving, Natalie H. Jenkins, Scott M. Stanley, William C. Bailey, Howard J. Markman, (Jossey-Bass, 2002)

What Women Want Men To Know, Barbara DeAngelis, Ph.D., (Hyperion, 2001)

Real Estate Riches; How To Become Rich Using Your Banker's Money, Dolf De Roos, Ph.D., (Warner Books, 2001)

Race For Success; 10 Best Opportunities For Black In America; George Fraser, (Merrill William & Co., 1998)

Sisters Are Cashing In; How Every Woman Can Make Her Financial Dreams Come True, Marilyn French Hubbard, (A perigee Book, 2000)

Smart Money Moves For African Americans, Kelvin Boston, (Putnam, 1996)

Divorce & Money; How to Make the Best Financial Decisions During Divorce, Attorneys Violet Woodhouse, CFP & Dale Fethering, Nolo Press, 2001

Publications

Black Enterprise
Ebony
Essence
Forbes
Fortune
In The Black
Kiplinger Personal Finance
Money Magazine
Smart Money
Worth Magazine

Newspapers

Barrons
Financial Times (London)
Investors Daily©
The New York Times
USA Today
The Wall Street Journal

Index

Symbols

$250,000 capital gains exclusion 263
401(K)
   13, 21, 54, 72, 81, 126, 145, 206, 250, 265
9 Step Reduction Plan 322

A

accountant 233, 264, 265, 305
action plans 35, 62, 64, 65, 70, 73, 77
addiction 66
affirmations 72
affirmative action 22
African American 18, 20, 22
alimony 181, 219, 224, 238
alimony and spousal support 253, 254
allowance 32
Alvis Davis 182
American dream 23
Angela Bassett 109
anger 15
annual renewable term 348
antenuptial agreement 292
anxiety 73
argue about money 31
arguments 11
Asian American 22
assets 110
assets and debts 96
ATM 80, 85
attitudes 11, 38, 58, 84
attorney or mediator 259
automatic inflation protection 344
automatic investment plan 325
automating bill paying 86

automobile insurance 341, 342
average fee for a lawyer 240
average income 21
Avoider 74
Aziela Jaffe 334

B

bag lady 42
Bag Lady-To-Be 125
Balancing a checkbook 73
balancing checkbooks 26, 85
bank accounts 110
banker 239, 305
bankruptcy 9
Barry Bonds 291
beliefs 35, 61, 81
beliefs, damaging 86
beliefs, gender 39
beliefs, money limiting 40, 41, 44, 46
beliefs, negative 27, 45
beliefs, new money 46
beliefs, non-gender 39
Ben Sweetland 324
Bill Clinton 158
Bill Cosby 174
Binger 12, 61, 65
"Black and Single: Meeting and Choosing a
   Partner 183
black children 20
black culture 20
"Black Men Not Looking For Sex" 182
blame game 101, 103
bounced checks 120
boundaries 17
"Breadwinner Wives and the Men They
   Marry" 181
budget 63
budgeting 61
building trust 109
Business Higher Education Forum 21
business ownership 268

385

Need More Help?

The Romance and Finance Couples' Money Counseling Group

What We Do

The Romance and Finance Couples' Counseling Group specializes in helping couples create that wealth-building team. We offer hands on step-by-step financial programs and educational tools to help you and your partner get on the same money page.

Services Offered

- Pre, and Post-Marital Financial Counseling

- Marital Financial Counseling

- One-on-One Couples' Counseling

- Interactive Workshops

- Tele-Seminars & Tele-Conferences

- Financial Seminars & Workshops from a Female and Male Perspective

Contact Us:

The Romance and Finance Couples' Money Counseling Group
4110 Redwood Road, Suite 103
Oakland, California 94619
Tel: 510-482-5129
Fax: 510-482-5130
Email: sisterceo@aol.com

MetaMedia Publishing

Life Changing information to empower you to the next level of your life

ORDER FORM

MetaMedia Publishing, Inc.
6114 LaSalle Avenue
Number 724
Oakland, CA 94611-2802

Telephone: (510) 482-5129
Email metamediapub@aol.com

Fax: (510) 482-5130

Yes, Please order my copy of *"What's Money Got To Do With It?—The Ultimate Guide On How To Make Love and Money Work In Your Relationship'"* **I understand that I may return any books for a full refund – no questions asked!**

I would also like to order ____ additional copies for my friends in need.

Total copies ____

Company Name: _____

Name: _____

Address: _____

City: _____ State: ____ Zip: ____ ____

Work Phone: _____ Home Phone: _____

Email: _____

Payment:
☐ Check
☐ Credit Card
☐ VISA   ☐ Mastercard   ☐ AMEX   ☐ Discover
Card Number: _____
Name on Card: _____ Exp Date: _____

Price: $23.95

Sales Tax:
California residents please add 8.25%

Shipping: First book: $6.00
                Each additional book add $3.00

# of books @ $23.95 ea:	_____
Subtotal:	_____
Applicable Tax:	_____
Shipping Total:	_____
Grand Total:	_____